Complexities of Higher Education Administration

Complexities of
Higher Education
Administration

Case Studies & Issues

Mary Lou Higgerson
Susan S. Rehwaldt

Southern Illinois University
Carbondale

Anker Publishing Company, Inc.
Bolton, MA

Complexities of Higher Education Administration
Case Studies and Issues

ISBN 0–9627042–7–X

Composition by Deerfoot Studios.
Cover Design by Marianna Montuori.

Anker Publishing Company, Inc.
176 Ballville Road
P.O. Box 249
Bolton, MA 01740–0249

ABOUT THE AUTHORS

Mary Lou Higgerson is a seasoned academic administrator with twenty years of experience as department chair, associate dean, and associate vice president for academic affairs. Her selection as an American Council on Education Fellow in 1986-87, provided her with an opportunity to work as a member of a campus president's staff and for the head of a university system. Higgerson holds a Ph.D. from the University of Kansas where she studied and conducted research in organizational communication. Her consulting and research interests have gravitated from corporate communication to the application of organizational communication techniques to higher education administration. Combining her knowledge of communication literature and skills with her administrative experience, Higgerson's focus in her writing, consulting, and training activities is on the application of communication and management theory utilizing video vignettes and case studies. Since 1990, she has taught a variety of topics for the American Council on Education in both the Fellows Program and seminars offered through the Department Leadership Program. Currently an associate professor of Speech Communication at Southern Illinois University at Carbondale, Higgerson teaches courses in organizational communication and the university as an organizational culture. Higgerson has co-produced training videos on communication strategies relevant for higher education administrators and has written articles which have appeared in such publications as *The Chronicle of Higher Education, Journal of College and University Personnel Association, Continuing Higher Education Review,* and *The Department Chair.*

Susan S. Rehwaldt's educational background is a combination of business and academic administration. She holds a bachelor's degree in business administration from Washington University (St. Louis) and an M.S. and Ph.D. in Education from Southern Illinois University at Carbondale. Her dissertation, funded by a research grant from the Midwest College Placement Association, focused on issues of gender discrimination in the corporate hiring process. Currently an assistant professor of communication, she teaches in the areas of business communication and technical writing. Dr. Rehwaldt has twenty years of varied experience in higher education administration: in student counseling/placement; as an assistant to a university president; and as a tenured faculty member with an additional administrative assignment as coordinator of the Office Systems program. She also served (concurrently) for three years as editor of a nationally circulated quarterly professional journal and, since 1989, has been a member of the board of Augsburg-Fortress Publishers (Minneapolis). Dr. Rehwaldt has created training seminars for students and alumni in job search strategies, two-career families, interview communication techniques, résumé writing, and other forms of communication related to the job search and career decision-making; has co-produced video vignettes; and has given many national presentations on current topics in academic administration. Her research and writing are focused on communication issues in the workplace. She has published a number of articles which have appeared in a variety of higher education publications including *The Journal of Studies in Technical Careers* and *The Department Chair.*

CONTENTS

FOREWORD

The importance of effective higher education administration can hardly be overstated. Poor administration almost always saps institutional energy and enthusiasm, generates undue complexity and extra work, and can create a sense of directionless floundering. Rightly done, administration empowers faculty and staff, enabling them to attend to the challenges before them without distractions. Students suffer or benefit accordingly.

These are almost patently obvious facts, but the academy has yet fully to acknowledge them. Our traditions seem to make us uncomfortable in celebrating leadership roles and successes. The very ambiguity in the greetings extended those accepting these roles is illustrative. Expressions of condolence compete with those of congratulations. Individuals in leadership positions can internalize these mixed messages, with moments of self-doubt and confusion as a result.

Whether we be already fully engaged in positions of academic leadership, presently preparing for assuming one leadership activity or another, or simply contemplating that possibility, the material in this book is a helpful resource. Thoughtful appropriation will promote more effective higher education administration and will help sustain those involved through the periods of doubt its complexities inevitably bring. Structured around a variety of case studies, the material lends itself to both individual and collective use.

Case studies are a valuable learning resource because they present the texture and particularity of the concrete. They are far closer than theories to the untidiness of the immediate situation, but distant enough to be free of actual consequences. That is, they convey the insistent and multiple demands for problem solving in this or that case—demands that more abstract theory can obscure. Yet, case studies are forgiving, for no one's career turns on the decision proposed, there are no damaging outcomes, and one is not burdened by confidences.

Without the pressures of the moment that require immediate response, the reader has the opportunity for lengthier reflection and consideration. Case studies are invitations to become engaged in the issues at hand. While cases are specific in their details, the issues are generalizable. Problems and problem people have multiple locations. Whether the case be considered by the individual in self-directed study or in a lively group discussion, a variety of possible analyses and approaches will soon present themselves. None will be self-evidently the 'correct' one. Some will be better, others worse, but there will be opportunity to reflect on why.

In a group discussion, no one is privileged. All have the same information and, at least initially, the same frame of reference. Differences will soon emerge and individual involvement will be enriched and enhanced by interaction with the perspectives and comments of others. Each participant will be a resource for the other. And yet, of course, in the end each must assume responsibility for his or her own learning and decisions.

There are multiple routes to higher education administration. One set goes through a degree program in a higher education department. Another entails an intensive summer experience in an institute. Still another involves no formal education at all, but rather learning on the job. This text can be a part of all routes. Disciplined use will result in an enhanced ability to analyze situations and to identify and assess responses, to consider both strategy and tactics in realistic situations, and to evaluate the likelihood of success.

The authors have considerable experience in a variety of administrative positions in higher education. The case studies they have crafted are recognizable and broadly accessible. The questions they pose focus the issues for productive resolution. Having over the years constructed and taught a number of cases myself, I know their value. I invite the reader to participate in this value—not to slip back into comfortable and passive observation, but to insert themselves into the situation. When this happens, this book can become an excellent resource for advancing and celebrating effective higher education administration.

John B. Bennett
Quinnipiac College
Hamden, CT

PREFACE

For over a decade, we have contemplated writing a case study book combining higher education administration and communication theory. The positive reaction to the case studies we created and used in formal classroom and workshop settings, and in more informal professional development seminars and counseling sessions, caused us to conclude that there was a need for such a collection of cases to facilitate professional development in both arenas.

Throughout our careers we have collected—mostly in our subconscious—anecdotal information, ideas, observations and alternatives. We also gained tremendous benefit from reflecting on how we would have handled each situation. We compared notes, read *The Chronicle of Higher Education*, talked with colleagues, saw themes emerging, and discussed these over numerous lunches. We gave presentations regularly, published in administrative and communication areas and added more lines to our vitae. However, a pivotal activity took place several years ago when we scripted four video vignettes to use for professional development activities. We were again so encouraged by the reaction of those attending our workshops and training sessions that we decided to write this book.

Participants, nationwide, in these various settings were overwhelmingly appreciative of the educational opportunity afforded by case study glimpses of "real life" administration. They were relieved to find that others wrestled with similar problems and were receptive to the information on communication techniques. They all welcomed the opportunity to improve their communication skills. Because we had noticed, once again, that our commentary accompanying these vignettes always fell into the same two categories (communication and administration), we were finally convinced that our backgrounds, disciplines, and academic experiences had prepared us to make the contribution we intend this book to provide.

A key to proceeding with the book was our realization (and workshop participants' and colleagues' agreement) that one does not have to "live it to learn it." A tremendous amount of learning takes place when one walks in the shoes of another and is forced to analyze the problems, wrestle with all the options, consider alternative solutions or courses of action, and finally make a decision. This book is meant to provide that experience.

To be certain that the cases were realistic and beneficial to students and professionals across institution types, we enlisted the assistance of numerous friends and colleagues. A special thanks is due to all of these reviewers who read early versions of our manuscript:

Marilyn J. Amey, University of Kansas
H. George Anderson, Luther College
Patricia Arey, Mississippi University for Women
John B. Bennett, Quinnipiac College
John S. Burns, Washington State University
William E. Cashin, Kansas State University
Linda J. Corder, University of South Dakota
Donna Corriveau, Illinois Board of Higher Education
John W. Creswell, University of Nebraska
K. Patricia Cross, University of California-Berkeley
Irene Hecht, American Council on Education
Mark Hickson III, University of Alabama
John C. Hollwitz, Creighton University
Gary L. Hunter, Miami University
Loren Jung, University of Missouri
George Keller, University of Pennsylvania
Barry McCauliff, Clarion University
Linda Moore, University of Akron
Donald Mundinger, Illinois College
Jerrald Pfabe, Concordia College
Hildegard Schmidt, Rosary College
Stephen Schmidt, Loyola University
Alan Seagren, University of Nebraska
Bruce Swinburne, University of Arkansas
Susan B. Twombly, University of Kansas
Mary Watson, Valdosta State College.

Mary Lou Higgerson
Susan S. Rehwaldt
Carbondale, Illinois
January, 1993

Index of Higher Education Issues and Administrative Tasks

INDEX OF COMMUNICATION SKILLS

Interpersonal skills
- Statics, tensions and abrasions
- Transition
- Who's on first?
- Domino effect
- Publish or perish
- Whose decision is this anyway?
- Supervisor's dilemma
- Silence gives license
- Puzzle pieces
- Hindsight is 20/20

Interview techniques
- Statics, tensions and abrasions
- An exceedingly chilly climate
- Mirror, mirror on the wall. . .
- Supervisor's dilemma
- Puzzle pieces

Interpreting facts and inferences
- An open and shut case
- Statics, tensions and abrasions
- Who's on first?
- An exceedingly chilly climate
- Publish or perish
- Mirror, mirror on the wall. . .
- Puzzle pieces

Managing conflict
- Transitions
- Statics, tensions and abrasions
- Domino effect
- Publish or perish
- Mirror, mirror on the wall. . .
- Whose decision is this anyway?
- Silence gives license
- Competitors or partners?
- Hindsight is 20/20

Message construction
- The new mandate: Assess!
- Transitions
- Statics, tensions and abrasions
- Who's on first?
- Mirror, mirror on the wall. . .
- Supervisor's dilemma

Index by Administrative Level and Constituency Group

(Positions and offices are listed in descending order.)

State board of higher education
- The new mandate: Assess!
- An attempt to finesse
- Competitors or partners?

Institution governing board
- An attempt to finesse
- An open and shut case

System head
- The new mandate: Assess!
- An exceedingly chilly climate

President
- Transitions
- An open and shut case
- An exceedingly chilly climate
- Hindsight is 20/20
- Silence gives license
- Puzzle pieces

Legal counsel
- An open and shut case
- An exceedingly chilly climate
- Hindsight is 20/20

Provost/vice president (academic affairs)
- The new mandate: Assess!
- Transitions
- An attempt to finesse
- An open and shut case
- Who's on first?
- Domino effect
- Whose decision is this anyway?
- Competitors or partners?

Directors/vice presidents (development, institutional advancement, public relations, and alumni services)
- An exceedingly chilly climate
- Puzzle pieces

Admissions, recruitment
- Whose decision is this anyway?

- Competitors or partners?
- Puzzle pieces

Dean
- Transitions
- An open and shut case
- Who's on first?
- Domino effect
- Supervisor's dilemma
- Competitors or partners?

Department chair
- Statics, tensions and abrasions
- Who's on first?
- Domino effect
- Publish or perish
- Mirror, mirror on the wall. . .
- Whose decision is this anyway?
- Silence gives license

Faculty senate or constituency groups
- The new mandate: Assess!
- An open and shut case
- Publish or perish
- Domino effect
- Whose decision is this anyway?

Faculty
- Statics, tensions and abrasions
- Publish or perish
- Who's on first?
- An open and shut case
- Mirror, mirror on the wall. . .
- Silence gives license

Students
- Statics, tensions and abrasions
- Who's on first?
- Hindsight is 20/20
- Silence gives license
- Competitors or partners?

INDEX BY INSTITUTION TYPE

Large public institutions: state supported with more than 15,000 students, including doctoral programs and an emphasis on research.
- The new mandate: Assess!
- Transitions
- An attempt to finesse
- Who's on first?

Large private institutions: primarily privately supported with more than 15,000 students, including doctoral program with an emphasis on research.
- An open and shut case
- Statics, tensions and abrasions

Mid-size public institutions: state supported with enrollments of 4,000 to 10,000 students, primarily undergraduate education with a few master's degree programs.
- An exceedingly chilly climate
- Domino effect
- Publish or perish

Mid-size private institutions: primarily privately supported with enroll-ments of 4,000 to 10,000 students, primarily undergraduate education with a few master's degree programs.
- Hindsight is 20/20
- Mirror, mirror on the wall…

Small public institutions: state supported with enrollments of fewer than 4,000 students focusing on baccalaureate education.
- Whose decision is this anyway?
- Supervisor's dilemma

Small private institutions: primarily privately supported with enrollments of fewer than 4,000 students focusing on baccalaureate education.
- Silence gives license
- Puzzle pieces

Community colleges: state supported institutions offering two-year asso-ciate degrees, continuing education credits, and other certificate programs.
- Competitors or partners?

INTRODUCTION

Academic administrators are well aware of the complexities and frustrations of managing a dynamic enterprise. Their success hinges on communication—both personal and institutional—within the context of financial, political and personnel issues. When administrators accurately perceive their environment and audience, analyze the problems before them, and communicate effectively, tough issues can be confronted, alternatives discussed and sound decisions made. When the communication process breaks down, or when administrators' perceptions of people and issues are not accurate or realistic, then potentially avoidable problems develop, often escalate, and can thwart administrative success.

This text is intended to be a resource for students and practitioners of academic administration. The case studies are intended to engage the reader as an active participant in very real situations that can be generalized across most institution types. This book can be used both in formal classroom situations and for self-directed instruction.

The case studies can be used in graduate courses in educational administration, organizational communication, and management to move students beyond theory into the complexities of administration, thereby helping students see the utility of communication as an administrative tool for problem solving. Likewise, the text can serve as a valuable resource for administrators and persons contemplating careers in academic administration who wish to gain insight into the challenges awaiting them, who want to grow professionally, and who would prefer to learn experientially by analyzing the actions of others rather than personally enduring the multitude of crises described in these case studies. Finally, individuals who are contemplating a career in administration can get a taste for the real life complexities of higher education administration before making a formal commitment to that career path.

SPECIAL FEATURES

About the Case. Each case begins with a brief introduction framing the issues to be addressed. The reader is given a general description of the principal participants and the dilemmas they face. Care is taken not to prejudice the outcome of the case study process or to imply that there is only one correct decision, action or solution.

Pause for Questions. Each case is punctuated with a series of questions. These queries stop the action at critical decision points throughout the case, offering the reader an opportunity to strategize with the administrators involved, to consider alternatives and to make decisions. Subsequent questions allow for an evaluation of the decisions made by either the case's actors or by the reader. New information is often presented after a series of questions—as is the usual case in real administrative situations.

The questions are not meant to project a *correct* answer; in fact, great care has been exercised to avoid that possibility. Rather, the questions keep the student/reader from slipping into a comfortable third-person observer role or from truncating an analysis of the problems before a complete understanding of all variables is obtained. Occasionally, the queries are followed by statements which suggest relevant communication concepts or administrative issues. These comments are provided to encourage the reader to probe more deeply, beyond the obvious alternatives and strategies.

Selected Readings. An annotated list of suggested readings provides information for those who desire additional material on particular administrative issues or communication skills inherent in the resolution of the case under discussion. The readings, from books and journals and ranging from the practical to the theoretical, can be used in formal classroom situations or for self-directed instruction.

These suggested readings also allow the instructor/reader to select a specific focus for a given case. For example, one case can initiate a discussion on curriculum, on faculty governance, or on state involvement in higher education. The readings allow the class or individuals to gain additional insight into whatever facet(s) of the scenario is appropriate, and to appreciate the broader questions and controversies associated with a given issue.

Multiple Indices. While a professor utilizing this text for a full term course may choose to have the students work through each case and each issue, those in other professional development settings may prefer to focus on a few specific issues. Or an individual may wish to select case studies on certain issues which are of particular relevance or interest. To assist all readers, the case studies and issues addressed are organized according to four variables:
- higher education issues and administrative tasks
- communication skills

- administrative level and constituency group
- institution type.

With these indices, for example, an instructor teaching a unit on program evaluation could identify the particular cases which are relevant by using the index on higher education issues and administrative tasks. Similarly, an individual wanting to learn more about communication strategies for initiating change could consult the communication skill index to locate the relevant cases and related annotated bibliography.

THE CASE STUDY METHOD

The case study method provides a risk-free methodology that can help individuals improve their administrative skills and sharpen their sensitivity to those organizational factors which can either facilitate or hinder their ultimate achievements. Working through case studies can likewise sharpen the reader's sensitivity to those communication skills which can either facilitate or hinder their careers. Whether used for group or individual instruction, the case study method is based on four important assumptions.

1. **Common experiences.** Situations experienced in academic administration are generalizable across institutions of higher education. While colleges and universities can vary in size, mission, and funding source, they have many similarities. All, for example, have faculty who need to be effective teachers and students who are focused on receiving an education and preparing for eventual employment or additional study. Because of the generalizability of these cases, those using this text can benefit from all the cases, regardless of whether a case was placed on the type of campus of particular interest to that individual reader.

2. **Risk-free environment.** The case study method gives individuals an opportunity to learn from the experience of others in a risk-free environment. In fact, the case study method actually accelerates the type of learning that typically accompanies professional work experience. For this opportunity to be fully realized, the student/reader must remain an active participant in the discussion process, sizing up situations described in each case, analyzing the alternatives available, and developing strategies in response to the questions asked.

3. **Theory to practice.** The case study method allows theory to be translated into practice. Information contained in published materials about the various approaches to faculty evaluation and the characteristics of positive performance counseling may seem like common sense. However, combining this theoretical information on human resource development with the communication skill needed to effectively conduct a

performance counseling session is much more difficult. The case study method starts with reality and uses theory, as prompted by the readings, to fine tune the various strategic actions and skills which may be useful in any given situation.

4. **Critical thinking.** This text does not supply the answers, because no simple answers transcend all institutional and personality types. It does, however, help the student/reader to identify and to analyze the issues, variables and options. Successful administrators seldom start with all the information necessary to solve a given problem, but they must be able to recognize and to articulate the important questions that need to be answered. Critical thinking skills are the combination of knowing the questions to ask, using the information assembled, applying the appropriate communication and management skills, and making decisions with clarity and vision. Studying real cases, in a group setting or individually, will improve a person's ability to think critically.

Working from these four assumptions, this text is designed to provide an opportunity for "experiencing," studying and pondering some of the complexities of higher education administration. This learning, whether done as part of a formal class, a professional workshop, or independently, will serve to sharpen one's leadership and communication skills for more effective administration in higher education.

To our colleagues and families
who encouraged us to write this book
and who provided the support we needed to finish it

MIRROR, MIRROR ON THE WALL...

About the Case

One of the toughest personnel problems that department chairs and deans face is the challenge of getting faculty ready for successful promotion and tenure review. The task is not limited to the review year, but must begin the moment a faculty member is appointed to a tenure track position. If standards and criteria for tenure and promotion are not made clear early, the result can be catastrophic for all concerned. This task is made even more difficult when faculty, upon reflection, see only positive images of their own professional personae. When problems do arise, they can also lead to hours spent in meetings, in formal grievance proceedings, and even in a courtroom.

CASE STUDY

George Overton was director of the School of Music at Anchor University, a private institution with an enrollment of about 10,000 undergraduate and 500 graduate students. Although the university was primarily an undergraduate institution, offering only a few master's degree programs, its faculty were expected to conduct research and to publish. Overton felt it was one of his responsibilities to try to interpret that expectation to the faculty in the School of Music, as well as to assist senior academic officers in understanding how that expectation, in fact, translated into activity for musicians.

Anchor's emphasis on research, Overton knew, grew out of the administration's desire to obtain recognition for the institution in research and to realize the benefits which accrue from increased external grant and contract activity. Most faculty received at least 25 percent release time for research activity. Campus policy, as printed in the faculty handbook (Attachment A), makes explicit the importance of research activities to the promotion and tenure decision process. Despite the clarity of the policy, the university initially had some difficulty trying to convince faculty that indeed research was important to the mission of the university and would be a significant factor in promoting faculty and in granting tenure.

George Overton had just finished his second annual evaluation of Professor Igor Pryor, a distinguished oboist who joined the faculty in the School of Music at Anchor University about two years ago. Overton was following a university policy (Attachment B) requiring an annual performance evaluation of all untenured faculty. This policy was implemented four years ago to help ensure that faculty understood the standards and criteria for tenure and promotion.

Today, most of the faculty seem more accepting and comfortable with the research requirement. In fact, the pendulum has begun to swing in the opposite direction in that a few faculty would prefer to focus exclusively on the research component of their assignment to the point of slighting their teaching responsibilities.

School of Music. Adding Igor Pryor to the faculty in the School of Music was seen by George Overton as an important hire in keeping with his school's commitment to building a strong *performance* faculty. Pryor also filled a critical opening in the school's Woodwind Quintet, a group that enjoyed an international reputation.

During his first two years at Anchor, Professor Pryor managed to win the acclaim of the other members of the Woodwind Quintet as a talented musician. In addition, Overton noted that Pryor exhibited considerable expertise in his efforts to promote the quintet's professional reputation. Professor Pryor orchestrated the booking for a one month tour of Europe last semester; he also maintained a rigorous performance schedule as a member of the area symphony orchestra and the university orchestra. In the area of performance, Professor Pryor proved to be even more impressive than had been anticipated.

Unfortunately, Professor Pryor paid little attention to anything other than performance. During the past two years, George Overton had received numerous complaints from students who reported that Professor Pryor was difficult to locate, did not keep regular office hours, and was not willing to schedule appointments with students. Some of the complaints suggested to Overton that Pryor may not be well prepared to meet his classes (i.e., Pryor did not create nor distribute a course syllabus) and his basis for assigning grades was not made clear to students.

Equally disturbing to Overton were the enrollment statistics. Only three of the six students once enrolled in oboe instruction for credit remained in the program. From this group, the director heard many complaints that Professor Pryor often canceled, without notice, their scheduled lessons.

When George Overton assigned Professor Pryor to teach a freshman music appreciation class with a large enrollment, he protested on the grounds that his travel schedule, as dictated by his membership in the Woodwind Quintet, caused him to miss too many classes. Professor Pryor argued that he should only engage in one-on-one instruction which can be scheduled around his performance schedule. The director later assigned the music appreciation class to another instructor.

Professor Pryor's work in the area of school and university service was not much stronger than his effort in teaching. He seemed to accept committee assignments willingly, but his attendance at committee meetings was sporadic. Even though Pryor was the school's only representative on the college's Faculty Advisory Council, Dean Steinberg had recently informed Overton that Pryor had attended only one of the six meetings held during the past semester. Neither Overton nor Steinberg was content with that attendance record.

Two Performance Evaluations. In accordance with the university policy, the director of the School of Music met individually each year with Pryor and all other untenured faculty who were in tenure track positions. Overton used those occasions to review their progress toward meeting the institution's standards for promotion and tenure. Overton was expected to document these performance evaluation meetings with a written record of what was discussed. Last year, when meeting with Pryor, the director decided to tone down his criticism of Pryor's teaching and service because Overton believed that every new faculty should have at least one year to become acclimated to the school and the institution. The director's letter documenting his first performance evaluation session (Attachment C) with Professor Pryor was brief and totally complimentary.

Last week Overton held his second performance evaluation session with Professor Pryor to discuss the work done by Pryor in his first two years at Anchor. In this session, Overton was somewhat more pointed in his remarks when discussing student complaints regarding Pryor's teaching and the need to balance the amount of effort given to teaching with the amount allocated to performance. Professor Pryor appeared to be so shocked and wounded by the reports of student complaints that the director felt obliged, once again, to soften his comments regarding his criticism of Pryor's conduct in his letter documenting the evaluation session (see Attachment D).

George Overton was fully aware that Pryor's progress toward promotion and tenure was problematic. Quite simply, without documentation of effective teaching, Overton recognized that Pryor would not be able to obtain tenure and promotion at their institution. Further, his nonchalance in committee work could serve to alienate colleagues who might otherwise be supportive of his tenure application. Because Pryor was valued by the school for his performance capability, Overton was anxious to help Pryor meet the standards required for tenure and promotion. The director was very surprised and puzzled by Pryor's reaction to the students' complaints. The director believed that Pryor had been given ample time to become acquainted with the teaching and service components of his appointment and to become acclimated to the university culture which clearly places students (and therefore teaching) as a top priority.

University policy required that the director of the School of Music and Professor Pryor, together, would meet with Dean Steinberg to discuss Professor Pryor's annual performance evaluation and progress toward promotion and tenure. Overton was worried that Professor Pryor did not either comprehend or accept Overton's comments regarding the importance of teaching. Last year, the required meeting with the dean was brief and positive. With the chair's good evaluation in hand, the dean had no basis for suspecting a growing problem.

Let's pause here. . .

1. *Evaluate the director's actions thus far in dealing with Professor Pryor. Did Overton handle Pryor's first year evaluation properly? Be specific in developing the rationale for your conclusions.*

2. *Critique Overton's first letter (Attachment C). Does this letter make subsequent annual evaluations of Pryor easier or more difficult?*

3. *Was Overton's second performance evaluation session with Pryor effective? Specify why or why not. Assume the role of the director and indicate how you would have conducted the evaluation session. Role play or script your evaluation session with Professor Pryor. Assume the role of the director and draft a more effective letter to summarize the outcome of your evaluation session with Professor Pryor. Consider what documentation you would have had ready for the second session. Critique the director's second letter (Attachment D).*

4. *What action might be taken by George Overton to alter Igor Pryor's attitude and performance in the area of teaching? Consider steps that might be taken aside from the formal evaluation session. Make certain that your suggested alternatives are consistent with university policy.*

5. *Given university policy which requires performance review by both the director and the dean, which administrator is primarily responsible for*

*communicating performance problems to a faculty member and for coun-
seling a deficient faculty member on ways to improve performance? You
may want to review the readings which discuss the roles and duties delegated to department chairs, directors and deans.*

The Director and the Dean. The director of the School of Music
made an appointment to talk with the dean before their scheduled evaluation session of Professor Pryor. Overton wanted to talk with Dean Steinberg in advance of their meeting with Pryor to seek the dean's support in
helping Pryor understand the importance of effective teaching to tenure
and promotion.

Overton scheduled his meeting with the dean only after considerable
thought and some anguish because Overton certainly did not want to
jeopardize Pryor's opportunities for obtaining tenure. He chose not to talk
with Dean Steinberg before this because he didn't want to prejudice the
dean against Pryor.

Overton gave the dean a brief history of Pryor's uneven progress
toward meeting tenure standards. The dean agreed with Overton's assessment of the situation and expressed his opinion that it was imperative that
Pryor clearly understand the precise standards for promotion and tenure
as early as possible in his probationary period.

Dean Steinberg was also concerned that George Overton's letter of
documentation following Pryor's second annual evaluation was written
with too positive a tone in view of the facts of the situation. Clearly, the
director's two letters, taken together, suggested that nothing was wrong
and that Pryor, after two years on the faculty, was making satisfactory
progress toward meeting the promotion and tenure standard. From firsthand experience, the dean knew that this type of false signal would create
a difficult, and grievable, tenure review in the event the faculty member is
denied tenure and can produce evidence suggesting that he was told he
was doing all he needed to do.

Let's pause again. . .

6. *Assume the role of Dean Steinberg and identify all possible strategies for conducting a performance counseling session with Professor Pryor. What is your
preferred approach and why? Can you anticipate Professor Pryor's reaction
to each of the issues you expect to raise? You may want to try out your strategy in a role play situation.*

7. *What documentation would you, as dean, have ready for this session with
Igor Pryor? Be specific in indicating what facts and information you plan to*

present to Pryor. Keep in mind that your session will be his first encounter with significant negative feedback.

The Meeting. After the typical introductory courtesies, Dean Steinberg sat down with Overton and Pryor to review Pryor's performance over the last two years. Dean Steinberg was certain that he needed to stress the importance of good teaching. He did not, however, believe that he could discuss the students' complaints as they were heard only by the director and were not mentioned in the director's letter summarizing Professor Pryor's evaluation.

Dean Steinberg said, "In looking at your record for the last year, I was amazed to discover the number of performances you made. It is clear that you're an outstanding oboist and a talented addition to the institution's Woodwind Quintet."

"Thank you," replied Pryor. "I take a lot of pride in my performance ability."

Dean Steinberg, picking up on Pryor's mindset, said, "That's obvious, and I want to be clear that your effort and achievement in the area of performance is recognized in the college. I must ask, however, how you manage such a full performance schedule while teaching classes?"

Professor Pryor seemed ready for that question and replied quickly, "Well, the director and I agreed that it's best if I teach only courses with small enrollments and those which require one-on-one instruction. After all, that's where my talent is and that's the reason I was hired. So in working with individual students on oboe, or small groups of students on performance theory, I can set the lesson times and class meetings around my performance schedule. It also has the advantage of giving music majors an opportunity to see what life as a musician is all about."

Dean Steinberg responded, "That's true, but most of our students do not aspire to become full-time professional musicians. Many are pursuing music education degrees. How many students are now studying the oboe with you?"

"Three," said Pryor, "but I have recruited four new students for the program who will begin next fall if the university comes through with the necessary scholarship money."

Dean Steinberg, turning to his right and directing this comment directly to George Overton, said, "I thought we had more than three students currently in oboe."

Overton answered, "There were six in the program a year ago, but at the moment only three are enrolled for credit."

"Why is that?" retorted the dean. "What happened to the other three?"

Professor Pryor, in a matter-of-fact tone, interjected, "The oboe is a very difficult instrument and not all who believe that they want to perform are really cut out to pursue it as a profession. Certainly one of my jobs as an educator is to help students make that often difficult decision."

Dean Steinberg resumed his previous posture and said to Pryor, "I am concerned that if you're working with only a few students, we may have difficulty in documenting your teaching effectiveness when your dossier for promotion and tenure comes up for review."

Professor Pryor, almost chuckling, said, "No, don't worry. I obtain both peer reviews and student evaluations of my teaching on a regular basis and they're all excellent. I have that information in my file."

"I'm glad to know that you've been collecting that," said the dean, "because I notice that you did not attend—either last year or this year—the workshop this college sponsors on how to prepare for promotion and tenure review. You know our objective in this college is to help faculty understand the criteria and standards for successful promotion and tenure reviews and to give whatever guidance we can in pulling together the documentation that will be expected so that all our faculty hires can be successful in securing tenure and promotion."

"Well," drawled Pryor, "as I recall, I believe I was out of town performing on the dates of those workshops."

Dean Steinberg, sitting up taller and getting right to the point said, "Do you have any questions about the process of promotion and tenure or the standards of the college or university?"

Professor Pryor, directing an appreciative smile toward George Overton, said, "No, I've been having my annual meetings with the director and he assures me that everything is moving along fine."

Dean Steinberg said, "Well, we have picked up on one concern in this office and I believe it's something that can be remedied fairly easily. As you know, you serve as the School of Music's only representative on the college's Faculty Advisory Committee. It is important that the School of Music be represented on that group, yet my recollection is that you were only able to make one of the meetings last semester. Your attendance record is really not up to the standard expected for such a service activity."

"Sorry," said Pryor, "but it's hard to be in two places at once—and I know that you hired me to play the oboe. So when I need to be out of town for performances or rehearsals, I can't put committee work first. "

Dean Steinberg, seeing an opening, said, "Well, we hire faculty not only to participate in just one activity, but also to be effective teachers, and to have a sense of collegiality. That means that faculty are expected to contribute service to their discipline, to the school, and to the college. I must tell you that I've heard some of your colleagues in the School of Music complain that you don't pull your weight with regard to assuming such service responsibilities."

"I hope you realize," replied Pryor, "that those faculty members are typically speaking from jealousy."

Dean Steinberg, doing a double-take, said, "Excuse me?"

"Oh yes," replied Pryor, "I have heard some of those comments too, but I must tell you I know exactly the few people who are grumbling. I believe that they are motivated by the fact they are jealous of my musical capability and my talent. They certainly do not perform as often as I."

Dean Steinberg added, "I'm not sure that is the case, but I do know that the School of Music was basically not represented last semester on this college's Faculty Advisory Committee."

"Well," said Pryor, somewhat grudgingly, "I see your point. Perhaps that committee assignment should be given to someone else."

Dean Steinberg countered by saying, "I will leave such committee assignments to the discretion of the music school's director, but you must understand the importance of service to the school and to the college, particularly as it is perceived by your colleagues."

Following the performance evaluation session, Dean Steinberg drafted a letter to Professor Pryor summarized the content of the meeting (Attachment E).

Let's pause one final time. . .

8. *Evaluate Dean Steinberg's performance counseling session with Professor Pryor. What worked and what didn't work? Review the dialogue and rewrite Dean Steinberg's part to correct statements you identified as ineffective.*

9. *Do you believe Professor Pryor has a better understanding of the standards for promotion and tenure and the expectations for his performance? Please specify why or why not. Is the session with Dean Steinberg likely to cause Professor Pryor to alter his behavior?*

10. *What follow-up might be done to remedy any remaining misunderstandings? Is follow-up to clarify tenure standards the responsibility of the director, the dean, or both?*

11. *Would the dean's letter (Attachment E) serve to put Pryor on notice? Is the letter sufficient? Edit the letter to strengthen it.*

12. *What else, if anything, should be done by the college dean? What else, if anything, should be done by the school's director to encourage Professor Pryor to alter his performance in the areas of teaching and service? Be certain that your recommended action is consistent with the university's policy. You may wish to review the various roles of deans and chairs.*

Attachment A

Anchor University
Policy on Promotion and Tenure

Anchor University is a comprehensive university. Therefore, it is essential that its faculty be dedicated to achieving excellence in teaching, research/creative activity, and professional contributions to preserve and strengthen the vitality of the university. Tenure and academic promotion is awarded to those faculty making continuing contributions in these areas. The preservation of quality requires that all persons recommended for promotion clearly satisfy the general criteria presented herein. Fairness requires that these criteria be applied as uniformly as possible.

A basic format for tenure and/or promotion dossiers will be given to the collegiate deans for distribution through department chairs and directors to faculty members eligible to be considered for tenure and/or promotion. A common format for representing the supporting information will help assure fairness in the decision-making process. As tenure and promotion require that a person's entire professional contribution be reviewed, the format calls for information on professional background, previous academic and professional experience, teaching and advising activities, scholarly contributions, and service activities. Some academic units may wish to add special categories.

A faculty member will be evaluated for promotion in any year at her or his request. A tenured faculty member below the rank of professor must have her or his dossier submitted for review by the basic academic unit at least every five years unless the faculty member requests in writing that it is not to be reviewed. A more frequent review of faculty performance for purposes of promotion is strongly encouraged. A faculty member will be reviewed for tenure at the end of a two-year probationary period if hired at the rank of professor; at the end of a four-year probationary period if hired as an associate professor; and at the end of a six-year probationary period if hired as an assistant professor. The decision emanating from such a request shall be considered as final. If the decision is negative, the faculty member will be notified in writing that the following contract year will be terminal.

The faculty member should assist in the preparation of his or her dossier. The faculty member should be allowed to submit whatever he or she considers relevant to promotion or tenure review in addition to any information or material required by the university, collegiate or departmental policies.

I. General Criteria

    A. **Teaching:** The first step in promotion is an evaluation of teaching effectiveness. Only after an affirmative judgment as to teaching effectiveness has been made can serious consideration be given to an evaluation of scholarship and professional service. Unless a determination is made that the candidate is an effective teacher, whether at the departmental or interdisciplinary level, promotion will not be granted. Teaching includes an up-to-date knowledge of one's discipline. In some instances, teaching may be indirect, primarily in support of student learning activities. Faculty members also influence teaching by designing courses and curricula. Textbooks and innovative instructional material may be considered contributions to teaching. In addition, faculty members influence teaching in less tangible but no less decisive ways through such activities as counseling students, through conversations with colleagues, etc.

Detailed and specific evidence of effective teaching should be included in the dossiers of faculty members being recommended for promotion. Evidence should include peer evaluations and student evaluations conducted over a reasonable period of time. Faculty colleagues should be asked to evaluate the objectives, methods and materials of courses designed and/or taught by the individual. Evaluations of teaching effectiveness should also be drawn from faculty who have taught with the individual or have frequently observed classes taught by the individual. Wherever possible, evaluations should also include evidence concerning the continuing performance of students taught by the candidate.

B. **Research/Creative Activity:** Research and creative activity are those activities which serve to advance the discipline or the state of the art. Evidence of research and creative activity, essential for promotion, includes written publications, non-print performances, funded grant applications, exhibits, artistic performances, and the like. Textbooks and innovative instructional materials having significant value beyond this campus may be considered contributions to research/creative activity. The dossier of an individual should provide substantiating evidence submitted by qualified observers within or outside the university (e.g., reviews of the candidate's books, artistic performances, etc.). If the candidate's field is one in which no colleague has expertise, it is essential that outside review of the candidate's scholarly activities be sought.

C. **Professional Contributions:** Faculty members are expected to make professional contributions through service to the department, the college, the university, and the discipline at large. The last item includes discipline-related community service. Professional services may include paid or unpaid consulting work. Administrative and professional work on behalf of the department or the university, for which there is no specific compensation or assignment, may be regarded as service. It is desirable that evaluations by qualified individuals indicating the quality and extent of the service rendered be submitted with the promotion dossier.

II. Minimum Standards for Academic Ranks

Each basic academic unit and collegial unit may have defined requirements which exceed those of the university. The minimum university requirements for each academic rank are given below:

A. **Assistant Professor:** Promotion from the rank of Instructor to Assistant Professor requires an ability to teach effectively and the academic degree defined by the academic unit for the position held by the candidate. Those tenured in the rank of Instructor may meet the minimum university criteria for promotion to Assistant Professor by: (1) demonstration of effective teaching; (2) successful completion of scholarly/creative activity which contributes to the discipline or field of study and offers promise for future achievement (e.g., completion of the required academic degree), or peer-reviewed publications, or peer-reviewed artistic /creative performances; and (3) demonstrated participation in service activities appropriate to the discipline and the academic unit.

B. **Associate Professor:** Promotion from the rank of Assistant Professor to the rank of Associate Professor requires: (1) a demonstrated record of effectiveness as a teacher; (2) a record of peer-reviewed publication and/or peer-reviewed creative activity which has contributed to the discipline or field of study, to the candidate's intellectual/artistic development, and to the quality of the academic unit; (3) a record of professional service appropriate to the discipline, the academic unit, and where possible, the college and/or the university; and (4) promise of growth in teaching and research or artistic/creative activity.

C. **Professor:** For promotion to the highest academic rank, the candidate's academic achievements and professional reputation should be superior. This rank can be earned only by the faculty member who has demonstrated continued growth in, and has a cumulative record of, teaching effectiveness, substantial peer-reviewed publications and/or peer-reviewed creative activity, and professional contributions and service.

Attachment B

Anchor University
Performance Evaluation Policy

All untenured faculty in tenurable ranks must be evaluated annually and informed regarding their professional performance. This evaluation shall be the primary responsibility of the academic unit chair or director, and it shall be made with regard to the criteria, standards, and guidelines cited in the university's promotion and tenure policy. Following the evaluation conducted at the academic department level, the faculty member shall receive a letter from the chair or director summarizing the content of the evaluation session. This letter will be copied to the college dean. The college dean will then hold a meeting with the faculty member in the presence of the department's chair or director to review the faculty member's progress toward meeting the tenure and promotion standard as established by the university and the college. This evaluation session shall include a statement of the programmatic needs of the college and academic unit relative to the faculty member under review. Following the evaluation session, the faculty member shall receive a written statement summarizing the content of the meeting from the college dean. A copy of this correspondence will be sent to the academic unit's chair or director.

Attachment C

Director's Evaluation Letter, Year One

TO: Igor Pryor
    Assistant Professor

FROM: George Overton
    Director, School of Music

RE: Annual Evaluation

It was a pleasure to meet with you and to discuss your many and significant achievements. The School of Music at Anchor University is most fortunate to have you on its faculty. Please keep up the excellent work.

cc: Dr. Jerome Steinberg, Dean
  File

Attachment D

Director's Evaluation Letter, Year Two

TO: Igor Pryor
          Assistant Professor

FROM: George Overton
          Director, School of Music

RE: Annual Evaluation

This memorandum is to document that you and I discussed your accomplishments and performance for the last calendar year, and have reviewed your progress in meeting the criteria and standards established for tenure and promotion.

You have informed me that you have recruited four new oboe students who will be coming to the university next semester. I realize that it is difficult to recruit students in your area, and I laud your efforts to do so.

During the last calendar year, you have been very active at recitals, most notably in your performance at Carnegie Hall. You have performed with the Woodwind Quintet in major cultural centers and have performed with various area symphony orchestras as soloist and conductor. Your work as a performer has been exemplary.

You have served the School of Music in many important ways; most notably, as manager of the Woodwind Quintet. Without your leadership the quintet would not have achieved the active concert position it now enjoys. In addition, you organized performance tours and directed the summer music camps. You have worked hard to fulfill the goals and aspirations of the School of Music.

You are one of the finest artists in the School of Music. I stand ready to assist you in every way possible in the future development of your work.

cc: Dr. Jerome Steinberg, Dean
    File

Attachment E

Dean's Letter

Dr. Igor Pryor
School of Music
Anchor University

Dear Professor Pryor:

Without question, you have managed to maintain an extensive performance schedule both as a member of the Woodwind Quintet and as a solo performer. I was pleased to learn that you have obtained several peer reviews on your performance with the Woodwind Quintet on the European tour and at the National Oboe Conference. The invitation extended for you to serve as the American representative of the Cambridge Classical Music Institute is further evidence of your growing reputation as an accomplished oboist. This activity will continue to expand your reputation as an accomplished musician.

Your description of the student evaluations of your teaching suggests that you will have no difficulty in substantiating your teaching effectiveness for your tenure review. I was pleased to learn that you did solicit peer reviews of your teaching, as well as your work in the music camps, as was suggested last year.

Since most of the peer reviews of both teaching and research/creative activity were sent directly to you, I suggest that you review these with your director in the near future. That will enable Director Overton to assist you in determining what additional documentation might be collected to advance the strongest case possible on your behalf.

You continue to serve the School of Music in several ways. Certainly, your work as manager of the Woodwind Quintet was integral to the success of the group's European tour. You represented the School of Music on the Faculty Advisory Committee which is an important contribution even though your attendance at committee meetings was disappointing.

Since you did not attend any of the university workshops on promotion and tenure, I was relieved to learn that you are comfortable with your understanding of the tenure and promotion procedures for the forthcoming tenure review. I was surprised to learn that you believe that you are not perceived favorably by some of your colleagues in the School of Music and that you fear this could result in an unjustified negative tenure vote. While I understand the inclination to attribute this to feelings of jealousy toward you because you have maintained such an active performance schedule, I cannot point to anything which might substantiate that fear. Indeed, I've seen several music faculty with strong performance records promoted and/or tenured over the past several years with a strong endorsement from their faculty colleagues. However, given your fear, I believe that it is most important that you review your documentation with your director as early as possible to be certain that the documentation is complete.

I enjoyed having an opportunity to review your activities and progress in collecting the documentation needed for a favorable tenure review. I hope that next year is both productive and rewarding.

Sincerely,

Jerome Steinberg, Dean

cc: George Overton, Director, School of Music
    File

SELECTED READINGS

Bennett, J. B. (1983). *Managing the academic department: Cases and notes.* New York, NY: American Council on Education/Macmillan.

This text presents short case studies on the responsibilities usually assigned to chairs. Section four of this text presents additional cases on the task of performance counseling.

Bennett, J. B., & Figuli, D. J. (Eds.). (1990). *Enhancing departmental leadership: The roles of the chairperson.* New York, NY: American Council on Education/Macmillan.

This text contains 26 essays which offer strategies and concrete guidance on many of the tasks and responsibilities typically assigned to the department chair. The essays on "Faculty evaluation: The roles of the department chair" by J. B. Bennett; "Chairpersons and faculty development" by K. E. Eble, and "Tactics and strategies for faculty development" by W. J. McKeachie are particularly relevant to this case study.

Eble, K. E., & McKeachie, W. J. (1986). *Improving undergraduate education through faculty development.* San Francisco, CA: Jossey-Bass.

The authors describe in detail the nature and purpose of faculty development programs and offer four specific case studies as illustrations of how to design and implement faculty development programs. In the final chapter, the authors link faculty development programs to the improvement of undergraduate education.

Gmelch, W. H., & Miskin, V. D. (1993). *Leadership skills for department chairs.* Bolton, MA: Anker Publishing.

Based on extensive research and practice, the authors offer a solid resource of practical information for department chairs.

Hartman, S. J., Griffeth, R. W., Crino, M D., & Harris, O. J. (1991). Gender-based influences: The promotion recommendation. *Sex Roles, 25,* 285-300.

The authors report findings from a study conducted to measure the effects of certain characteristics on promotion decisions. They studied: rater gender, ratee gender, the gender stereotype of the job, and the gender stereotype of the ratee's personal characteristics.

Hickson, M. III, & Stacks, D. W. (1992). *Effective communication for academic chairs.* Albany, NY: State University of New York Press.

This text includes essays written by communication scholars. Of particular relevance for this case study are the essays "Assessing faculty" by R. M. Smitts and "The performance appraisal interview: Guidelines for department chairs" by M. Stano.

Magnusen, K. O. (1987). Faculty evaluation, performance, and pay: Applications and issues. *Journal of Higher Education, 58,* 516-529.

The often elusive link between evaluation of faculty performance and the resultant salary recommendation is explored, focusing on a job-related evaluation process used by a college of business within a large state university system. Magnusen's analysis exposes the difficulties inherent even in a well conceived, carefully constructed evaluation process.

Miller, R. I. (1986). Academic promotion and tenure. *The Journal of the College and University Personnel Association, 37*(4), 19-26.

Miller discusses the six factors that continue to have an impact on promotion and tenure policies and procedures. These factors are: the economy of the state or region, political decisions, institutional planning, personnel planning, demographics and creativity. He suggests criteria to evaluate promotion and tenure policies and procedures.

Morris, V. C. (1981). *Deaning, middle management in academe.* Urbana, IL: University of Illinois Press.

Based on personal experience, Morris provides a realistic portrayal of the "middle manager" position of the academic dean. Written with wit and clarity, Morris analyzes the inner structure of campus management to depict the human side of personnel management, public and student relations, budget planning, affirmative action, faculty politics, salary disputes and tenure decisions.

Ormrod, J. E. (1986). Predictors of faculty dissatisfaction with an annual performance evaluation. *The Journal of the College and University Personnel Association, 37*(3), 13-19.

The author reports the findings of a study conducted to determine those factors which characterized faculty members most dissatisfied with the evaluation of their performance. She studied years of service, level of evaluation, impact on salary, and inconsistency among evaluators.

Russo, C. J., Ponterotto, J. G., & Jackson, B. L. (1990, Summer). Confidential peer review: A supreme court update and implications for university personnel. *Initiatives, 53,* 11-17.

A recent U.S. Supreme Court decision found that a university is not entitled to a common law privilege to withhold confidential peer review documents from a federal agency investigating allegations of employment discrimination. This decision has potentially far reaching implications for personnel decision on college campuses. The authors review the University of Pennsylvania case in detail, including the court's discussion of the first amendment and academic freedom, and draw conclusions for consideration by institutions of higher education.

Seldin, P. (1993). *Successful use of teaching portfolios.* Bolton, MA: Anker Publishing.

Written for an audience from the highest-level administrators to teaching faculty, the author provides information about the use of teaching portfolios from the institutional as well as the personal level. Sample portfolios and suggestions for using them for teaching improvement and for personnel decisions are provided.

Seldin, P. (1991). *The teaching portfolio.* Bolton, MA: Anker Publishing.

In this concise handbook for faculty and administrators seeking to improve teaching effectiveness, Seldin identifies key issues, red-flag warnings, and landmarks for success through the creation and maintenance of a "teaching portfolio." The emphasis is on how to construct and use a portfolio.

Seldin, P., & Associates. (1990). *How administrators can improve teaching: Moving from talk to action in higher education.* San Francisco, CA: Jossey-Bass.

The authors begin with the premise that effective teaching is under-rewarded in higher education. Special care is given to make clear the rule that administration must try to encourage and to foster teaching improvement.

Trotter, P., & Risdon, P. (1990). Performance counseling. *CUPA Journal, 41*(3), 21-24.

The authors advance the argument that performance counseling should take into account the three components that affect a faculty member's performance: department and professional goals; professional competencies; and factors that impede professional development. They define professional competencies to include: communication skills, interpersonal skills, decision-making and management skills, and skills in working with groups.

Tucker, A. (1992). *Chairing the academic department: Leadership among peers (3rd edition).* New York, NY: American Council on Education/Macmillan.

A text for anyone seeking more information about the roles and responsibilities often assigned to department chairs. Of particular relevance to this case are the chapters included in Part V, "Workload assignments, faculty evaluation, and performance counseling."

Tucker, A. & Bryan, R. A. (1991). *The academic dean: Dove, dragon, and diplomat (2nd edition).* New York, NY: American Council on Education /Macmillan.

This text offers a description of the roles and responsibilities assigned to academic deans. Specific chapters are devoted to the relationship of the dean to department chairs, to provosts and vice presidents, and to the faculty and students.

2

STATICS, TENSIONS AND ABRASIONS

About the Case

Conflicts can arise when different perceptions exist regarding the faculty's role and responsibility. These differences may be the product of culture, gender, socio-economic condition, and previous experience. Administrators frequently must resolve conflicts between students and instructors. To do this in a fair and equitable manner, educators must be prepared to investigate the complaints, to evaluate the evidence, and to judge the conduct of those involved. Listening to the initial statement of the problem, asking the right questions, and communicating so as to understand and to arrive at the desired outcome requires a combination of analytical ability and interpersonal communication skills. In this case, the associate provost at a large private institution is the first to become aware of the disturbing situation.

CASE STUDY

The associate provost, R. J. Talbot, sat quietly behind his large mahogany desk considering the tale being related to him by one of the institution's students. As was his custom in such situations, he listened and took short, to-the-point, notes. Dr. Talbot had considerable experience listening to student complaints, having served as associate provost for academic affairs at Clifton University for almost ten years.

Clifton, often compared to Northwestern University in Illinois, was a large private institution located in the sun belt. It was experiencing a strong enrollment increase, notwithstanding a recent hike in tuition. Private institutions are not vulnerable to the wrath of taxpayers when they raise tuition, but they are subject to the laws of supply and demand as they seek to market a product that some fear is rapidly becoming overpriced. Richard Talbot was himself a product of the private school system and was not concerned that Clifton had priced itself out of the market. He harbored a personal theory that private institutions had to keep their tuition rate sufficiently higher than state institutions in order to differentiate their educational product from that offered by the public sector.

Dr. Talbot had handled a large number of student complaints. Undergraduates at Clifton were typically good students with more than enough self-confidence. They prided themselves on being able to handle most campus situations, but also knew when to ask for outside assistance. Usually, student problems bubbled up through the administrative hierarchy from the classroom through the department and college, and would reach the provost's office only after the complaint had been given full consideration, but unacceptable resolution, at the dean's level. Occasionally, students seeking immediate relief from their problems would attempt to short-circuit the appeal route and start in the Office of the Provost. In those instances, Dr. Talbot typically listened and then helped the students understand why it was in their best interests to follow the normal appeal process, which paralleled the chain of command in making their concerns heard and in trying to get issues resolved.

Indeed, even as Dr. Talbot had waited for the student to arrive, he knew that this situation was different from any he had encountered previously at the university. The student had called in advance to make an appointment. Dr. Talbot had long ago observed that most students seeking prompt resolution through some action on the part of the provost's office would simply appear at his door. In contrast, when making this appointment, the student had indicated that she needed to discuss a matter which was "critical to her education and to her future." Dr. Talbot's secretary had forewarned him that this student had seemed cautious, and indeed nervous, in setting up the appointment.

The student, a tall slim brunette, introduced herself as Heather McIntyre, a junior in Clifton's College of Engineering and Computer Studies. She extended her hand and Dr. Talbot found himself the recipient of a strong, firm handshake. Ms. McIntyre seated herself and immediately launched into a description of what she described as a "serious problem." In relating the events leading up to this meeting, Dr. Talbot found the student to be quite articulate, but obviously shaken by the events as she described them.

The student began in a quiet voice, "One of my professors, Dr. Ahmad, hates me. I have him this semester for a required course. I just know that he's going to give me a lower grade than I deserve in Engineering 378. Worse yet, I have to take two more required courses from Dr. Ahmad before I graduate. I don't know what to do about the situation. I love engineering; I want to stay in mechanical engineering. I'm doing well in the courses, but if Dr. Ahmad fails me in three required courses, I'll be washed out of the program."

Dr. Talbot asked, "Why do you believe Dr. Ahmad hates you?"

"We just didn't get off to a good start this term," the student replied. "The very first time that I asked a question in class, it was obvious that he thought I was stupid. He never answered my question. In fact, he was somewhat insulting, implying that I was wrong to take up class time with my dumb question."

Dr. Talbot probed further, "Do you remember what you asked?"

Heather McIntyre answered politely, "No sir, not verbatim. But I do remember that it was a legitimate question. He was lecturing on the basic principles of heat transfer. I was asking for clarification about some part of his lecture that I did not understand."

Dr. Talbot interjected another question. "Was this your only run-in with Dr. Ahmad?"

"Oh, no! "said Heather. "After that, I tried to remain quiet in class, but about two weeks ago, I was having difficulty with one of his lab assignments. He distributes the lab sheets on Tuesday and we were to turn in our completed assignments on Thursday. Rather than lose any points for not understanding what he wanted us to do, I scheduled an appointment to see Dr. Ahmad during his regular office hours on Wednesday morning. When I went to his office, I asked him to explain what we were to do on the lab assignment for that week. I told him that I was a good student, but that I wasn't sure what he wanted us to do in the last part of the lab activity. He immediately stood up and started waving his arms. He was outraged! Then he shook his finger in my face and told me that I was insolent in my behavior toward him. He also said that my attitude had better change fast or that I was going to fail the course. I still don't understand what made him so angry. All I knew to do was apologize, but he kept shouting at me. There were other students waiting to see him. I was very embarrassed. Our whole meeting lasted only a few minutes. I kept apologizing and finally left without ever getting an answer to my question."

"How did you do on that lab assignment?" asked Talbot.

"I got a C," Heather noted, "because I missed a lot of points on the last section—the one that I didn't understand. In fact, I still do not understand how it is possible to standardize testing procedures across different material samples."

"How are you doing in the course overall?"

"Well, I got an A on the midterm," she said, "but it was an objective exam that was graded by Dr. Ahmad's graduate assistant. All my other lab assignments are B's and A's."

"Well, this doesn't seem like the end of the world, does it?" The associate provost said, forcing himself to remain attentive. Grades of B or C did not seem too catastrophic to him anymore. Many students who came to his office were appealing academic suspension. They were not good students and had transcripts to verify their activities in the classroom. Heather, on the other hand, apparently had very good grades, a good work ethic, and still thought she had a problem. He tuned in again to her narrative.

Ms. McIntyre replied, "No, but what worries me is that Dr. Ahmad is still very angry with me. Last Tuesday afternoon, one of my classmates went in to get help on this week's lab assignment. He told me that Dr. Ahmad asked him if he knew me. He said that Dr. Ahmad called me a 'troublemaker.' Dr. Ahmad also told him that my attitude had better change or I would fail the class. I don't understand what I ever did that was so wrong, but Dr. Ahmad seems determined to remain angry at me for it—whatever it is. He is even starting to write strange comments on homework assignments and other papers that are turned in and returned with grades."

"What types of comments?"

Heather McIntyre reached into her book bag and extracted a file folder. "Here, I brought the papers I got back this week." She opened a green file folder and extracted a number of sheets covered with incomprehensible mathematical calculations. Talbot regretted his solid liberal arts background, and vowed to drop by more engineering and science classrooms in the future.

Dr. Talbot took the papers from Heather and read the following comments from the margins: "Arrogance is no substitute for accuracy, C+." On another paper was written: "Your naiveté is evidenced in your work, C." On a third paper: "You had better check with your advisor about dropping this course, D."

"Have you talked with Dr. Ahmad about these comments?"

"No!" said Heather. "I was too afraid to approach him. That's why I came to see you. I don't know what to do. I don't have the nerve to go to his office again—but I have to pass this class—and those two next year. I don't say a word in class anymore. I am at a loss what to do next. I have apologized a number of times. When it was so obvious that Dr. Ahmad was angry with me, I apologized to him in front of the class, hoping it would neutralize what had suddenly become a very bad scene. I also apologized to him in his office when he got so angry because I asked for clarification about the lab assignment. I told him that I didn't mean to make him angry, but he wouldn't believe me. I thought that it might help if I wrote a more formal letter of apology so he might understand that I truly didn't intend to make him angry, but that did not work either."

"Did Dr. Ahmad acknowledge your letter?"

Ms. McIntyre nodded her head and said, "Yes sir, he crumpled it up into a ball and gave it back to me. I brought it with me in case you wanted to read it."

Dr. Talbot read the badly wrinkled letter (Attachment A). When he had finished reading the letter, he looked up and asked: "May I keep this?"

Heather McIntyre answered with a faint smile, "Sure."

Dr. Talbot had one more question. "Have you talked with anyone else at Clifton about this matter?"

Again the engineering student answered in the affirmative. "Yes. I talked with Ms. White. She is the college's academic advisor. She believes I made a terrible mistake. Ms. White told me that Dr. Ahmad is very defensive about his faculty status. He is less tolerant of interruptions and questions by students than most faculty. Ms. White believes that I offended him by asking questions which somehow implied that his lecture wasn't clear or his directions on the lab assignment were incomplete."

Dr. Talbot, beginning to feel like an interrogator asked, "Does her explanation seem plausible to you?"

"No, not really," answered Heather. "Dr. Ahmad answers questions asked by my classmates, like the one who also made an appointment to ask about the lab assignment. Jack told me that he didn't have any trouble when he asked Dr. Ahmad about the assignment. I really don't believe my tone implied anything that would give Dr. Ahmad reason to be defensive with me. He just hates me and I don't know what to do about it."

"Do I have your permission to discuss this matter with the dean of the College of Engineering and Computer Studies?"

"Sure," replied Heather, "if you think it would help. But please don't do anything to make Dr. Ahmad more angry with me. I still have to take two more required courses from him next year if I decide to stay in mechanical engineering."

Dr. Talbot, now standing to indicate that their discussion was coming to a close, said, "Let me review the matter with the dean and see if we can't come up with a way to resolve this misunderstanding. I'll get back to you in a few days. Be sure that my secretary has your campus address and phone number."

Heather said with obvious sincerity, "I hope you can do something, Dr. Talbot. You're my last hope. Thank you for your time."

The Next Day. Dr. Talbot's secretary brought him an envelope from the records office. It contained the information that he had requested regarding Ms. McIntyre (Attachment B). Having looked over the information about the student's academic record, Dr. Talbot now felt ready to talk with the dean of the College of Engineering and Computer Studies.

Let's pause here. . .

1. *If you were Dr. Talbot, what factors would you be considering as the basis of the apparent conflict between Ms. McIntyre and Dr. Ahmad?*

2. *What needs to happen for the conflict between Ms. McIntyre and Dr. Ahmad to be resolved?*

3. *Do you agree with Dr. Talbot's decision to discuss this matter with the dean of the College of Engineering and Computer Studies? What are the potential risks and benefits for Dr. Talbot in talking with the dean? What other options were available to Dr. Talbot? Specify the potential risks and benefits associated with each of your alternatives.*

4. *Is there any other information which Dr. Talbot should gather before his meeting with the dean? If so, please specify exactly what information you would want if you were Dr. Talbot and where you could expect to find it.*

5. *Has Dr. Talbot discovered a larger issue than the conflict between Ms. McIntyre and Dr. Ahmad? What other activities might be affected by this situation in the long-term, and in the short-term? Could this situation, for example, impact student recruitment and retention, the institution's reputation, faculty retention, and campus morale?*

6. *Give some thought to how you would broach the subject with the dean. Would you, for example, discuss the matter over the phone or schedule a meeting? Would you provide the dean with a written copy of your notes from your initial meeting with Ms. McIntyre?*

Meeting with the Dean. Dr. Talbot made an appointment with Dean Kenichi Obata, and walked across campus to the College of Engineering and Computer Studies still pondering the puzzle of Heather McIntyre. Dean Obata was incredulous at the story and quickly assured Dr. Talbot that he considered Dr. Ahmad to be an outstanding teacher. This posture did not surprise Talbot since Dean Obata was always quick to defend and protect his faculty. In fact, it appeared to be a conditioned response to any implied criticism.

Dr. Ahmad, the dean noted, had been at Clifton University for only two years and was still working toward tenure. "Hamed Ahmad was born in the Middle East but moved with his parents to the United States when he was in high school. He has his Ph.D. from MIT and had many job offers when he graduated. Clifton was lucky to get him."

Dean Obata continued, "You know, R. J., students who are having academic problems often find great solace in placing the blame on the instructor. Maybe that is the basis for the comments you have picked up about Hamed."

"I couldn't agree with you more, Ken," responded Dr. Talbot, adding, "but Heather McIntyre is not a poor student. In fact, she has a very respectable academic record."

"Heather McIntyre," echoed the dean.

Dr. Obata became perceptively more focused when he learned the identity of the student reporting this concern. In all candor, the dean exclaimed, "But she's one of our best students. Why would she complain to your office?"

Talbot replied, "Please understand. Ms. McIntyre was not complaining. She is worried about her grade and is seeking help to resolve a conflict she doesn't know how to handle. She told me that she apologized to Dr. Ahmad even though she didn't understand what she could have done to offend him. She even wrote a formal letter of apology which, by the way, he refused to accept. She doesn't know what else to try. If Ms. McIntyre is truly one of your better students, it seems to be in our best interest to help resolve this conflict between her and Dr. Ahmad."

The dean nodded solemnly in agreement.

Associate Provost Talbot said, "We could both talk with him, but I believe that he's likely to be less defensive if you approach him. Perhaps you can learn Dr. Ahmad's perception of what has happened in his interactions with Ms. McIntyre? What did she say or do to upset him so? You may also want to talk with your academic advisor because when Ms. McIntyre told her of this conflict, it didn't seem to surprise Ms. White. Perhaps there's more to the story than either of us knows at this point."

Dean Obata emitted a long sigh and said, "Sure. Give me a few days and I'll get back to you when I know more about it."

Let's pause again. . .

7. *Critique the associate provost's approach to the dean. Was the associate provost's purpose accomplished? Give some evidence to support your conclusion. Is the matter resolved?*

8. *Had Ms. McIntyre been a C- student, would the associate provost have handled the matter any differently? How? Why? What if Ms. McIntyre had been a C- student, but the daughter of a prominent attorney or Clifton alumni?*

Gathering Information. Shortly after meeting with the associate provost, the dean called Ms. White. He asked her about any students' comments she may have heard regarding Dr. Ahmad's teaching. Ms. White told him that most of the students seem to manage just fine in Dr. Ahmad's class, but there were a few who seem to get off to a bad start with him.

Dean Obata said, "I know of Ms. McIntyre's difficulty in working with Dr. Ahmad."

"Yes," she acknowledged, "I hated to see that happen. Once students have a falling out with Dr. Ahmad, they don't seem to ever get back in his good graces. Ms. McIntyre, as you know, is a great student so it's a real shame."

"Tell me about the other students who have had some difficulty with Dr. Ahmad."

Ms. White answered slowly as she contemplated that question, "Well there aren't that many. Let's see. Last semester Jane Anderson told me that he never acknowledged or answered her questions in class. He would say, 'that's in the text,' or 'I already covered that,' or 'you better start paying attention.' She said that he got very upset when she tried to see him during office hours for extra help. I only heard one other student complain about Dr. Ahmad. That was Beth Holbrook. Two years ago, shortly after his arrival, one day Beth came in and talked with me in my office. Her encounter was not too unlike the one described by Heather McIntyre. The only difference was that Beth was a senior when we hired Dr. Ahmad so she only took one course from him before she graduated."

Dean Obata asked, "What was Beth's grade in the course?"

"Let me pull that up on the computer..." The dean could hear the familiar clicking sounds of the computer keyboard as Ms. White accessed Beth Holbrook's transcript. "Oh yes, here it is. Beth got a D in her one course with Dr. Ahmad."

"Beth Holbrook was a good student. Is that right?" asked the dean, not willing to trust his memory.

Ms. White, studying the computer screen again, answered, "Oh yes. If it hadn't been for her course with Dr. Ahmad, this shows that she would have finished with A's or B's in all of the required engineering courses."

"Are those the only students you can recall complaining about Dr. Ahmad?"

Ms. White responded quickly, "Yes, I believe that's it. Like I said, there are just a few who don't seem to hit it off with him. If I think of any others, I'll let you know."

Dean Obata closed the conversation, "Thank you for your help. Do let me know if you come up with anything else or remember any other students."

Let's pause again. . .

Assume the role of Dean Obata as you consider the following issues.

  9. *Having the facts as Dean Obata knows them, you are to hypothesize an explanation of what might be driving the conflict between Dr. Ahmad and Ms.*

McIntyre. Be sure to substantiate your conclusions with facts when possible, and not pure conjecture.

10. *Given the information which you, as dean, have gathered, how do you intend to approach Dr. Ahmad? Would you, for example, talk with him or send him a letter documenting the specific nature of your concern? What factors will influence the strategy you have devised—your relationship (as Dean Obata) with Dr. Ahmad, his personality and track record, or the sensitivity of the issue? Be sure to specify the reasons for selecting the strategy you would utilize.*

11. *Script your introductory comments to Dr. Ahmad and your responses if he repeats his previously stated perceptions of Ms. McIntyre. Script any questions you expect to raise and the factual information you intend to present. If you decide to send a formal letter, generate a draft of it.*

Meeting with Dr. Ahmad. The dean has chosen to invite Dr. Ahmad to his office for a discussion of his teaching—at least that is the way the dean's secretary phrased it in setting up the appointment. Dr. Ahmad cordially greeted the dean, shook hands, and demonstrated his respect for the dean by waiting for the dean to ask him to be seated.

Dean Obata opened the discussion with a jovial, "You're about to finish your second year at the university and I wanted to talk with you about how things are going. Are you enjoying your life as a faculty member at this institution?"

Dr. Ahmad smiled and responded, "Oh, yes. My classes are challenging for me and my research is coming along very well."

"Tell me about the courses you teach. How are they going?"

Dr. Ahmad again responded with a grin and said, "Great. I'm really pleased with how well they are going. The principles of thermodynamics and heat transfer are not easy to convey to students. I still remember the first time I was introduced to conduction and convection. It all seemed somewhat obscure, but I pressed on. The students here are catching on quickly to some really difficult concepts."

Dean Obata noted, "We have some excellent students."

Dr. Ahmad nodded and said, "Yes, I've been most impressed."

Moving gently to the topic of the meeting, Dean Obata said, "I understand that you have one of our brightest women students in your Mechanical Engineering Applications class at the moment, a Ms. McIntyre."

Dr. Ahmad frowned and said, "She is not a good student."

Dean Obata pushed for more information. "Oh? Why do you say that?"

Dr. Ahmad continued, "She does not work hard. She is insubordinate. And most important, she is too busy questioning my authority as a faculty member to learn from me."

"What do you mean?"

Dr. Ahmad answered, "She questions me. She tries to say that I'm not being clear and does so in front of the whole class. She challenges my explanations of well-accepted engineering principles. She seems more determined to undermine my authority as the instructor of the course than to learn from me. No, she is not a good student and she is not doing well in my class."

One last pause. . .

12. *Evaluate Dean Obata's effectiveness in talking with Dr. Ahmad. Was Dean Obata correct to approach Dr. Ahmad or should he have delegated the problems and tasks to Dr. Ahmad's department chair? Under what conditions could this faculty/student conflict have been resolved by the department chair? Role play or script your approach.*

13. *As Dean Obata, where would you lead the discussion at this point?*

14. *What alternatives are available to Dean Obata in terms of resolving this situation?*

15. *Should the associate provost be involved in further resolution of this matter? Why or why not?*

Attachment A

Dear Dr. Ahmad:

It is very clear to me that you are extremely upset and angry with me. While I honestly do not know what I could have said or done to offend you, I do wish to apologize. I can assure you that I never intended to make you angry or upset. I sincerely hope that you will accept this letter of apology and forgive me for whatever has caused you to be so angry with me.

Sincerely,

Heather McIntyre

Attachment B

Clifton University
Student Report
Records Office

Name: Ms. Heather McIntyre

Home address: 107 Court Side Lane
Milford, XX xxxxx

Home phone: (xxx) 268-1997

Parents: Paul McIntyro and
Megan Phillips

Campus address: Brookside Manor, Apt. 6D
Sunset City, XX xxxxx

Campus phone: 645-2121

Total credit hours earned to date: 78

Total GPA to date: 3.67 (4.0 scale)

Upon admission:
ACT: 30   SAT: 1425
High school rank: 1 of 473 (Valedictorian)
National Merit Semi-finalist

Scholarships and Awards:
First year: Named Dean's List
Second year: Named Dean's List
Third year: Recipient of the Sanford
Laboratory Scholarship
for Academic Excellence

SELECTED READINGS

Balenger, V. J., Hoffman, M. A., & Sedlacek, W. E. (1992). Racial attitudes among incoming white students: A study of 10-year trends. *Journal of College Student Development, 33*, 245-252.

The authors report the findings of a study designed to analyze the attitudes held by incoming white students toward blacks over the 10-year period from 1978 to 1988, to determine if the racial attitudes held by whites has become more positive or negative.

Belenky, M. F., Clinchy, B. M., Goldberger, N. R., & Tarule, J. M. (1986). *Women's ways of knowing: The development of self, voice, and mind.* New York, NY: Basic Books.

Based on intensive interviews and shadowing with many women, the authors describe the multitude of obstacles that women must overcome in developing the power of their own minds. The "ways of knowing" that women have cultivated and learned to value are described.

Bok, D. (1991). The improvement of teaching. *Teachers College Record, 93*(2), 236-251.

Bok outlines practical steps for improving the quality of teaching at universities. Included among these guidelines are requirements for proficiency in English and adequate preparatory training.

Bossman, D. (1991). Cross-cultural values for a pluralistic core curriculum. *Journal of Higher Education, 62*, 661-681.

Bossman comments on the meaning and implication of cross-cultural studies, value orientation, and pluralism to the goals of a core curriculum. He concludes with five recommendations for assessing the core curriculum.

Boyer, E. L. (1987). *College: The undergraduate experience in America.* New York, NY: Carnegie Foundation for the Advancement of Teaching/Harper & Row.

The report examines the way in which the structures and procedures of colleges affect the lives of students. In addition to describing the current condition of higher education in America, the report offers suggestions for improving and strengthening higher education. Chapter 8 on "Faculty: Mentors and Scholars" has particular relevance for the issues addressed in this case.

Finifter, D. H., Baldwin, R. G., & Thelin, J. R. (Eds.). (1991). *The uneasy public policy triangle in higher education.* New York, NY: American Council on Education /Macmillan.

The authors discuss the impact of public policy on the issues of diversity, quality, and budget in higher education. Of particular relevance to this case study are the chapters entitled: "The Goal of Diversity: Access and Choice in

Academia" by Robert Zemsky and "Barriers to Diversity and the Myth of Equal Access" by Reginald Wilson.

Hall, R. M., & Sandler, B. R. (1982). *The classroom climate: A chilly one for women?* Washington, DC: Association of American Colleges, Project on the Status and Education of Women.

Using information obtained from empirical research, survey reports and individual responses to a "call for information" issued in conjunction with this project, Hall and Sandler describe both the subtle and not so subtle ways in which men and women students are often treated differently. The authors also suggest specific actions which might be taken to create a learning climate that would foster the intellectual development of all students.

Hall, R. M., & Sandler, B. R. (1984). *Out of the classroom: A chilly campus climate for women?* Washington, DC: Association of American Colleges, Project on the Status and Education of Women.

The authors offer a detailed description of those actions and events that take place outside the formal classroom but which impact students' personal and intellectual growth. The focus of the report is not on policies and programs, but rather on many common campus experiences which depict how some students are frequently treated outside the classroom in their relationships with faculty, administrators and staff, and male peers.

Harris, J., Silverstein, J., & Andrews, D. (1989). Educating women in science. In C. S. Pearson, D. L. Shavlik, & J. G. Touchton (Eds.), *Educating the majority: Women challenge tradition in higher education* (pp. 294-310). New York, NY: American Council on Education/Macmillan.

The authors describe the male bias that continues to exist in science and scientific pedagogy. The authors posit the belief that science and its pedagogy must be feminized so as to include values and methodologies associated with the female gender.

Henry, S. D. (1991). Higher education and cultural pluralism: A reawakening of ethics. *CUPA Journal, 41*(3), 13-19.

Henry discusses historical patterns related to cultural pluralism and ethics in the environment of higher education, and identifies three ethical issues facing higher education: the writing skills test, the selection of faculty, and the liberal education curriculum. He sees the focus on cultural pluralism as a positive force for an expanded discussion of this topic.

Kuh, G. D. (1990). Assessing student culture. *New Directions for Institutional Research, Number 68,* 47-60.

The author summarizes literature on student cultures and reviews approaches to assessing student culture which is believed to have a significant impact on many aspects of college life, including student learning.

Manning, K., & Coleman-Boatwright, P. (1991). Student affairs initiatives toward a multicultural university. *Journal of College Student Development, 32,* 367-374.

The authors present a model to assist in understanding an institution's progress toward a true multicultural environment, and discuss conflict as inevitable, positive, and essential to achieving the goals of multiculturalism.

Moses, Y. T. (1989). *Black women in academe: Issues and strategies.* Washington, DC: Association of American Colleges, Project on the Status and Education of Women.

The author describes the climate for black women students, faculty, and administrators in both predominantly white institutions and in historically black colleges and universities in terms of race and gender stereotyping. Recommendations tailored to the needs of black women are included.

Pearson, C. S., Shavlik, D. L., & Touchton, J. G. (1989). *Educating the majority: Women challenge tradition in higher education.* New York, NY: American Council on Education/Macmillan.

This text begins with the premise that educating women involves more than admitting them to institutions originally designed for men. The 29 chapters contributed by leaders in higher education are organized into four sections: (1) understanding women's diversity and commonalities; (2) learning environments shaped by women; (3) re-conceptualizing the ways we think and teach; and (4) transforming the institution.

Reynolds, A. (1992). Charting the changes in junior faculty: Relationships among socialization, acculturation, and gender. *Journal of Higher Education, 63,* 637-652.

The author uses case studies to demonstrate some of the changes that junior faculty encounter as they build relationships with their faculty colleagues and their institutions in the years prior to the tenure decision.

Sandler, B. R. (1986). *The campus climate revisited: Chilly for women faculty, administrators, and graduate students.* Washington, DC: Association of American Colleges, Project on the Status and Education of Women.

The focus of this report is on the subtle ways in which women faculty, administrators, and graduate/professional students are treated differently from their male counterparts. The effect of this differential treatment is to communicate that women are not considered to be first-class citizens of the academic community. Specific recommendations for changing this chilly climate for women are presented in the report.

Seldin, P. (1993). *Successful use of teaching portfolios.* Bolton, MA: Anker Publishing.

A superb resource for administrators and faculty seeking information about the implementation and use of teaching portfolios. Includes cases of institutions using portfolios for teaching improvement and personnel decisions, as well as sample portfolios from across disciplines.

Seldin, P. (1991). *The teaching portfolio: A practical guide to improved performance and promotion/tenure decisions.* Bolton, MA: Anker Publishing.

An excellent handbook for faculty and administrators seeking to improve teaching effectiveness. As a teaching improvement technique, teaching portfolios identify key issues, red-flag warnings, and suggest landmarks for success.

Seldin, P., & Associates. (1990). *How administrators can improve teaching: Moving from talk to action in higher education.* San Francisco, CA: Jossey-Bass.

The authors begin with the premise that effective teaching is under-rewarded in higher education. Special care is given to make clear the rule that administration must try to encourage and to foster teaching improvement.

Touchton, J. G., & Davis, L. (Compilers). (1991). *Fact book on women in higher education.* New York, NY: American Council on Education/Macmillan.

This text contains, in one comprehensive volume, data on women faculty, students, administrators, staff and trustees. It provides current data culled from the Equal Employment Commission, National Research Council, Bureau of the Census, National Center for Education Statistics, and Bureau of Labor Statistics. The text is organized into seven topical areas: demographic and economic trends which are significant to higher education; transition from high school to college; enrollments; degrees earned; faculty; administration, trustees, and staffs; and student financial aid.

Wines, W. A., & Napier, N. K. (1992). Toward an understanding of cross-cultural ethics: A tentative model. *Journal of Business Ethics, 11,* 831-842.

Starting from the premise that ethics is the systematic application of moral principles to concrete problems, the authors describe the ethical dilemma that results when moral values are applied to decisions made in cross-cultural settings.

3

COMPETITORS OR PARTNERS?

About the Case

In the same way that customers may trust that computer software and hardware manufacturers will always work closely together, people often assume that community colleges and four-year institutions of higher learning work together to plan the various curricula and courses. Students who elect to begin their postsecondary education at a community college are often unaware of the difficulty they may encounter should they elect to transfer credit to a four-year institution. In many states, community colleges and four-year baccalaureate institutions are often competitors. Both offer the first two years of college to all who enter. Even in instances where the number of incoming transfer students is greater than the number of incoming freshmen, four-year institutions are reluctant to shed traditional mission statements. Frequently, these institutions continue to compete for incoming freshmen and fail to work cooperatively with community colleges in an effort to improve their recruitment of transfer students.

CASE STUDY

West Orange Community College. Franklin Pearson, the dean of instruction at West Orange Community College (WOCC) glanced at his calendar and experienced a strange premonition. His next appointment was with Caroline McDermott, the college's director of admissions. While the dean was not certain of the topic for the upcoming meeting, he had an uneasy feeling that Ms. McDermott had come to report yet another obstacle to WOCC's efforts to work cooperatively with the state's four-year institutions.

He had long wrestled with the issue of diplomatic cooperation between the state's community colleges and the state's four-year degree-granting institutions. The community colleges, Pearson believed, had been established as a way to make higher education more accessible to more of the state's population, and were also intended to serve a growing number of nontraditional students. He himself was very sympathetic to these students who often needed to retool in order to secure better employment, or who were trying to obtain a higher education degree while struggling as a single parent.

Pearson knew that each year an increasing number of students found the lower tuition and the convenient locations of the state's community colleges to be very attractive. He was sure that this trend was emotionally threatening to administrators at the state's four-year institutions. Pearson was proud that WOCC gave struggling students the opportunity to pursue postsecondary education while living at home and/or without leaving their jobs. WOCC students could delay paying the higher tuition charged by the four-year institutions until at least their third year of college. A significant number of parents and prospective students from the local area mentioned this to him at every WOCC open house he had ever attended. Pearson was proud of WOCC's impact on the community and its people.

Pearson was a student of the entire higher education process and watched with interest as the state's four-year institutions gradually changed from institutions which attracted most of their students to the campuses as freshmen. Now educators, and even the press, were referring more and more often to some of these institutions as "senior" institutions with increasing numbers of students transferring to them.

Pearson knew that this movement had created controversy and confusion within those institutions since their original missions, as viewed internally, had not changed appreciably. Specifically, the faculty and administrators at the four-year institutions failed to alter their practice and failed to take any steps to acknowledge their changing mission and role in the state's higher education scheme. Four-year institutions continued to emphasize the recruitment of freshmen and did little to accommodate the special needs of the growing number of transfer students. Externally, in many cases, the state as well as students and their parents modified their views of the purpose of these baccalaureate institutions where four-year programs of study were built on the premise of a critical mass of majors beginning at the freshmen level. As a result of these long-held assumptions and organizational structure, Pearson could see that the state's community colleges and the four-year institutions were now blatantly competing head-to-head to recruit incoming freshmen.

In an attempt to make higher education more affordable and accessible, the state was offering its population, Pearson believed, a two-tier system of higher education. Pearson did not believe that his state had done an effective job of differentiating the role of each, which had the effect of creating serious competition between the community colleges and four-year institutions. In view of these developments, Pearson hired Caroline McDermott, who had six years of student recruitment experience, to work in West Orange's admissions office and manage all recruiting activities.

Let's pause here. . .

1. *Can you clarify what the goals of West Orange Community College are? What are the goals of this state's four-year public institutions?*

2. *What are the costs—and not only in terms of the finances—when missions change and goals are not met? List the factors, internal and external, that can force changes in an institution's mission. How can the leadership of an institution remain cognizant of changing conditions which necessitate changes in the basic goals of the institution?*

Pearson and McDermott both believed that community colleges fared very well in this competition with so-called senior institutions for the recruitment of incoming freshmen. The community college had a number of advantages over four-year institutions. WOCC's tuition was much lower, and students could also save additional money by commuting from home. In addition, WOCC students did not have to leave whatever part-time or full-time employment they had in order to pursue their education. All this made for a very healthy recruitment environment for McDermott and her staff.

The only dark spot in this otherwise bright picture, so far as Pearson and McDermott could see, was the transfer requirements created by the four-year institutions. Because community colleges did not set these requirements, they found themselves continually reacting to decisions made by others. Pearson and McDermott had often discussed this major dimension of the education equation that was out of their control. Community colleges did not set the transfer requirements at four-year institutions and continually found themselves in uncomfortable reactive modes.

McDermott and Pearson both understood the importance of being able to assure students that the two years of coursework completed at WOCC in English, mathematics, the humanities, and the sciences, would enable students to achieve junior standing upon transferring to a four-year state school. She knew that WOCC students, as very focused consumers, were not interested in taking more time and spending more money than necessary to complete their college education.

Prospective students would often asked McDermott if WOCC courses would be accepted by senior institutions in order to meet the freshmen and sophomore pre-major requirements. She knew that WOCC's success in recruiting students hinged on her answer to these important questions. If WOCC could not assure students on this point, its recruitment success could be in jeopardy.

South Central University. In order to deal with the issues of transferability of WOCC courses, Pearson and select faculty from WOCC worked with South Central University (SCU), the four-year public institution closest to WOCC, along with other senior institutions in the state to gain an understanding of course equivalencies. Faculty at the four-year institutions were invited to review the courses taught by WOCC and specify their equivalency to courses offered by SCU. These agreements, he noted, were nearly always initiated by the community college and were often slowly and painfully reached. Worse yet, the four-year institutions would often change their general education requirements without any advance notice to the community colleges. These changes were usually costly to the community colleges in terms of reputation, student morale and enrollment.

Pearson was particularly frustrated with SCU's ability to change its degree or course requirements without notifying any of the state's community colleges. Ideally, the community colleges and the four-year institutions should have been consulting with each other regarding the educational opportunities afforded the typical transfer student. Pearson would have been delighted to receive advance notification of ancillary changes now being made without consultation. But, because these four-year institutions viewed the community colleges as competitors for the same student populations, he felt that they had little motivation to work on clear and effective inter-institutional agreements.

Frustrating Developments. As Dr. Pearson finished this thought, he heard a knock at the door. Caroline McDermott had arrived for their ten o'clock meeting. After a brief exchange of pleasantries, the director of admissions moved directly to the purpose of their meeting.

Trying to keep the frustration from her voice, McDermott said, "Well, it's happened again. South Central University changed its general education requirements! Effective this term, their general education requirement for English increased from six to nine credit hours. Also, the mathematics requirement in general education is no longer satisfied with our three-credit course in algebra. South Central added other non-algebra topics to the math requirements. Of course, this means that WOCC students who transfer to SCU will have to take at least two more general education courses because their courses at WOCC will not fulfill all of South Central's requirements as we had advised them they would."

Pearson recognized both her frustration and the seriousness of the issue. He said, "I assume that we had no forewarning that this change had been approved and would be implemented with the start of this new term."

He had barely finished when McDermott responded with, "As usual, absolutely none!"

Pearson, thinking like a dean of instruction, said, "We'll need to reevaluate our curriculum and see what we might do in our general education transfer program—and in our algebra course in particular—to get back in line with what is now being required at SCU."

"Yes," agreed McDermott, "but at this point, we don't know what changes may have been made by the other four-year institutions in the state. For all we know, they may still be requiring an algebra course as their general education mathematics requirement."

Pearson continued to focus on the needs of the WOCC students and noted, "The largest percentage of our students will eventually transfer to SCU and we will need to offer a math course soon which that institution will accept as equivalent to its basic math requirement. I am also concerned about those who intend to transfer to other schools. When do you think we might learn what curricular changes have been implemented into the requirements of the other four-year institutions?"

McDermott, becoming tense, "Typically, we find this information in the newest undergraduate catalog for each of the four-year institutions which we receive as soon as they are printed. My staff is working through the ones we've received this month to see if any such changes can be identified." Pearson indicated that he wanted to be kept apprised of developments as her staff worked through the catalogs. McDermott left Pearson's office feeling that she had been correct in sharing this news with him, but also feeling that neither of them had a clue about what to do to rectify or at least improve the situation.

Pearson turned to the window after McDermott left. He considered that this most recent change implemented by SCU was yet another example of the difficulty that plagued WOCC and other community colleges throughout the state. He also knew that this latest change in the general education requirements of SCU must have been approved at least one year before it was printed in the just-issued undergraduate catalog. He felt sure that if SCU had notified the community colleges of the pending change in general education requirements, fewer students would have been caught in the middle.

Pearson knew that the state's community colleges must work out a more harmonious relationship with the state's four-year institutions. More specifically, Pearson was most anxious that West Orange Community College work out a more harmonious relationship with South Central University. How? He wasn't sure.

_____

Let's pause again. . .

3. *How could West Orange Community College approach South Central University about the issue of transferability of its courses? How might WOCC approach the other four-year institutions in the state? Who at WOCC is in the best position to initiate discussion with SCU? Detail the arguments that might be used to persuade four-year institutions to be more cooperative regarding such curricular changes. To change a competitive situation into a cooperative one, common objectives and benefits must be identified.*

4. *Which position at West Orange Community College should carry these issues to South Central University and to the other four-year institutions in the state? Why? Consider the responsibilities typically delegated to each level of administration for policy making and policy implementation.*

5. *Would anything be gained by joining forces with the other community colleges in the state? If so, how might that be accomplished? Would such a joint venture jeopardize the recruitment efforts of West Orange Community College?*

6. *What role might a state board or commissioner of higher education play in this area? Compare, for example, the role of a state board that is limited by statute to serve in a coordinating or record-keeping capacity with a board that has ultimate responsibility for prescribing the mission and the program inventory to the public institutions in the state.*

_____

SELECTED READINGS

Clagett, C. A., & Huntington, R. B. (1992). Assessing the transfer function: Data exchanges and transfer rates. *Community College Review, 19,* 21-26.

> The authors summarize the complexity of obtaining and reporting information on transfer rates from community colleges to baccalaureate institutions, and report on a voluntary data exchange of individual student information now taking place in Maryland. The necessity of defining certain variables (transfer goals, transfer programs, student course load, and degree completion) illustrates why transfer rates are not easily obtainable.

Cohen, A. M. (1992, February). Calculating transfer rates efficiently. *Community, Technical, and Junior College Journal, 62*(4),32-35.

> The author explains the importance of transfer data and defines key terms and methodologies, and the scope of the Ford Foundation grant given to collect data on student transfer from community colleges to four-year institutions.

Cross, K. P., & Fideler, E. F. (1989). Community college missions: Priorities in the mid-1980s. *Journal of Higher Education, 60,* 209-216.

> Comparing data from a 1984-85 administration of the Community College Goals Inventory (CCGI) at ten community colleges with responses obtained from eighteen community colleges in 1979, the researchers determined that the top goals and priorities for community college have changed very little. The authors contend that the future challenge for community college administrators will be to respond to social change with institutional integrity and continuing commitment to the communities that they serve.

Deegan, W. L. (1992, April/May). Proven techniques: The use and impact of major management concepts in community colleges. *Community, Technical, and Junior College Journal, 62*(6), 26-30.

> The author reviews the use and impact of various management concepts at community colleges and discusses the relevance of management theory and practice to the issues and problems cited by community college presidents.

Dougherty, K. J. (1992). Community college and baccalaureate attainment. *Journal of Higher Education, 63,* 188-213.

> Dougherty responds to charges of a "baccalaureate gap" between entrants of community colleges and of four-year institutions, analyzing the attrition rate at community colleges and four-year institutions, difficulties related to transferring, and the impact of "transfer shock" in the form of poor grades of students who elect to transfer. He concludes with recommendations to improve the transfer rate as well as attrition and retention patterns.

Dressel, P. L. (1987). Mission, organization, and leadership. *Journal of Higher Education, 58,* 102-109.

The author identifies eleven reasons for reorganization: new functions; separating of growing complex functions; new technologies; bypass individuals; outside funding to support new unit; internal and/or external pressure; greater diversity; focus on purposes and goals; to imitate or emulate changes at other institutions; personal views of new administrator; to attract attention. He then discusses the importance and interrelationships of the mission, structure and function of the institution.

Editors of the *Chronicle of Higher Education.* (1991). *The Almanac of Higher Education: 1991.* Chicago, IL: University of Chicago Press.

This volume provides descriptions and demographic data on higher education, including information on the trends and changes in higher education.

Fleck, R. A., Jr., & Shirley, B. M. (1990, Winter). Expert systems for transfer credit evaluation: Problems and prospects. *College and University, 65,* 73-83.

Following a discussion of the transfer credit process, the authors review progress made toward the development and use of "expert systems" which convert decision-making related to transfer credit evaluation into a more structured process.

Garrett, R. L. (1992). Degree of centralization of governance of state community college systems in the United States, 1990. *Community College Review, 20*(1), 7-13.

The author reports on a study conducted to assess the degree to which the governance structure of each state's community college system is centralized. State systems are rank ordered according to their assessed centralization index value.

Grubb, W. N. (1991). The decline of community college transfer rates: Evidence from national longitudinal surveys. *Journal of Higher Education, 62,* 194-217.

Grubb identifies and discusses three reasons why the transfer of students from community colleges to four-year institutions continues to be important. Using data from these studies, Grubb studies transfer and completion trends among students entering community colleges. He concludes with an analysis of the causes of the decline in the community college transfer rate.

Jones, J. C., & Lee, B. S. (1992). Moving on: A cooperative study of student transfer. *Research in Higher Education, 33,* 125-140.

This summary of a cooperative study of the effectiveness of student transfer centered on a community college in California, a campus of the University of California, and a campus of California State University. Key issues identified were preparation, persistence and performance. The results of the study revealed a clear profile of the successful transfer student.

Knoell, D. M. (1990, October/November). Guidelines for transfer and articulation. *Community, Technical, and Junior College Journal, 61,* 38-41. [Excerpted from *Transfer, articulation, and collaboration: Twenty-five years later.*]

Developed from the findings of a national study funded by the Ford Foundation on transfer, articulation, and collaboration, the author presents 29 guidelines for transfer and articulation that impact every level of decision-making from governmental entities to faculty.

Phelps, D. G. (1990/1991, December/January). Access, equity, and opportunity. *Community, Technical, and Junior College Journal, 61,* 34-37.

In this speech presented to board members and administrators at the 49th Annual Conference of the Association of Texas Community Colleges, Phelps summarizes the changing demographics of students served by community colleges and challenges those who shape the direction taken by these institutions to "face reality" and accept the fact that the so-called "traditional" student no longer exists.

Prager, C. (Ed.). (1988). Enhancing articulation and transfer. *New Directions for Community Colleges, Number 61.* San Francisco, CA: Jossey-Bass.

Prager assembles a collection of essays addressing the issues associated with articulation between two-year and four-year institutions and the resulting impact on transfer students.

Ringle, P. M., & Capshaw, F. W. (1990). Issue-oriented planning: Essex Community College. *New Directions for Institutional Research, Number 67,* 69-82.

Ringle and Capshaw describe an issue-oriented approach to planning and illustrate its flexibility for allowing an institution to respond to internal and external challenges. The application and usefulness of this approach at Essex Community College is detailed for the reader.

Roueche, J. E. (1988). The university perspective. *New Directions for Community Colleges, Number 64,* 53-60.

The author traces the forces that led to the emergence of community colleges and describes the ways in which universities inevitably influence the program and curricula of community colleges.

Stimpson, C. R. (1992, July/August). Some comments on the curriculum: Can we get beyond our controversies? *Change, 24,* 9-11, 53.

The author discusses the issues associated with building a curriculum that regains public trust and challenges faculty and administrators to move beyond the present controversies to a renewed ethic of professionalism that rises above ideologies and disciplines.

To-Dutke, J., & Weinman, E. (1991). Developing articulation agreements between two-year and four-year colleges: A program-to-program curriculum-based approach. *College Student Journal, 25,* 524-528.

The authors provide a description of a specific model used by Montclair State College to develop articulation agreements between two-year and four-year institutions.

Townsend, B. K. (Ed.). (1989). *New Directions for Community Colleges, Number 65.* San Francisco, CA: Jossey-Bass.

A collection of essays of various scholars regarding the issues and processes associated with building a "distinctive image" for community colleges.

Turner, C. S. V. (1992). It takes two to transfer: Relational networks and educational outcomes. *Community College Review, 19,* 27-33.

Following a review of literature which demonstrates how the transfer process may impede community college students from earning baccalaureate degrees, the author articulates the need for interinstitutional linkages which will require the breaking of current routines and practices.

4

Publish or Perish

About the Case

Perceptions, interpersonal relationships, and other behavioral patterns evolve gradually over time. People can react differently to the same stimulus— be it another person, an event, or an object. In this case, one person and that individual's actions are viewed in very divergent ways by others. Some see only the good, some only the bad, and one observer is in the process of changing some long-held assumptions. When perceptions or emotions blur reality, problems eventually develop. The other facet of this case involves the way this pivotal person sees himself. A change in the institution's mission alters the professional relationships among faculty. Well-intended encouragement from some faculty colleagues and the department chair translates into intense pressure to achieve.

CASE STUDY

The Accusation. Dr. Alexander Roderick, the chair of the English department at Great Rivers University, was deeply engaged in a discussion with Dr. Eleanor Phillips, a tenured associate professor in English. "Those are serious charges you are making against Tim Anderson. You could be sued for slander," he said in a low, firm voice.

"I can only be guilty of slander if I am lying. I am not lying, and I can prove it. Nor am I making these charges lightly. Tim has consistently padded his credentials in a fraudulent way. You're not willing to look at the facts because Tim's the department's favorite son," she countered. "You and the other members of the 'old guard' have always protected him."

"That's not true," retorted Roderick. "Tim has done very well here despite having to contend with some overzealous colleagues. What possible basis could you have for making such an outrageous accusation?"

"I'll tell you what I have found," said Phillips. "As you know, this is my third year on the department's personnel committee, which means that I look at and evaluate the accomplishments submitted by every faculty member each year. The accomplishments forwarded by Tim Anderson each year contain fraudulent exaggerations. In the past he has claimed to have been a "guest lecturer" in classes where he was merely one of several faculty invited to attend in order to field questions. This year, however, Tim reached an all-time low."

Roderick, clearly uncomfortable with this entire conversation, said, "I am not going to enter a discussion over semantics."

"Alexander, this is not a matter of semantics, it's a matter of ethics and accurate reporting," countered Phillips. "Tim also has claimed that he made a presentation at national professional organizational meetings when, in fact, his only role was to attend a meeting as a member of a caucus group. He's been doing these things for years, but now he's gone one step further. This year he claimed that he had a manuscript accepted for publication which I know for a fact has not been accepted."

Roderick was now fascinated with the direction in which the conversation had turned. "How in the world would you know that?" he asked. He could sense immediately that Phillips felt quite sure of herself regarding her response to his question. "I'm a reviewer for the journal he listed as having accepted the publication and I checked with the editor," she said. "His manuscript was reviewed and rejected."

Without thinking, Roderick blurted, "What right do you have to check on something like that? Besides, maybe Timmy intends to revise and resubmit it."

Phillips was neither convinced nor dissuaded by the chair's explanations. She continued, "Maybe so, but he should not list the manuscript as having been accepted. You better look at the information I've compiled and be ready to take some action. If you're not prepared to restore an ethical standard in this department, I'll take this to someone who will."

With that comment, Phillips dropped the file folder which she had been waving about for emphasis on the chair's desk, turned around swiftly and walked out.

The Reaction. Alexander Roderick was numb as he began to read and comprehend the file left by Eleanor Phillips. On the one side, he felt greatly annoyed with her for making such a big issue over the terminology used by Tim Anderson in his summary of his accomplishments for the year. After all, he reasoned, there was not really a significant difference between being a "guest lecturer" in a course and a "guest expert" invited to answer questions. It seemed to the chair that both duties had the same purpose (i.e., the education of students).

At the same time, he was deeply unsettled by Phillips' allegation regarding the rejected manuscript. Roderick had to acknowledge to himself that Phillips was absolutely correct, at least on that issue. Even if Tim had intended to revise and resubmit the manuscript, he should not list it as having been accepted. Roderick's stomach tightened as he found a letter in the file from the journal's editor making clear that Tim's manuscript had been reviewed and summarily rejected.

The "Favorite Son." Today was not the first time the chair had heard Phillips refer to Tim Anderson as the department's "favorite son." He had always dismissed the comment as being petty and driven by professional jealousy. Now, as he wrestled with new facts and his own conscience on the matter, Roderick had a clearer understanding of what the term "favorite son" might mean. He had to confess, if only to himself, that there was probably an emotional component involved in the department's evaluation and assessment of Anderson.

Timothy Carleton Anderson had earned his baccalaureate and master's degrees in the English department at Great Rivers. Tim had been the department's model student. Without exception, all of the older faculty who had taught him in class adored him and applauded his intellectual capability. But Tim's history with Great Rivers started long before his freshman year. Tim's grandfather had been, for years, the revered dean of Great Rivers' College of Arts and Sciences. In fact, the building that housed the English department today was named for Tim's grandfather when he retired over eighteen years ago.

Further, Tim Anderson's family had been connected with Great Rivers for generations. The Anderson clan had endowed a special speaker series, hosted cultural events, and established substantial scholarship awards. They continue to live in the area and are willing to speak out on a variety of issues, particularly when Great Rivers needs to garner community support.

The English department always felt honored and somewhat flattered that Tim Anderson had elected to pursue a major with them. Since the department only offered a master's degree, Tim went out of state for three years to earn his doctorate. Each summer, however, he returned to Great Rivers University where the department hired him as a term instructor to teach an introductory writing class. No one was particularly surprised when Anderson was offered a permanent tenure-track position with the university as he neared completion of his dissertation.

Anderson is now in his third year as a faculty member of the English department. From the beginning, Tim's return was welcomed by those whom Phillips referred to as the "old guard." In contrast, younger faculty hired since Tim's undergraduate days greeted him with some suspicion.

The Chemistry of the English Department. Much to the annoyance of Roderick, these younger faculty have watched Tim's every move. They were quick to complain when Tim's contract was extended through two academic years even though he had not yet completed his dissertation.

Originally, Anderson had been hired on what was called a contingency contract. The terms specified that he would start at the instructor rank and be promoted automatically to the rank of assistant professor upon the completion of his doctorate. According to the contract, he was to accomplish this before the close of that academic year. Phillips and a few others argued that Tim's contract should not have been renewed because he had failed to complete the dissertation. In response, Roderick and the senior faculty members argued that the department would be foolish not to renew the contract for another year since Tim had been one of the more productive young members of the department. Clearly, Roderick agreed with the older faculty and, accordingly, Tim's contract was renewed. The next year, the argument was repeated, a little more heatedly, but again the contract was extended.

Complicating this discussion was another important issue related to faculty activities: productivity. Productivity was increasingly important to the English department because the leadership at Great Rivers was changing the institution's mission. Research was rapidly becoming a more important evaluative component. An institution which at one time primarily emphasized teaching, Great Rivers now had promotion and tenure standards for its faculty which required substantial effort and success in research as well as in teaching. For this reason, the "old guard" had pointed to Tim Anderson with some pride. While his dissertation was moving along more slowly than had been anticipated, and still was not complete, each year Tim had produced a longer list of scholarly publications than any other junior faculty in the department, including Phillips.

Alone with his thoughts, Roderick wondered if Tim had been pressured by the department's expectations of him to exaggerate, and then to falsify, his accomplishments. Roderick was confident that the "old guard" would not be as outraged by Tim's action as Phillips had been. While he felt that it might be time to counsel young Tim on how to present his accomplishments more carefully, he was fearful that Eleanor Phillips would not be satisfied until formal charges were filed against Tim Anderson for unethical conduct.

Let's pause here. . .

1. *Assume the role of Dr. Alexander Roderick, the chair of the English depart-*
   ment. What actions, if any, would you take at this time? Specify both your
   objective and the action that you might take to accomplish this objective. Have
   you considered the perceptions of the various players in detailing the chair's
   actions?

2. *Should Tim Anderson's reputation and success as a "model student" influ-*
   ence the current situation? Why or why not?

3. *Is Dr. Phillips acting as an ethical member of the department in her concern*
   over Tim's credentials? Was it proper for her to check on Tim Anderson's
   manuscript with the journal editor? Consider the ethical responsibilities of
   faculty to promote academic honesty in students and colleagues. At what
   point does the responsibility become an intrusion on the rights and privacy of
   others?

4. *In what situations are department chairs obliged to surrender their personal*
   evaluations and pursue matters with some measure of objectivity? What pre-
   cautions or steps can an administrator take to ensure objectivity in decision-
   making? Is it possible, in some instances, to err by remaining too neutral or
   passive?

One Week Later. After a week of informal conversation, Roderick's expectations were confirmed. The "old guard" was convinced that Tim simply didn't know any better. They found the recommendation that formal charges be filed against him to be outrageous. How could the department file formal charges of unethical conduct against someone who merely didn't know or understand the acceptable practices? Phillips, on the other hand, insisted that any conscientious faculty member should know that it was unethical to falsify professional accomplishments.

Flashback. With the informal debate ensuing among the department faculty in their offices and in hallways, Alexander Roderick recalled another incident from the annals of the English department. About six years ago, the department graduated Anthony Tucker, a very personable master's degree student who came from a very impoverished home. The department had worked hard to recruit Tucker and felt a deep commitment to seeing him graduate and achieve successful employment.

This particular student was carefully nurtured through his master's degree program by the faculty. They assisted him in hurdling any and every obstacle to ensure that he graduated in a timely manner. As he neared graduation, two of the faculty worked with Anthony to help him

find employment. They assisted him in preparing his resume´ and introduced him to various contacts they had in the publishing field. When
Anthony took an entry-level position with a large Midwestern book pub-
lisher, the whole faculty was elated.

However, a few months after Anthony's graduation, the president of
Great Rivers received a letter from a scholar in California informing the
university that significant portions of Anthony's master's thesis had been
plagiarized from this person's doctoral dissertation. This was a serious
blow to the English department faculty. For months, they wrestled with
their own consciences as to whom was at fault. Had Anthony alone
behaved unethically? Or in their own haste, had they failed to make certain that Anthony understood all definitions of plagiarism? Had their eyes
been fixed on the goal and not on the process?

As Alexander Roderick listened to the faculty's heated debate over
Tim Anderson, he experienced the same uneasy feelings he had had
throughout the Anthony Tucker episode.

Where Do We Go From Here? The informal debate over Tim
Anderson's future became quite formal the next Friday morning when
Eleanor Phillips met with Alexander Roderick. She told him that she had
checked the faculty handbook and learned that university policy permitted an individual faculty member to file charges of unethical conduct
against another faculty member. Placing the handbook on Roderick's
desk, Phillips announced that she would be filing formal charges against
Tim Anderson according to university policy. That meant, she said, that
the charges would be filed with Roderick for his reaction and subsequent
recommendation to the college dean. The dean's recommendation would
eventually be presented to the academic vice president. Roderick knew
that Phillips was acting in accordance with the faculty handbook and had
expected her, at some point, to take this action.

Tim Anderson was acutely aware of the ongoing debate swirling
around him. He had even heard that Phillips planned to file formal
charges against him. Anderson had apologized with all sincerity to Roderick and to various members of the English department faculty for his
past actions. He understood that he did not have much of a defense
against Phillips' charges, but expressed his hope that he might be given a
second chance. He even offered to accept a zero salary increase to rectify
any unfair salary compensation he may have been given in the previous
two years based on his falsely enhanced productivity.

While Alexander Roderick knew that he would be obliged to forward
the charges filed by Dr. Phillips to his dean, he also knew that neither the
dean nor the academic vice president would be at all pleased to receive
them. Both the dean and the vice president were well aware that the
Anderson family had always been a valuable friend to the institution. Any

public airing of the charges would be costly to the respected Anderson name and to Great Rivers.

Let's pause again. . .

5. *Describe a possible course of action which might have convinced Phillips that it was not necessary to file formal charges against Anderson. How would such an action affect the informal issue of faculty conflict and ethical expectations? Assume the role of the chair, and indicate what you would do to achieve an informal resolution to the conflict before it escalated into formal charges.*

6. *At what point should the chair talk with the dean or others outside the department about this matter? Would it be advisable to forewarn the dean of the charges likely to be filed against Tim Anderson? Who else should be apprised of the growing conflict? Explain the reasons for your decisions.*

The Code of Ethics. Roderick picked up the faculty handbook, but did not turn to the section on formal grievance procedures. Instead, he turned to the American Association of University Professor's (AAUP) code of ethics and slowly reviewed the paragraphs which summarized the ethical responsibilities of the professoriate (Attachment A). Something had gone very wrong in his department. Faculty were pitted against each other. Tim had made some mistakes. Roderick, himself, was torn by his reaction to Tim's problems. The AAUP made it sound so simple, so obvious. Nothing in the English department seemed simple or obvious to Roderick.

Let's pause again. . .

7. *Consider the role of ethics in the chain of events in the English department. Critique the actions of Phillips, Anderson and Roderick in terms of the AAUP's statement as found in the faculty handbook (Attachment A).*

8. *Assume you are chair and had just reviewed the Code of Ethics. What actions would you take?*

Parallel Action. Even though Tim Anderson hoped that things could be resolved in order for him to stay at Great Rivers, he realized the severity of the situation and began applying for positions at other institutions. While Roderick understood Tim's reasons for doing so, it presented him with a new and equally difficult problem.

On the very day that he received Phillips' letter lodging formal charges of unethical conduct against Tim Anderson, Roderick also received a request from Tim to submit a letter of reference in support of his candidacy for a position at a comparable university in the South. Looking over the position description for the vacancy, he noted among the qualifications the stipulation that the applicant possess "professional integrity sufficient to serve as a role model for first-generation college students." To Roderick, it seemed that this nightmare simply would not go away.

One final pause. . .

9. *If you were in Dr. Roderick's place, would you agree to write a letter of reference for Tim Anderson under the circumstances? If so, describe what posture you would take in serving as a reference for Tim Anderson.*

10. *Specifically, to what extent is the chair obligated to mention the pending charges of unethical conduct that had been filed against Tim Anderson in a letter of recommendation? The chair recognizes that to do so may severely handicap employment opportunities for Anderson. To what extent is the chair obliged to disclose this information during any telephone follow-up of this letter of recommendation? Assume the role of the chair and script what you would say if the caller asks for an assessment of Tim Anderson's integrity? What would you do in the event that the caller doesn't mention this sensitive topic?*

11. *How does Tim's status, with regard to his yet incomplete dissertation and his one-year contract, impact the situation? How does it limit the chair's alternatives for assisting Tim?*

12. *Assume the position of department chair and draft a letter of recommendation for Tim Anderson.*

Attachment A

Great Rivers University
Faculty Handbook

Following is the Statement of Professional Ethics as published in the *American Association of University Professors Policy Document and Report, 1990 edition,* pages 75 and 76. This statement was approved by the faculty as part of its governing policy.

Professors, guided by a deep conviction of the worth and dignity of the advancement of knowledge, recognize the special responsibilities placed upon them. Their primary responsibility to their subject is to seek and to state the truth as they see it. To this end, professors devote their energies to developing and improving their scholarly competence. They accept the obligation to exercise critical self-discipline and judgment in using, extending, and transmitting knowledge. They practice intellectual honesty. Although professors may follow subsidiary interests, these interests must never seriously hamper or compromise their freedom of inquiry.

As teachers, professors encourage the free pursuit of learning in their students. They hold before them the best scholarly and ethical standards of their discipline. Professors demonstrate respect for students as individuals and adhere to their proper roles as intellectual guides and counselors. Professors make every reasonable effort to foster honest academic conduct and to ensure that their evaluations of students reflect each student's true merit. They respect the confidential nature of the relationship between professor and student. They avoid any exploitation, harassment, or discriminatory treatment of students. They acknowledge significant academic or scholarly assistance from them. They protect their academic freedom.

As colleagues, professors have obligations that derive from common membership in the community of scholars. Professors do not discriminate against or harass colleagues. They respect and defend the free inquiry of associates. In the exchange of criticism and ideas professors show due respect for the opinions of others. Professors acknowledge academic debt and strive to be objective in their professional judgment of colleagues. Professors accept their share of faculty responsibilities for the governance of their institution.

As members of an academic institution, professors seek above all to be effective teachers and scholars. Although professors observe the stated regulations of the institution, provided the regulations do not contravene academic freedom, they maintain their right to criticize and seek revision. Professors give due regard to their paramount responsibilities within their institution in determining the amount and character of the work done outside it. When considering the interruption or termination of their service, professors recognize the effect of their decision upon the program of the institution and give due notice of their intentions.

As members of their community, professors have the rights and obligations of other citizens. Professors measure the urgency of these obligations in the light of their responsibilities to their subject, to their students, to their profession, and to their institution. When they speak or act as private persons, they avoid creating the impression of speaking or acting for their college or university. As citizens engaged in a profession that depends upon freedom for its health and integrity, professors have a particular obligation to promote conditions of free inquiry and to further public understanding of academic freedom.

SELECTED READINGS

Atkinson, R. C., & Tuzin, D. (1992). Equilibrium in the research university. *Change, 24,* 21-31.

The authors define three missions of the institutions (propagation of knowledge, creation of knowledge, and application of knowledge), while noting a number of signs that the research university is in crisis (i.e., books on this topic, people are losing faith, scientific fraud exposed, and scarcity of research funds). This has led to what the authors call "a sense of estrangement" between teaching and research, and between undergraduates and faculty. Taking a critical look at undergraduate education, the need for freshman to declare a major, and the general education curricula, the authors show how research specialization impacts on these areas.

Bennett, J. B. (1983). *Managing the academic department: Cases and notes.* New York, NY: American Council on Education/Macmillan.

In this text, Bennett presents short case studies on the responsibilities usually assigned to chairs. Section Four of this text provides more cases dealing with the task of performance counseling.

Bennett, J. B., & Figali, D. J. (Eds.). (1990). *Enhancing departmental leadership: The roles of the chair.* New York, NY: American Council on Education/Macmillan.

This text contains 26 essays which offer strategies and concrete guidance on many of the tasks and responsibilities often assigned to the department chair. The essays on "Faculty evaluation: The roles of the department chair" by John B. Bennett; "Chairpersons and faculty development" by Kenneth E. Eble; and "Tactics and strategies for faculty development" by Wilbert J. McKeachie are particularly relevant to this case.

Blackburn, R., & Wylie, N. (1990). Current appointments and tenure practices. *CUPA Journal, 41, 3,* 9-21.

The authors, responding to concerns of junior faculty regarding their tenure, offer an analysis of faculty success in receiving tenure at twelve institutions over a seven-year period.

Bok, D. (1988, Summer). Can higher education foster higher morals? *Business and Society Review, 66,* 4-12.

As president of Harvard University, Bok defines the elements of a comprehensive program of moral education in higher education: courses in applied ethics; discussions of rules of conduct with students and fairly administering them; programs of community service; high ethical standards in institutional decision-making; and a campus climate that supports ethical standards. His challenge to the academic community is clear and forceful—and worthy of individual or collective consideration.

Boyer, E. L. (1990). *Scholarship reconsidered: Priorities of the professoriate.* Princeton, NJ: Carnegie Foundation for the Advancement of Teaching.

Boyer argues that the renewed interest in increasing and preserving the quality of undergraduate education will be achieved only by the way scholarship is defined and rewarded. Boyer advances the term "scholarship" as a broader, more appropriate concept than the old "teaching versus research" debate. Boyer suggests that the work of faculty encompasses four separate, though overlapping, functions: scholarship of discovery; scholarship of integration; scholarship of application; and the scholarship of teaching.

Brown, R. S. (1986, September/October). Can they sue me? Liability risks from unfavorable letters of reference. *Academe, 72,* 31-32.

The law is not clear in these areas. Although the writer of an unfavorable letter of reference can be sued, the truth is a strong defense which therefore allows a letter writer to be candid. The reference seeker must establish that the reference is untrue.

Creswell, J. W., Wheeler, D. W., Seagren, A. T., Egly, N. J., & Beyer, K. D. (1990). *The academic chair's handbook.* Lincoln, NE: University of Nebraska.

This handbook offers specific strategies for department chairs in working with faculty and in developing their own leadership capabilities. The strategies presented evolved from interviews with 200 successful academic chairs from 70 campuses. Of particular relevance to this case is Chapter 5 entitled, "Help newly-hired faculty become adjusted and oriented."

Essex, N. L. (1990). When administrators evaluate: Precautions to take when recommending job applicants. *Educational Horizons, 68*(3),158-160.

The author recommends that extreme care be exercised when responding to inquiries regarding the suitability of a prospective employee. He offers ten guidelines to assist administrators when faced with having to produce a statement of reference.

Morris, V. C. (1981). *Deaning, middle management in academe.* Urbana, IL: University of Illinois Press.

Based on personal experience, Morris provides a realistic portrayal of the "middle manager" position of the academic dean. Written with wit and clarity, Morris analyzes the inner structure of campus management to depict the human side of personnel management, public and student relations, budget planning, affirmative action, faculty politics, salary disputes, and tenure decisions.

Ommeren, R. V., Sneed, D., Wulfemeyer, K. T., & Riffe, D. (1991, Fall). Ethical issues in recruiting faculty. *CUPA Journal, 41*(3), 29-35.

This article focuses on the ethics of hiring practices in higher education, surveys faculty recently hired, itemizes issues involved in the hiring process, and concludes with recommendations for job applicants, search committees, and administrators.

Reynolds, A. (1992). Charting the changes in junior faculty: Relationships among socialization, acculturation, and gender. *Journal of Higher Education, 63,* 637-652.

The author uses case studies to demonstrate some of the changes that junior faculty encounter as they build relationships with their faculty colleagues and their institutions in the years prior to the tenure decision.

Sykes, C. J. (1988) *ProfScam: Professors and the demise of higher education.* Washington, DC: Regency Gateway.

The author asserts that the culture of the American professoriate is the reason for the collapse of higher education in the United States. This professional culture offers encouragement in the form of rewards for the publication of trivial research findings, communicates in impenetrable jargon to mask the lack of substance, and exudes hostility to good teaching.

Tucker, A., & Bryan, R. A. (1991). *The academic dean: Dove, dragon, and diplomat (2nd edition).* New York, NY: American Council on Education/Macmillan.

This text offers a description of the roles and responsibilities assigned to academic deans. Specific chapters are devoted to the relationship of the dean to department chairs, to provosts and vice presidents, and to the faculty and students.

Tucker, A. (1992). *Chairing the academic department: Leadership among peers (3rd edition).* New York, NY: American Council on Education/Macmillan.

Part II of this book includes five chapters which describe and discuss the various roles and responsibilities typically assigned to the department chair. Also discussed are the chair's roles in decision-making, bringing about change, and delegating work to faculty committees. Of particular relevance to this case study are the chapters in Part V, "Workload assignments, faculty evaluation, and performance counseling."

Vander Waerdt, L. (1987, October 7). How to maintain your integrity and avoid liability for giving honest references. *The Chronicle of Higher Education, 34,* B2-B3.

This lawyer summarizes court findings and offers straightforward advice for administrators to provide honest negative information when asked to evaluate colleagues.

5

TRANSITIONS

About the Case

This case portrays the difficulties encountered by a seasoned dean when a new vice president for academic affairs is hired. The new vice president's agenda makes change inevitable for a university which has enjoyed a certain stability and predictability from its senior administrators. The focus of this case is on the response of the dean of the College of Fine Arts to the institution's new criteria for judging program effectiveness in an environment of reduced state funding. More specifically, the College of Fine Arts is judged by the new vice president as being extremely cost-ineffective. Initially, the dean must balance his need to create and maintain a positive working relationship with the new vice president with his duty to advocate strongly for his college.

CASE STUDY

Frances Adams was in her tenth year as the dean of the Midwest University's (MU) College of Fine Arts (CFA). Like most deans on the MU campus, Dr. Adams came to the institution as an untenured assistant professor after completing her doctorate in music education at a prestigious Eastern university. Following her promotion to the rank of professor she was named director of the School of Music, a position she held for eight years before being named dean.

Many colleagues believed that Dean Adams would be a competitive candidate at some future date for the vice presidency at MU. She was noted for her sensitivity and responsiveness to the wishes of the faculty who individually and collectively held their dean in high regard. She had also been highly visible on campus contributing to several significant campus-wide initiatives, including a committee charged with recognizing the outstanding faculty researcher and serving as chair of the university's centennial celebration.

The College of Fine Arts is comprised of four departments: art and design, music, theatre, and dance. Enrollment in all departments has declined, but not at a greater rate than experienced in similar programs across the country. More recently, the college made a greater attempt to better define those ways in which their courses could service other departments and program majors. For example, faculty in the area of dance, along with faculty from the School of Social Work, are discussing the possibility of offering some basic movement courses for students who plan to work with senior citizens.

In general, the faculty in the college are good instructors devoted to educating students and to providing the surrounding area with the only available cultural offerings within a radius of 150 miles. The theatre productions at Midwest University—as well as the music and dance performances—are extremely well attended. It is not unusual for all the tickets to be sold well in advance of opening night. For these reasons, Oakville, the home of Midwest University, is often called the "cultural oasis" of this Great Plains state.

The University. Midwest University is a large, doctoral granting, public institution located 150 miles from the nearest major city, in a town with a population of 35,000. While Oakville has some light manufacturing industry, farming and the university are the two major economic endeavors within the surrounding region. Except for those individuals who were recruited to the area by the university, the town is populated by persons native to the region. Superimposed on this environment is a heavy religious fundamentalism among the native population.

For the past seven years, MU enrollment has ranged between 18,000 and 20,000 students. Almost five percent of the students commute from neighboring towns; 65 percent live in university residence halls with the remainder living in off-campus housing. Graduate students are recruited nationwide and comprise roughly 25 percent of the total student enrollment. Most undergraduate students are state residents and are, primarily, the first persons in their families to attend college.

This mix provides the community with a blend of professional people with advanced degrees (typically from outside the region), blue collar workers involved in light industry and in technical and office support positions at the university (typically those native to the area), self-employed agricultural workers, and 20,000 young persons between the ages of 18 and 30. Oakville has a limited tax base, finite town resources, and a disproportionate number of young adults.

MU, considered by educators to be a strong regional public institution, was founded in response to the well-articulated educational needs in that part of the state. Consequently, the university enjoys a warm relationship with people from the surrounding area. For decades, senior university administrators played a significant role in the economic development and management of Oakville and its surrounding communities.

The university has successfully recruited talented faculty and administrators who move to Oakville and often stay until retirement. For this reason, there has been little turnover in the central leadership of the university during the past 25 years.

The President. The current president, Dr. Frederick Wickham, was recruited to the university as chair of the English Department more than 30 years ago. Having served the university as dean of the College of Liberal Arts, and as vice president for academic affairs before assuming the position of president, Dr. Wickham knows and cherishes every aspect of the university. At age 67, President Wickham has taken several actions to ensure the future of the university beyond his scheduled retirement in three years.

One such move was his decision to hire a new vice president for academic affairs from outside the university. Because Midwest University was accustomed to selecting senior administrators from within, this hire served notice to the campus community that change was imminent. From the faculty's perspective, this action of the president broke a valued tradition. While the president knew that anyone brought in from the outside at the rank of vice president would be met with suspicion, he deemed it an important step and an administrative necessity.

The president observed that MU was facing long-term financial difficulties as the state confronted some unpleasant realities. Income revenue in the state had decreased sharply over the past few years while the unemployment rate and the state's population receiving welfare assistance continued to grow. President Wickham judged it to be extremely important to the future of the university to have leadership experienced in taking positive action in times of tight fiscal resources. He believed that this was preferable to the comfort and complacency which would be experienced had he promoted someone with a long history at the university. Dr. Wickham felt that the *quid pro quo* was worth it.

The Vice President. The newly arrived vice president for academic affairs, Dr. Roger Hufford, has lived up to every expectation. He moved quickly and in hitherto unexpected ways, demonstrating a superb talent for managing and generating fiscal resources.

By working closely with the Office of University Relations, the vice president made new and significant links with business leaders in the nearest major metropolitan area. The university received two sizable contracts to do human resources training for Fortune 500 corporations. In addition, the vice president showed much finesse in working with the alumni and other friends of the university. After just six months in the position, the contributions received from telefund activities doubled that received the previous year.

During his first eight months on campus, Hufford set a completely new agenda for the university. He worked closely with the Office of Institutional Research to obtain comparative data on the relative cost-effectiveness of each graduate and undergraduate academic program. He was the first academic vice president to look closely at the expenditures within academic affairs by department in relationship to that unit's overall productivity.

This analysis revealed an inequitable and varied workload across campus. In some departments, faculty routinely taught one, three-credit course per semester while in other departments, faculty taught three or four, three-credit courses per semester. The load variation was attributable to release time for other activities. In many departments, faculty had their teaching loads reduced to allow more time for research or to compensate for a heavy committee assignment. In other departments, however, all research and service activities were simply additions to the full teaching load of three or more classes.

Armed with a detailed comparative analysis of faculty workloads, department productivity, and program cost-effectiveness at MU, the vice president planned to hold meetings with each academic dean to review the data on each college relative to the university norm and the vice president's personal expectation for that college. As might be predicted, the message to each dean and subsequent discussion would be as varied as the data on each college.

The Issue. The data from MU's Office of Institutional Research, gathered at the request of Vice President Hufford, show the College of Fine Arts (CFA) to be a very costly entity when compared against university averages. The college seems to be at the wrong end of each continuum being studied in the vice president's current analysis. Program enrollments are low, yet faculty workloads are high.

Dean Adams knows that the programs offered in the College of Fine Arts are deceptively equipment intensive. For example, students majoring in theatre not only learn to act, but also to operate computerized light and sound boards, to design costumes and to construct sets. In addition, students apply these acquired skills within the context of an actual performance. This requires that the Theatre Department run a production program which allows students numerous opportunities to practice in order to utilize and perfect these skills. However, to offer a series of shows each semester requires additional costs associated with the box office and publicity aspects of theatre. Taking this into consideration, Dean Adams was not shocked by the data on the College of Fine Arts provided to her by the vice president during their first meeting (Attachment A).

In this initial meeting with the vice president, Dean Adams was surprised by the attitude of the vice president regarding the data—he either did not understand or would not accept Adam's explanations. Adam's felt the music curriculum could serve as the basis of her explanation, but soon discovered it was virtually impossible to convince the vice president, for example, that one-on-one instruction and small class enrollment was essential to the effectiveness of the instrumental music program.

In the face of such explanations (read "excuses"), Vice President Hufford, a geologist by training, insisted that he understood the need to give slower music majors some individualized attention, but believed that such "extra" assistance should be provided during office hours or as part of a group laboratory experience. The meeting ended cordially but with neither individual satisfied with its results. A second meeting was scheduled for the following week.

In preparation for her second meeting with the vice president, Dean Adams collected additional information on the College of Fine Arts (Attachment B). The data assembled by Adams demonstrated that, overall, the college's enrollment had increased during the past five years. Furthermore, the overall increase in the total credit hours generated by the college made it clear that the departments in the College of Fine Arts provided course work to students in *other* degree programs as well. Indeed, every CFA department taught at least one course which was required of all MU students as part of the university's general education curriculum.

Let's pause here. . .

Assume you are dean of the College of Fine Arts. You have only a few days to make some very important strategic decisions. The following discussion questions should help you retrace the action thus far and calculate your next move.

1. *What are the issues of the impending conflict? What might you, as dean of the College of Fine Arts, have done to anticipate and to minimize the existing differences of opinion with the vice president? How might you, as dean, address the vice president's financial concerns regarding your college? Be sure to explain why your prescribed plan of action would be likely to work given the other personalities involved and the present campus environment.*

2. *Would you, as dean, seek to involve the president in this ongoing discussion? If so, what role would you have the president take? Be clear in explaining how you would have the president learn of this conflict and what you believe*

he should do, if anything, about the ongoing disagreement. If you prefer not to involve the president, explain why you feel this should be avoided.

3. *At this point, would you, as dean, inform the faculty in your college of your discussion with the vice president? List both the risks and gains associated with informing the CFA faculty of the unsettled nature of your disagreement with the vice president. If yes, how would you communicate with the faculty on this matter?*

4. *How would you rate the dean's data (attachment B)? What arguments can the dean make using these data? How do you think the vice president will react to these arguments? What other data might be assembled for the dean's use? Are there other arguments you would make on the college's behalf? Consider what external constituencies might be used or invoked to provide additional leverage for the position being advanced.*

Meeting Two. At the second meeting, much to the dean's dismay, the vice president seemed to perceive the dean's new information as irrelevant to the central issue at hand. As Dean Adams persisted in her explanations, she could tell that the vice president was becoming somewhat annoyed with what he perceived to be the dean's unwillingness to accept the clear facts regarding her college. The vice president wanted the dean to become a team player, and to implement the needed changes.

The vice president rejected the dean's data and noted that despite the "modest" increase in enrollment and student credit hours generated, the college cost per credit hour was "obscene" when compared with the university average. Dean Adams attempted, again, to explain the need for individualized instruction and small class sizes for students majoring in the fine arts, but the vice president snapped back by saying that "perhaps the university, then, can no longer afford to offer degree programs in the fine arts." After an hour-long meeting, which was frustrating to both individuals, the dean left the vice president's office sure that she had not been heard, but not sure what to do next.

That same day, the vice president's secretary called Dean Adam's office to schedule a third meeting on this same subject. The meeting was set for Friday, just three days after the second meeting. Adams has to decide whether to capitulate in order to minimize her losses or to attempt to devise a new strategy.

Let's pause one last time. . .

5. *Why were the data presented by the dean at the second meeting rejected by the vice president? What gaps are left between what the vice president was asking*

and what the dean was presenting? Consider how the dean's arguments and data would need to be presented in order to be persuasive to the vice president. How can the dean adapt his communication to the vice president's perspective?

6. *Have the discussions to date between the dean and the vice president altered or limited the options remaining for the dean? If so, explain why and how. Compare the vice president's initial perception of the dean with his modified perception following the two meetings described in this case.*

7. *Would the College of Fine Arts be better served if its dean stopped trying to explain its status quo to the vice president and agreed that the academic programs in the college will have to become more cost-effective if they are to survive in the present environment? Consider at what point advocacy becomes counterproductive.*

8. *If the dean were to accept the vice president's assumptions about the programs in the College of Fine Arts and attempt to make all of its programs more cost-effective, how should this change be communicated to the faculty? Should, for example, the dean recommend to the faculty ways in which the college programs might be made more cost-effective or simply explain the new parameters for achieving cost-effectiveness and ask the faculty to generate solutions? To what extent should the dean communicate directly with the faculty and to what extent should she rely on department chairs to communicate relevant information to the faculty? You may find it helpful to review the roles and responsibilities assigned to chairs and to deans.*

9. *Does the dean have any alternatives other than: (a) to continue her discussions with the vice president in an effort to have the vice president better understand the college; (b) to accept her "marching orders;" or (c) to devise ways to make the programs in the college more cost-effective? If so, please explain what other alternatives remain for the dean?*

10. *As Dean Adams, what course of action would you take at this point? Is there a better way to educate the vice president without offending or alienating him? By assessing the vice president's personality from the facts presented in this case, can you predict the probability of your success?*

11. *Has the vice president acted appropriately for his position? Could the vice president have averted the outcome of this growing conflict without jeopardizing his plan for the university? You may find it helpful to review the conditions conducive to initiating change.*

Attachment A: Vice president's data

College of Fine Arts (CFA) – Midwest University (MU)
Faculty Productivity
A Fiscal Year (FY) Report

	Instruction Lower Division (100-200 level courses)	Instruction Upper Division (300-400 level courses)	Instruction Graduate	Total
Student Credit Hours Generated	18,414	19,812	3,144	41,370
Faculty Cost	$391,953	$1,152,172	$475,239	$2,019,364
Cost per credit hour (CFA)	21.29	58.16	151.16	48.81
Cost per credit hour (MU)	23.39	41.10	105.78	43.40
Administrative Cost				$1,411,362
Cost per credit hour (CFA)				34.12
Cost per credit hour (MU)				24.59
Support Cost	$488,017	$732,035	$126,497	$1,346,549
Cost per credit hour (CFA)	26.50	36.95	40.23	37.38
Cost per credit hour (MU)	18.75	21.25	35.43	25.10
Institutional Support				$753,587
Cost per credit hour (CFA)				18.22
Cost per credit hour (MU)				17.87
Operation and Maintenance				$1,138,687
Cost per credit hour (CFA)				27.52
Cost per credit hour (MU)				25.50
Total All Costs				$6,669,549
Cost per credit hour (CFA)				161.22
Cost per credit hour (MU)				98.75

University Definitions Used to Generate College Productivity Data

The following definitions were developed to provide uniform treatment of the inputs of student credit hours, state appropriations expenditures, and reported faculty/staff effort. These definitions provide structure and guidelines for the allocation of direct and indirect costs associated with providing instruction to students.

1. Student Credit Hours Generated — The total credit hours generated for all enrollments continuing after the deadline to drop a course for each term are accumulated by course number and by educational level of the student (lower division, upper division, and graduate).

2. Faculty Cost — Salaries paid to people who teach in all ranks is broken down according to course number and level, and applied to appropriate colleges.

3. Administrative Cost — The salary of administrative staff who support the instructional activity becomes part of the cost of instruction even though these individuals do not directly teach or generate student credit hours. This cost is charged to the college in which the individuals work.

4. Support Cost — The college's fiscal year budget for such items as equipment, travel, supplies, telecommunications, student wages, and contractual services. The support costs must eventually become part of the cost of instruction.

5. Institutional Support — Each department benefits from centralized services which support instruction. Examples of these services would be the university library, the museum, the campus health service, student placement, admissions and records, and counseling. Each college's share of these overhead costs is computed by determining the college's share of the total university budget.

6. Operation and Maintenance — This category includes those services to campus grounds and facilities. The cost charged to each college is determined by the routine service needed exclusively by that college in addition to the college's share of general operating and maintenance expenses. For example, the Physical Education course which requires the exclusive use of one swimming pool causes the cost of maintaining that pool to be charged to the College of Education. That college also will be charged a percentage of the general building upkeep in which it is located.

Attachment B: Dean's data

College of Fine Arts
Historical Data

Number of Student Majors by Academic Year (AY)

Department Degree Level	Current AY minus 4	Current AY minus 3	Current AY minus 2	Current AY minus 1	Current AY
Art and Design					
Undergraduate	270	265	300	305	310
Graduate	33	35	35	36	37
Dance					
Undergraduate	41	43	40	44	45
Graduate	7	8	6	7	6
Music					
Undergraduate	120	115	112	110	108
Graduate	20	19	17	17	14
Theatre					
Undergraduate	64	65	69	68	70
Graduate	15	16	16	15	16
COLLEGE TOTALS					
Undergraduate	495	488	521	527	533
Graduate	75	78	74	75	73

Credit Hours Generated by Fiscal Year (FY)

Department Degree Level	Current FY minus 4	Current FY minus 3	Current FY minus 2	Current FY minus 1	Current FY
Art and Design					
Undergraduate	16,136	16,089	17,122	17,165	17,215
Graduate	1,636	1,663	1,659	1,675	1,689
Dance					
Undergraduate	6,456	6,556	6,423	6,587	6,599
Graduate	293	303	289	330	365
Music					
Undergraduate	11,723	11,587	11,526	11,446	11,336
Graduate	586	572	551	569	503
Theatre					
Undergraduate	3,036	3,043	3,058	3,052	3,076
Graduate	571	587	583	547	587
COLLEGE TOTALS					
Undergraduate	37,351	37,275	38,129	38,250	38,226
Graduate	3,086	3,125	3,082	3,121	3,144

SELECTED READINGS

Atkinson, R. C., & Tuzin, D. (1992). Equilibrium in the research university. *Change, 24,* 21-31.

The authors define three institutional missions (propagation of knowledge, creation of knowledge, and application of knowledge) while noting a number of signs indicating that the research university is in crisis. This has led to what the authors call "a sense of estrangement" between teaching and research, and between undergraduates and faculty.

Bensimon, E. M. (1990). The new president and understanding the campus as a culture. *New Directions for Institutional Research, Number 68,* 75–86.

The focus is on how a new president can become part of the campus culture. The content is organized around the issues of understanding the campus culture and recognizing the means of knowing an institution as a culture.

Bieber, J. P., Lawrence, J. H., & Blackburn, R. T. (1992). Through the years—Faculty and their changing institution. *Change, 24,* 28-35.

The authors discuss the dilemma faced by faculty as they attempt to relate to a constantly changing institution. The conclusions were derived from interviews with faculty at the University of Michigan.

Bryson, J. M. (1989). *Strategic planning for public and nonprofit organizations: A guide to strengthening and sustaining organizational achievement.* San Francisco, CA: Jossey-Bass.

The author describes a variety of models and approaches to help leaders and administrators fulfill institutional missions and satisfy departmental or institutional goals. Of particular relevance to this case is Chapter 3, "An effective strategic planning approach for public and nonprofit organizations," in which Bryson describes an eight-step strategic planning process.

Colvin, T. J., & Kilmann, R. H. (1990). Implementation of large-scale planned change: Some areas of agreement and disagreement. *Psychological Reports, 66,* 1235-1241.

The authors, studying 400 experts, identified key areas—both positive and negative—related to change. They discovered widespread agreement on five issues related to change: creating a shared vision; publicly acknowledging employees' contributions; achieving agreement among top administrators; evaluating effectiveness at frequent intervals; and encouraging employee involvement. They also noted five possible actions related to change for which there was little consensus among the experts.

Deegan, W. L. (1992). Proven techniques: The use and impact of major manage-ment concepts in community colleges. *Community, Technical, and Junior College Journal, 62*, 26-30.

The author reviews the use and impact of various management concepts at community colleges and discusses the relevance of management theory and practice to the issues and problems cited by community college presidents.

Dressel, P. L. (1987). Mission, organization, and leadership. *Journal of Higher Education, 58*, 102-109.

The author identifies eleven reasons for reorganization: new functions; sepa-rating of growing complex functions; new technologies; bypass individuals; outside funding for to support new unit; internal and/or external pressure; greater diversity; focus on purposes and goals; to imitate or emulate changes at other institutions; personal views of new administrator; and to attract atten-tion. He then discusses the mission, structure, and function of the university—noting that an institution which is not clear regarding its mission and objectives will not be improved by a simple reorganization.

Ehrle, E. B., & Bennett, J. B. (1988). *Managing the Academic Enterprise: Case studies for deans and provosts.* New York, NY: American Council on Education/Macmillan.

In this text, the authors present 25 original case studies and solutions to the most common problems faced by deans and provosts. In Chapter One, the authors set the stage by describing the roles and relationships of academic deans and provosts.

Hambrick, D. C., & Fukutomi, G. D. S. (1991). The seasons of a CEO's tenure. *Acad-emy of Management Review, 16*, 719-742.

Though written with the corporate CEO in mind, the discernible "seasons" of an executive's tenure have relevance for the senior-level administrator in higher education. The five seasons defined by the authors are: response to mandate; experimentation; selection of an enduring theme; convergence; and dysfunction. These seasons prompt distinct patterns of behavior which influ-ence organizational performance.

Hollingsworth, A. T., & Boone, L. W. (1990). Decision time: The dilemma for insti-tutions of higher education. *CUPA Journal, 41*,1-10.

The authors present a general decision-making model and describe the three criteria (productivity, adaptability and flexibility) which are essential to orga-nizational effectiveness. Institutions must change well-established organiza-tional decision processes if they are to be viable in responding to changing environmental conditions.

Hurst, P. J., & Peterson M. W. (1992). The impact of a chief planning officer on the administrative environment for planning. *Research in Higher Education, 33,* 1-17.

To be effective, institution-wide planning must have the support of key administrators. Presidents, vice presidents, and deans must achieve sufficient consensus regarding their objectives to make reaching these goals a possibility. This paper studies the role of the chief planning officer in this equation with the findings of this survey research open to a variety of interpretations.

Keller, G. (1983). *Academic Strategy: The management revolution in American higher education.* Baltimore, MD: The Johns Hopkins University Press.

In this book, Keller describes the nature of the management revolution that now impacts higher education, and explains how institutions can use a strategic planning process to improve the overall quality of decision-making. The text is a blend of descriptive information and prescriptive advice for the leadership in higher education.

Levin, H. M. (1991). Raising productivity in higher education. *Journal of Higher Education, 62,* 241-262.

The author offers an analysis of the issues associated with the need to improve productivity in higher education . The author proposes a systematic approach to raising productivity that requires a clear statement of goals and priorities, a list of established incentives, and an information generating system that would encourage the search for effective alternatives.

Morris, V. C. (1981). *Deaning, middle management in academe.* Urbana, IL: University of Illinois Press.

Based on personal experience, Morris provides a realistic portrayal of the "middle manager" position of the academic dean. Written with wit and clarity, Morris analyzes the inner structure of campus management to depict the human side of personnel management, public and student relations, budget planning, affirmative action, faculty politics, salary disputes, and tenure decisions.

Mouritsen, M. M. (1986). The university mission statement: A tool for the university curriculum, institutional effectiveness, and change. *New Directions for Higher Education, Number 55,* 45-52.

The author provides a discussion of the importance of having institutional culture, values, and integrity clearly articulated in the mission statement which can then become the catalyst for change. The specific experience at Brigham Young University is used to illustrate the benefits accrued from a clear declaration of mission.

Schmidtlein, F. A., & Milton, T. H. (Eds.). (1990). Adapting strategic planning to campus realities. *New Directions for Institutional Research, Number 67.* San Francisco, CA: Jossey-Bass.

In this text, the authors provide descriptions of the planning processes used at five diverse institutions from a research university to a community college. In the final chapter, Schmidtlein offers his definition of planning and discusses the importance of relating planning to institutional character and adapting planning to current issues.

Tucker, A., & Bryan, R. A. (1991). *The academic dean: Dove, dragon, and diplomat (2nd edition).* New York, NY: American Council on Education/Macmillan.

In this text, the authors offer a description of the roles and responsibilities typically assigned to academic deans. Specific chapters are devoted to the relationship of the dean to department chairs, to provosts and vice presidents, and to the faculty and students.

Tucker, A. (1992). *Chairing the academic department: Leadership among peers (3rd edition).* New York, NY: American Council on Education/Macmillan.

Part II of this book includes five chapters which describe and discuss the various roles and responsibilities typically assigned to the department chair. Also discussed is the chair's role in decision making, bringing about change, and delegating work to faculty committees.

Walker, D. E. (1979). *The effective administrator.* San Francisco, CA: Jossey-Bass.

Drawing on more than two decades of personal experience, the author offers a realistic understanding of the political nature of the campus community in order to develop a more effective administrative style. The author also demonstrates how his approach can be used to improve campus communication, prevent confrontation, define problems pragmatically, and involve faculty, staff, students, and other groups in decision-making.

6

AN EXCEEDINGLY CHILLY CLIMATE

About the Case

The potential for a major public relations problem and the possibility of legal complications are part of the campus environment, and should not be lost on today's administrators. How the college president decides to act on hearsay information will impact internally on the college climate and externally on its image. This case is centered on the institution's response to extremely sensitive and potentially damaging information. The president must balance the need for prompt and responsible action with the need to avoid prejudicing allegations—while appearing to be sensitive and fair to all involved.

CASE STUDY

The Conflict. Edward Nelson, the president at Wild Rock College, a picturesque campus which is part of the large state college system, was looking out of the window at the lovely dogwood blossoms which decked the campus in remarkable beauty each spring. There were only six more weeks to the end of the semester when he would begin a three week vacation at his favorite fishing retreat in Canada. He turned from the window as his secretary, Laura Emory, entered his office along with Phil Brown, his public relations assistant. Phil always appeared disheveled and grim, but this time he looked absolutely haggard.

Without offering any salutations, Phil informed Nelson, "I just heard by way of the grapevine that our new vice president for administration has repeatedly propositioned two of the young women on his staff. I understand that one has already contacted an attorney and the other is trying to decide what to do."

"So much for a peaceful spring," said the president, more to himself than anyone else. "How can we be certain that the women are telling the truth? Why should we believe that Malcolm Ozwald would do something like that?"

"There are two of them and I think we have to assume that *both* can't be lying," responded Phil. "The one that contacted the attorney did so in an effort to keep her job. She believes Malcolm is going to fire her because she rejected his advances. The other one is hoping to avoid the need to go public or hire an attorney, at least for now—again for career reasons."

"Okay, assuming that this is all true, what next?" sighed the beleaguered president.

Let's pause here. . .

1. *What is next? Does the president have to take any action at this point? What are the potential gains and liabilities of acting now? What, if anything, should the president do? Be specific.*

2. *Was the public relations assistant acting responsibly to have come to the president so quickly with this hearsay information? Should Phil have waited until he had more direct evidence? Consider the language used by Phil Brown and whether it was appropriate to report information obtained through the "grapevine"?*

3. *To whom and how should this information be reported? With whom might the president consult?*

The Institution. Wild Rock College is a campus of approximately 7,500 students, one of ten campuses scattered across the state. It has enjoyed an excellent reputation in the state as a primarily undergraduate public institution with a few strong master's degree programs. Wild Rock has built a positive image in the surrounding community which has enabled the institution to attract large numbers of freshmen despite the growing presence of community colleges within the state.

Edward Nelson has been president for six years. He came to Wild Rock from a public university where he had been dean of its large College of Liberal Arts and Sciences for the previous eight years.

Prior to Edward Nelson's tenure, public relations had been treated in an informal manner. However, Edward Nelson felt that an institution's public image was critical to such important tasks as student recruitment, fundraising, faculty recruitment and retention, and the placement of graduates. Hiring Phil Brown as his assistant was one of the first staffing decisions made by Nelson upon his arrival at Wild Rock. Brown has a bachelors degree in public relations and had worked for 15 years in the college's alumni office.

A Phone Call. President Nelson directed his secretary, Laura Emory, to call the system office. "I need to talk with Mac," he said wearily. Mac was Dr. Jason Macmillan, the head of the ten-campus state college system which included Wild Rock. Dr. Macmillan had his own office in the state's capital city. Nelson has worked with "Mac" the entire six years he's been at Wild Rock, and they have a high regard for one another.

President Nelson, speaking into the phone, said, "Mac, sorry to bother you this late in the day, but a matter has come up that I think you should know about. Phil Brown, my assistant, has brought some very disturbing information to my attention. According to his sources, Malcolm Ozwald, our new vice president for administration, has propositioned two young women who work in his office. One, we think, has already talked to a lawyer and the other may do so in the immediate future."

Macmillan understood the ramifications immediately and commented, "Whether Malcolm has been this indiscreet or not, your institution's image could be tarnished. Do you remember the public reaction to the incident at Prairie Valley College last fall? The one where a faculty member in zoology was found guilty of sexually harassing students for grades? I thought the negative publicity would never stop."

"I know we are in a delicate position," lamented the president, "and my assistant, Phil, will do all he can to achieve maximum containment. However, somewhere between Ozwald's guilt or innocence, and damage control or 'taking the high road,' is our best position. Any past experience with something like this?"

"Well, you are right about the parameters. Yes, I have had some experience," answered Dr. Macmillan. "It was years ago though. Back then, we would issue a strong, but private, warning to the offender and sweep the incident under the rug and pretend it never happened, or at least assume that the young women involved were not totally without fault for inviting such advances. But times and conditions have changed. Now there is a heightened public awareness to the issue of sexual harassment. Just last year, you may recall, we fired the dean of the College of Engineering at River View for a similar indiscretion. I was very uncomfortable with those who gave no credence to the accusers, but I was likewise unhappy that George had to resign. He was a terrific dean, well respected by the faculty, and besides, he brought lots of external funding to that campus."

"Any advice on how to proceed?" asked the president.

"No, not really. Just use your best judgment, Ed. Every situation is different. I would, however, like to be kept informed."

"You can be assured that I will do that, Mac. I'll call you each step of the way. Thanks for all your guidance. Goodbye."

Let's pause again. . .

4. *What is going through the president's mind? Did the president take a risk by talking with the system head about the information reported on Vice President Ozwald? What purpose did the conversation with the system head serve?*

5. *In general, what information should be reported up the line? How and when should information about a potential public liability be shared with superiors? Is there a need first to document or verify what has been learned? In this instance, how might the president verify the grapevine information? Or should the president even make an effort to verify such information?*

The President Wants Action. Upon hanging up the phone, the president turned to his secretary, "Laura, get Paul Perkins over here immediately. Tell him I need to see him *now!*"

While waiting for Perkins, the local attorney on a permanent retainer to the campus, President Nelson kept mentally reviewing what he had learned about Malcolm Ozwald during the screening and interviewing process a short ten months ago. Dr. Ozwald had received rave reviews from colleagues at the last two institutions where he worked. However, the president now remembered his own apprehension about hiring someone who had left his last two assignments after only about two years at each location.

At the time, however, his fears were alleviated though his personal telephone conversations with Ozwald's references. Without exception, each had assured Nelson of Ozwald's ability to handle the job and that his family was the reason behind each move (i.e., desire to move closer to a father who had suffered a stroke, a better climate for his wife's asthma, etc.). Worse yet, the president remembered that he had hired Ozwald over the strong opposition of the "old guard" of this campus who were standing strongly and vocally behind an internal candidate with similarly good credentials.

President Nelson was thinking how, just last week when speaking to the alumni, he had again taken credit for bringing a person with such a solid financial background to the campus. Another scattered thought racing through the president's mind was that the vice president for academic affairs recently went through a messy divorce—which, coupled with these allegations, had the potential to make his administration look sleazy.

President Nelson's thoughts were interrupted by the arrival of Paul Perkins, the well-respected lawyer whose prestigious firm had represented the campus for a number of years. Paul confidently entered the room, shook hands with the president and said, "Laura tells me you have a new problem on your hands. How can I help?"

"Paul, thanks for coming over. You know Phil Brown, my assistant?" The president began to give a quick summary of the situation to date. "Phil tells me that Malcolm Ozwald is chasing the women in his office—you know, propositioning them. I must admit that he has hired some very pretty staffers. Well, anyway, Phil says that two of them are ready to take action against him. One has already hired a lawyer."

Paul turned to Phil and started to rattle off questions. "Have the women filed formal complaints with the university? Who is their attorney?"

Phil Brown said, "Only one has an attorney, and I heard it was Brian Jacobs."

"What exactly are their accusations against Dr. Ozwald? What are their names and ages?" the attorney asked.

Phil Brown repeated the information he had given the president and added, "The gals are Susan Richardson and Maria Gomez. They both look incredibly young. I'm sure that neither is over 21. They both grew up in this area and are relatively recent high school graduates. They have basic secretarial training and entry-level computer skills. Malcolm hired them both shortly after he arrived."

The president began to warm-up to the problem. He interrupted to ask, "Can I fire the jerk?"

"No sir," answered Attorney Perkins.

The lawyer turned back to Phil Brown. "Have *you* talked with these women?"

Brown replied softly, "Well, no."

Perkins asked in frustration, "Has *anyone* talked with these women about Ozwald?"

Brown answered more slowly, "Well, no, not exactly. They talked with a friend of theirs who, in turn, alerted me to the situation."

"Okay, can I suspend him indefinitely without pay?" asked the president.

Phil Brown began to get visibly nervous at the possible consequences of his report of campus gossip.

"No," Perkins retorted firmly and continued, "Malcolm has not been publicly accused and he has not been tried for any crime."

"Can I suspend him indefinitely *with* pay?" asked President Nelson.

"Probably," said Perkins, "but that action brings certain liabilities with it, and I don't know if you are willing to pay that price."

Let's pause again. . .

6. *Is the president jumping to a premature conclusion with his assumption of guilt? Would he be thinking like this if the women involved were in their forties? What if only one woman was reporting this same accusation?*

7. *What kinds of information does the president need at this point? How might this information be obtained?*

Cooler Heads Begin to Prevail. The attorney turned to Phil again, "How widespread is this problem? Does Malcolm have eyes for every female in his office? Have these women encouraged this kind of attention? Does he ever travel with either of them? Have these women been romantically involved with male colleagues before?"

Phil answered, "I'm not sure. My source only knows about these two and their negative reactions. I've been told that at least one is prepared to go to court, if necessary. I haven't picked up any information that suggests either of these girls has been involved with other men."

Attorney Perkins looked directly at Phil and said, "Don't misunderstand me. I believe that you were correct to bring this matter to the president's attention."

He turned to the president and continued, "But none of us should lose sight of the fact that all of your information appears to be thirdhand and from only one source. How reliable is your source? Did your source realize that there would be a report filed with the president's office and that some follow-up would be probable?"

Phil answered, "Well, he certainly knows where I work and for whom, if that's what you mean."

The attorney shifted his attention back to the president. "Could Laura bring in your copy of the campus policies on sexual harassment and severance procedures? I want to review what the policies have to say about termination for cause." President Nelson used the intercom to ask Laura to bring in a copy of the policy manual.

Paul Perkins asked the president, in a softer tone than he used with Phil Brown, "You had no hint of this tendency from your background checks on Malcolm before you hired him?"

"No," said Nelson. "Believe me, I'm not that desperate for vice presidents."

Laura returned with a large, orange-colored three-ring notebook with paper clips marking the two policies (Attachments A and B). "Laura, thanks, and please retrieve Vice President Ozwald's personnel file for me. I want to reread his reference letters and my phone notes." Laura departed again.

President Nelson commented to the attorney, "Maybe I can talk to those women and try to cool them down. They don't seem to be angry at the institution—after all, we are their employer."

Let's pause again...

8. *Should anyone talk with the women at this point? If so, whom should it be?*

9. *Is there anyone else to call to get pertinent information? Whom, if anyone, would you call? What information would you request?*

10. *Review Attachments A and B. What provisions of the policy statements are relevant for the president?*

Malcolm Ozwald. President Nelson continued to exhibit signs of impatience. He called to his secretary, "Laura, buzz Vice President Ozwald and tell him that I need to meet with him immediately. I want to see him *now*. Pronto!"

President Nelson, turning to his assistant and to the attorney, said, "Okay, before he gets here, let's review our options. From what you say, I can't shoot him and I can't fire him. I assume that I can talk with him and get his side of the story. If I talk with him immediately, I may catch him off guard. If he has time to prepare his responses, he will be less likely to be candid with me. Now, if he confesses, what do I do? If he stops short of confessing, but clearly does not deny his, ah, shall we say interest in the women, then what? The most likely scenario is that he will deny that any of this happened. Then what can I do?"

Paul Perkins sat down next to the president and started to make a list of concerns on his yellow pad.

Let's pause again...

11. *What is Perkins putting on his yellow pad? What are the legal concerns in acting on unsubstantiated information? What are the president's options?*

12. *Is the president moving too fast? On what factual basis is the president acting? What are the potential risks and benefits of meeting with the vice president at this point?*

Scripting the Confrontation. With that session concluded, the president said to Phil and Paul, "I want one of you to stay here with me as a witness while I try to get to the bottom of this. If he is innocent, that's one thing, but if he is guilty, then that's another problem altogether. Phil, you stay. You've got the inside information and maybe we can bluff him into thinking we have a lot more. Paul, Ozwald is likely to think he's been tried and found guilty if you were here. But please wait in my conference room. Depending on how this goes, I may need you to join us."

Paul Perkins, still trying to slow what appeared to him to be a runaway train, gave the president a few last words of advice. "Be sure you stick to the facts as you know them. Don't accuse him of anything. Remember, you're unlikely to be able to ascertain the whole story or resolve this matter in one meeting. While you are talking with him, I am going to review your institution's sexual harassment policy. Have these women talked with anyone in your Affirmative Action office?" The two men shook their heads indicating that they did not know.

And one last pause. . .

13. *As president, what would you have done? Would you have talked with the women who were making the accusations or would you have done as President Nelson did, and bring in the accused? Would you have chosen to follow yet a different course of action? If so, outline your strategy. Do the provisions outlined in Section II.B.8 of the Sexual Harassment Policy influence your posture at this early stage?*

14. *Is the president's action consistent with the provisions outlined in Section II.A.5 of the institution's Sexual Harassment Policy (Attachment A)? Is it consistent with Section II.B.3 of the policy?*

15. *Is it a crime to "proposition" someone? Obtain a copy of the sexual harassment policy for your campus and use it to generate a strategy for dealing with this situation.*

16. *What other institutional policies are important in this situation? Have you considered personnel policies regarding dismissal for "cause" or policies on ethical conduct?*

17. *What is the place of ethics in this discussion? If Ozwald breaks down and confesses his guilt to the president, what should President Nelson do? Should the potential legal liability control all of the president's actions in relation to the young women and in reaction to Ozwald? When might ethical or humane concerns loom larger than legal concerns?*

Attachment A

Wild Rock College
Sexual Harassment Policy

Wild Rock College is committed to creating and maintaining a community in which students, faculty, and staff can work together in an atmosphere free of all forms of harassment, exploitation and intimidation. Sexual harassment, like harassment on the basis of race or religion, is a form of discrimination expressly prohibited by law. It is a violation of Title VII of the Federal 1964 Civil Rights Act and Title IX of the Educational Amendments of 1972.

The college will take whatever action is needed to prevent, stop, correct, or discipline behavior that violates this policy. Disciplinary action may include, but is not limited to, oral or written warnings, demotion, transfer, suspension, or dismissal for cause.

I. General Policy Statements

    A. Definitions and Examples

        1. Sexual harassment is defined as unwelcome sexual advances, requests for sexual favors, verbal or other expressive behaviors, or physical conduct commonly understood to be of a sexual nature when:

           a. Submission to, or toleration of, such conduct on or off campus is made either explicitly or implicitly, a term or condition of instruction, employment, or participation in other college activities;

           b. Submission to, or rejections of, such conduct is used as a basis of employment or academic decisions or assessments affecting the individual's status as an employee or student; or

           c. Such conduct has the purpose or effect of unreasonably interfering with an individual's status as a student or an employee or creates an intimidating, hostile, or offensive work or educational environment.

        2. Sexual harassment may involve the behavior of a person of either sex toward a person of the opposite or the same sex. Examples of behavior that would be considered sexual harassment include, but are not limited to, the following:

           a. Physical assault;

           b. Direct or implied threats that submission to sexual advances will be a condition of employment, work status, promotion, grades, or letters of recommendation;

c. A pattern of conduct, annoying or humiliating in a sexual way, that includes comments of a sexual nature and/or sexually explicit statements, questions, jokes, or anecdotes; or

d. A pattern of conduct that would annoy or humiliate a reasonable person at whom the conduct is obviously directed. Such conduct includes, but is not limited to, gestures, facial expressions, speech, or physical contact understood to be sexual in nature or which is repeated after the individual signifies that the conduct is perceived to be offensively sexual.

B. Consenting Relationships

1. Consenting romantic and sexual relationships between a faculty member and a student or between a supervisor and an employee, while not expressly forbidden, are discouraged. A faculty member or supervisor who enters into a sexual relationship with a student or an employee, where a professional power differential obviously exists, must realize that if a charge of sexual harassment is subsequently lodged, the burden will be on the faculty member or supervisor to prove immunity on grounds of mutual consent.

2. Relationships between a graduate student and an undergraduate, when the graduate student has some supervisory responsibility for the undergraduate, belong in this category. Among other relationships included are those between a student or employee and an administrator, coach, advisor, program director, counselor, or residential staff member who has supervisory responsibility for that student or employee.

C. Protection of the Complainant and Others

No student, faculty member, or staff member may be subjected to any form of reprisal for seeking information on sexual harassment, filing a sexual harassment complaint, or serving as a witness in a proceeding involving a complaint of sexual harassment. Any retaliatory action will be a violation of this policy and will be grounds for disciplinary action.

D. Protection of the Accused

Accusations of sexual harassment are grievous and can have serious and far-reaching effects on the careers and lives of accused individuals. Individuals who believe they have been falsely accused of sexual harassment may use the procedures of this policy to seek redress.

E. Responsibility of Supervisors

Supervisory personnel are charged with maintaining an atmosphere that discourages sexual harassment and ensuring that the college policy is enforced in their areas. Supervisors are directed to discourage all behavior that might be considered sexual harassment and to respond promptly to sexual harassment complaints. College officials who knowingly condone an incidence of sexual harassment or instances of reprisal for reporting such complaints will be subject to disciplinary action.

II. Complaint Resolution Procedures

Following are the guidelines that have been adopted for the orderly and prompt resolution of sexual harassment complaints at Wild Rock College.

A. Confidential Information Seeking

1. The information-seeking process gives individuals an opportunity to discuss in confidence a complaint in which they may be involved as a complainant, a respondent, a witness or a supervisor of one or more of the parties to the complaint. Individuals who believe they have been victims of sexual harassment should not delay in seeking assistance or advice. Persons to whom incidents of alleged sexual harassment have been confided are encouraged to refer the individual to one of the sexual harassment information centers.

2. Information Centers. The college has designated the following offices as sexual harassment information centers:

   a. Affirmative Action Office

   b. Counseling Center

   c. Personnel Office

3. Advisors. Information Centers are staffed with advisors who can provide information about sexual harassment. Each advisor is prepared to:

   a. Serve as an informational resource to individuals who have questions about sexual harassment;

   b. Provide individuals the opportunity to discuss, in confidence, the specifics of a complaint;

   c. Offer suggestions about informal actions that might be taken by an individual to remedy the situation;

   d. Provide the individual with information about the college policy on sexual harassment and related procedures and deadlines;

    e. Provide the individual with copies of applicable state and federal laws;

    f. Outline various options available for resolving a complaint; and

    g. Tell the individual whom to contact if she/he wishes to initiate a sexual harassment grievance.

4. Request for Information

    a. Requests for information may be made by telephone, in person, or in writing. No individual will be required to reveal his or her identity in seeking information. No administrative action will be taken on anonymous complaints of sexual harassment.

    b. Speaking with an advisor does not constitute a formal complaint or grievance and will be treated in the strictest confidence.

    c. After receiving information, an individual with a potential complaint may: 1) choose not to pursue the complaint; 2) decide to take action directly, verbally or in writing, with the alleged offender by requesting the individual to cease the offending behavior; 3) report the matter to the alleged offender's supervisor, asking that steps be taken to ensure that the offending behavior cease; 4) request assistance of a conciliatory, provided by the Office of Affirmative Action, in reaching a settlement of the complaint; and/or 5) proceed directly to the filing of a sexual harassment grievance.

    d. As appropriate, an information center advisor will make follow-up contact with the individual within a reasonable period of time to ascertain whether the matter has been satisfactorily resolved.

5. Responsibilities of Supervisors in Responding to Complaints

    a. If a complaint, whether written or oral, is brought to the attention of an alleged offender's supervisor, the department head, or the dean, then the officer has the responsibility to:

        1) Interview the person making the complaint, then interview separately any other persons who may have knowledge of pertinent facts, including the accused person;

        2) Seek assistance from the Office of Affirmative Action when needed;

3) Take corrected action to resolve the problem, if appropriate; and

4) File a written report with the complaint resolution officer regarding the resolution reached.

b. All supervisory personnel are charged with maintaining an atmosphere that will discourage sexual harassment and with responding promptly to sexual harassment complaints. Supervisors are responsible for ensuring that the college policy on sexual harassment is enforced in their areas.

B. Grievance Procedure

1. General Procedures

a. An individual who believes that he/she has been a victim of sexual harassment may file a formal grievance under these procedures. Individuals who believe they have been falsely accused or subjected to retribution may use the same procedures to seek redress.

b. The college reserves the right to take appropriate action when the victim is unwilling or unable to serve as a complainant but is willing and able to serve as a witness.

c. Justice and law require that an accused person right of due process, as well as the right to academic freedom, be fully assured to parties to the action. The college will make every effort to protect these rights and will undertake no action that threatens or compromises them.

d. A complainant may withdraw a charge after it has been filed, if the respondent agrees to the withdrawal.

2. Written Complaint

a. A formal sexual harassment grievance begins with a written complaint form, supplied through the sexual harassment information centers, which is to be filled out by the complainant. The written complaint should state the complainant's description of the incident clearly and concisely. The complaint form must be signed by the complainant and should be submitted to the Office of Affirmative Action not later than one-hundred twenty (120) calendar days following the last alleged incident of harassment.

b. After receiving a written complaint, the affirmative action officer will meet with the complainant as soon as possible, generally no more than five (5) work days after receiving the complaint form, to review the complainant to find the issues. The complainant will be asked to name witnesses to the incident, describe what steps have been taken to resolve the matter, and state what relief is being sought through the complaint process. The complainant will be told that the respondent will be notified in writing of the complaint at this stage. The notification will disclose the identify of the complainant to the accused individual.

3. Notice of Charge

   a. A notice of charge will be issued to the respondent. The notice will contain a copy of the written complaint and will be sent to the respondent by the affirmative action officer within ten (10) work days of the receipt of the sexual harassment complaint form. The complainant will be given a copy of the notice. The affirmative action officer will notify appropriate line administrators of the respondent's unit about the nature of the charges raised.

   b. The respondent will have ten (10) work days in which to make a written response to the charge. The response, written on a standard form, should attempt to answer each claim in the complaint. The grievance process will proceed, with or without the respondent's response, at the end of the ten (10) work day period.

4. The Hearing Panel

   a. The next step will be a formal hearing by a panel appointed to determine whether or not the college policy on sexual harassment has been violated.

   b. Within twenty (20) work days of receipt of the written complaint, the affirmative action officer will coordinate the selection of a three-member panel to hear the grievance. The hearing panel will consist of one member selected by the complainant, one member selected by the respondent, and a third member selected by these two panel members.

5. The Responsibilities of the Hearing Panel are:

   a. To conduct a fair and impartial hearing that will protect the rights of all parties involved;

   b. To receive and consider all relevant information that fair and reasonable people would generally consider reliable and that has a direct bearing on the particular factual question to which it is addressed;

c. To ask of the complainant, the respondent, and any other persons, relevant questions that might assist the panel in determining the facts;

d. To ensure that the complainant and respondent have full opportunity to present their claims, along with relevant information which may help establish their claims, and to question the other party, and all witnesses, in an orderly fashion;

e. To decide by majority vote on all questions of fact, recommendations of relief and disciplinary action, and any requests that are made during the hearing; and

f. To review the complaint within ten (10) work days after its appointment.

6. Findings and Recommendations

a. A panel will conclude its deliberations and complete its written recommendations within ten (10) work days after the conclusion of the hearing.

b. The panel will submit its written recommendations to the president, the complainant, the respondent, and the affirmative action officer. In making its recommendations, the hearing panel should arrive at one of two conclusions:

1) A decision that the facts do not support the allegations with a recommendation that the charges be dismissed and that all college records pertaining to the case be amended to indicate their dismissal; or

2) A decision that there was a violation of the sexual harassment policy. If the hearing panel believes the policy has been violated, its written statement will also indicate and include its findings of fact; it will also recommend appropriate relief of the complainant and may include recommendations for disciplinary action. The findings of fact and recommendations will be based solely on the information presented at the hearing.

7. Review of the Affirmative Action Officer

a. Within five (5) work days of receiving the panel's report, the affirmative action officer may recommend to the president that the hearing panel's recommendations be adjusted to take into account any record of previous sexual harassment by the respondent, or to achieve a consistency with past practice. Any recommendation for revision, along with written reasons for the revisions, will be affixed to the hearing panel's decision.

b. If the hearing panel's report is excessively delinquent, the affirmative action officer may submit an independent recommendation to the president for disposition or further proceedings as may be necessary.

8. Review by the President

a. The president will review the matter and render a written decision to the complainant, the respondent, the members of the hearing panel, and the affirmative action office no later than ten (10) work days after receiving the recommendations of the hearing panel and the affirmative action officer. The president will also inform the respondent's supervisor of the outcome of the grievance. The president may modify the recommendations of the hearing panel if he or she concludes that the substantive rights of any party have been prejudiced because the decisions or recommendations are: 1) unsupported by the evidence; 2) in violation of constitutional provisions, academic freedom, or the procedures described in the college policy on sexual harassment; or 3) arbitrary or in excess of the panel's powers.

b. The president will decide: 1) the actions to be taken regarding each recommendation and 2) the time frame in which these actions will take place.

c. The president will direct the appropriate vice president and line administrators to implement these decisions. Disciplinary action taken against college employees will be administered in accordance with the applicable college personnel policies, state statutes and/or contractual agreements.

d. Records of the hearings, the recommendations of the panel, and the final resolution of the complaint will be retained by the affirmative action officer.

9. Appeals

The president's action may be appealed in accordance with the appeals procedure contained in the bylaws of the Board of Regents.

Attachment B

Wild Rock College
Severance Policies

I. Non-reappointment

    A. Term appointments: A term appointment is employment for a specified period of time and may be renewed. However, reappointment to such a position does not create a right to subsequent employment or presumption of a right to subsequent employment. Since term appointments expire at the end of the term stated in the notice of appointment, no separate notice of non-reappointment need be given for such appointments.

    B. Continuing appointments: Notice of non-reappointment for untenured faculty on continuing appointment or for administrative professionals on continuing appointments shall be given in writing as follows:

        First Year Appointment—no less than three months notice.

        Second Appointment Year—no less than six months notice.

        Third and Subsequent Appointment Years—no more than one year notice.

        No notice period need exceed the length of the appointment.

    C. Termination of appointments: Dismissal for adequate cause is an action taken in response to unsatisfactory behavior and performance of a tenured faculty member, or an untenured faculty member, or an administrator serving on a continuing appointment in his or her professional capacity, referring to such matters as unethical conduct, incompetence, failure to perform reasonable assignments, or neglect of duty.

SELECTED READINGS

Adams, W. C. (1992, Spring). Helping your organization triumph over negatives. *Public Relations Quarterly, 37,* 12-16.

The author offers public relations assistance to chief executive officers in building a defense against negative publicity. He notes four realities that must be faced: (1) the worse the charge, the more newsworthy the story; (2) careers may depend on answering promptly; (3) lawyers will want no one to say anything; and (4) the situation can be turned into an advantage.

Astin, H. S., & Leland, C. (1991). *Women of influence, women of vision.* San Francisco, CA: Jossey-Bass.

A text for those who wish to read more about the influence of women in higher education administration. The authors trace how women leaders who sought for educational and social justice in America from the 1960s through the 1980s changed the way the roles of men and women are viewed within today's society and organizations.

Close, J. (1991, February). Speaking out to the public: Ten crisis communication strategies. *Best's Review, 91,* 86f.

Citing a crisis in public confidence, the author challenges corporate leaders to win back the trust of their constituents. He suggests using a combination of communication and actions, noting ten crisis communication strategies to serve as the basis for possible action.

Cooper, D. A. (1992, January). CEO must weigh legal and public relations approaches. *Public Relations Journal, 48,* 39-40.

The author notes the often conflicting advice a CEO may receive in a crisis from a lawyer and a public relations expert. The author assists the reader to understand why these two consultants often have different points of view as to the proper approach to handling a problem.

Finifter, D. H., Baldwin, R. G., & Thelin, J. R. (Eds.). (1991). *The uneasy public policy triangle in higher education.* New York, NY: American Council on Education /Macmillan.

The authors discuss the impact of public policy on the issues of diversity, quality, and budget in higher education. Of particular relevance to this case study are the chapters entitled: "The goal of diversity: Access and choice in academia" by Robert Zemsky and "Barriers to diversity and the myth of equal access" by Reginald Wilson.

Fritzsche, D. J. (1991). A model of decision-making incorporating ethical values. *Journal of Business Ethics, 10,* 841-852.

A model, to assist persons studying ethical behavior in business, is presented which includes the decision-maker's personal values and elements of the organization's culture. The author hypothesizes that this combination produces decisions which may be significantly different than decisions effected by personal values alone. The author's analysis is offered in both narrative and in model form.

Guillebeau, J. (1989, Fall). Crisis management: A case study in the killing of an employee. *Public Relations Quarterly, 35,* 19-21.

This brief article offers an hour-by-hour summary of actions taken by a small college to minimize the potential for unfavorable publicity following the killing of an employee. Guillebeau offers the reader some insight into the utility of a public relations function within an institution of higher education.

Harper, L. F., & Rifkind, L. J. (1992). Competent communication strategies for responding to sexual harassment. *CUPA Journal, 43*(2), 33-40.

Sensitive communication between people in the workplace is needed, according to the authors, to establish a positive work environment and to respond to sexual harassment situations. Looking particularly to higher education settings, the authors discuss the issues of different communication cultures: one for each sex; "sex role spillover" and its impact on many situations; and the implications of living and working in a "noncontact culture."

Knouse, S. B., & Giacalone, R. A. (1992). Ethical decision-making in business: Behavioral issues and concerns. *Journal of Business Ethics. 11,* 369-377.

The author identifies three "behavioral antecedents of ethical behavior" (individual differences, interpersonal variables, and organizational variables), and then offers ten propositions to aid in understanding corporate ethical behavior. These ten hypotheses lend themselves to discussion and possibly to insight as to how the organization's ethical environment evolves.

Sandler, B. R. (1986). *The campus climate revisited: Chilly for women faculty, administrators, and graduate students.* Washington, DC: Association of American Colleges, Project on the Status and Education of Women.

The focus of this report is on the subtle ways in which women faculty, administrators, and graduate/professional students are treated differently from their male counterparts. The effect of this differential treatment is to communicate that women are not considered to be first-class citizens of the academic community. Specific recommendations for changing this chilly climate for women are presented in the report.

Sexual harassment: Issues and answers. (1992). *CUPA Journal, 43*(2), 41-52.

This special section includes information on steps to follow in developing a policy on sexual harassment, a sample sexual harassment policy from the University of Florida, some definitions and rules governing the conduct of faculty, and some suggestions for dealing with a sexual harassment complaint.

Summers, R. J. (1991). Determinants of judgments of and responses to a complaint of sexual harassment. *Sex Roles, 25*, 379-392.

The author's research methodology examines factors that may influence judgments concerning complaints of sexual harassment (i.e., the victim's feminist orientation, professional competition between the victim and perpetrator, and the sex of the decision-makers). The researcher hypothesized that male decision-makers would be less favorable toward the woman making the sexual harassment complaint, and that males would favor less severe punishment and would be more willing to console the perpetrator. The findings show the influence of gender and the part played by a competition factor working between the complainants.

Taback, H. (1991, October). Preventing a crisis from getting out of hand. *Risk Management, 38*, 64-69.

The author identifies the six stages of an organization's crisis management plan: risk identification, advanced preparation, risk escalation, emergency response, disaster recovery, and return to normalcy. He also offers a "risk assessment master matrix" to help an organization identify and manage its level of risk.

Touchton, J. G., & Davis, L. (Eds.). (1991). *Fact book on women in higher education.* New York, NY: American Council on Education/Macmillan.

This text offers, in one comprehensive volume, data on women faculty, students, administrators, staff, and trustees. It provides current data culled from the Equal Employment Commission, National Research Council, Bureau of the Census, National Center for Education Statistics, and Bureau of Labor Statistics. The text is organized into seven topical areas: demographic and economic trends which are significant to higher education; transition from high school to college; enrollments; degrees earned; faculty; administrators, trustees and staffs; and student financial aid.

7

AN OPEN AND SHUT CASE

About the Case

A clear cut admission of guilt, virtual agreement by all parties on the essential facts of the case, set procedures to handle research misconduct, and a well-tested institutional grievance procedure ensuring due process did not make for smooth deliberations and agreement on what constitutes justice. While guilt was never an issue, the sanction conferred and the question of due process did become central issues. Both slow and fast responses added to the institution's potential for error. Compassion and institutional integrity clouded the penalty issue. This case illustrates the subjectivity of judging a case through the required levels from campus committee to the president, applying sanctions within a seemingly objective environment, and avoiding the plethora of opportunities for error.

CASE STUDY

The Confession. Last October, Dr. Edwin Venorsky telephoned his dean to admit that he had committed certain improprieties in his research while serving as a full-time tenured faculty member in the College of Science at Brockton University. Brockton University is a well-known private research institution with an undergraduate student enrollment of about 22,000 and a graduate enrollment of approximately 8,000. The university's science faculty had enjoyed decades of recognition not only for their scientific research, but also for the talented graduates who had likewise received recognition from the scientific community. Venorsky, a microbiologist, had been at Brockton for 14 years and had an outstanding reputation as an aggressive researcher in terms of his ability to secure external funds to support his progressive research projects.

Meeting a short time later with the dean, Dr. Venorsky reiterated his admission of having committed certain research improprieties and expressed a genuine desire to assist the university in correcting them. Venorsky relinquished the key to his research laboratory and supplied the dean with a file of information substantiating his confession.

The Inquiry and Investigation. The dean forwarded the matter to Brockton's Committee on Research Misconduct in accordance with the institution's policy (Attachment A). Aided significantly by documents provided by Venorsky, the committee quickly moved from the inquiry stage—functioning essentially like a grand jury, ascertaining that indeed scientific misconduct had in all probability occurred—to the investigative stage.

The committee now conducted a close examination of Venorsky's research activities, reviewing not only his research papers, but also his published and unpublished laboratory reports. In addition, the committee interviewed numerous individuals whom they believed could provide relevant information concerning Venorsky's research. Edwin Venorsky, himself, was invited by the committee to appear and be interviewed, but he declined.

The Preliminary Report. In February, the committee submitted a preliminary report to the provost, Dr. Joan Brecht, confirming Dr. Venorsky's admission of research improprieties and recommending the termination of Venorsky's employment as the appropriate sanction.

After receiving a copy of the research misconduct committee's preliminary report, Edwin Venorsky changed his mind and asked to appear and to testify personally before the committee. Two days after Venorsky submitted his request to testify before the committee, he suffered a mild stroke. His attorney remained in communication with the committee and reiterated Venorsky's urgent desire to address the committee regarding the sanction it recommended in its preliminary report. To accommodate Dr. Venorsky's unexpected health complications and wishes, the committee agreed to postpone the filing of its final report until Venorsky was well enough to meet with them. All appropriate university officials were notified of the request to delay the procedures as was required by Brockton's scientific misconduct policy. All concurred with the committee's decision to accommodate Venorsky.

Four months later Edwin Venorsky informed the committee, through his attorney, that he was well enough to testify before them. In addition to his own testimony before the group, Venorsky also produced several witnesses. These colleagues talked about his long affiliation with the university, their personal regard for his academic abilities, and their belief that the proposed sanction described in the preliminary report was too severe.

Dr. Venorsky presented no evidence to significantly refute any of the substantive findings of misconduct by the committee, nor did he offer any explanation for his misconduct.

The Final Report. The committee's final report, dated July 22, reiterated its earlier finding that Venorsky's activities had involved "serious research misconduct." Among the most serious findings, according to the committee, was his reuse of old data in several published articles and the presentation of these data as new, and therefore confirming, findings. The committee's final report noted that Venorsky had not adequately refuted, either orally or in writing, the committee's findings of research misconduct.

However, the committee did acknowledge the testimony of witnesses produced by Venorsky in his defense substantiating that he had made a "significant contribution to the teaching effort of the College of Science." The final report suggested that these contributions should not go unrecognized.

Further, the committee urged that every consideration be given to Venorsky's personal circumstances and that ample time be given to him both to restore his health and to find new opportunities to continue the productive aspects of his career. And finally, the committee recommended that Edwin Venorsky's rank of full professor and his tenure status be rescinded, but that he remain under a term contract as a lecturer with Brockton University until he could secure appropriate professional employment elsewhere.

The Provost and President Act. After careful consideration of the final report, Provost Brecht forwarded a communication, dated July 27, to President Sandoxis recommending that Dr. Venorsky's position as a tenured faculty member be terminated immediately. The provost did not recommend that Venorsky be retained as a lecturer with a term contract.

The president sent a copy of the provost's letter to Edwin Venorsky along with a short transmittal note. In this cover note, President Sandoxis invited Dr. Venorsky and his attorney to meet with him to present any concerns or information which they believed might be relevant to the provost's recommendation before a final decision was made by the president.

In a subsequent meeting with the president on August 2, Dr. Venorsky and his attorney presented a printed transcript of the testimony of the witnesses who had spoken of Venorsky's academic capabilities and personal attributes. Edwin Venorsky expressed his heartfelt belief to the president that since the misconduct would not have been uncovered had he not admitted to the improprieties, the institution had an obligation to weigh these few instances of scientific misconduct against the professor's overall integrity. He again voiced his sincere regret for having perpetrated these instances of scientific misconduct and his genuine interest in helping the university to correct the improprieties. Dr. Venorsky also asserted that his unfortunate actions had been promoted by increasing institutional pressure to secure external funds and to achieve national and international recognition through published research.

One week following the meeting with Venorsky, on August 8, President Sandoxis issued a letter to the professor informing him that his tenured position with the university would be officially terminated effective September 1. The letter also advised Venorsky that the termination could be appealed to Brockton's governing Board of Trustees, a group of 28 prominent and influential graduates and friends of Brockton University, a self-perpetuating unit with members serving seven-year terms. The president is an *ex officio* member of the governing board.

The Appeal. Edwin Venorsky elected to appeal the president's decision to the Board of Trustees. His appeal—as stated in the president's letter—was limited to the action of termination. In his appeal, Venorsky argued that the sanction was too severe considering that the scientific misconduct would never have been uncovered had he not originally confessed to it.

Also, the appeal pointed out that the decision to terminate deviated from the committee's recommended sanction as detailed in its final report. Dr. Venorsky noted that the committee, having heard firsthand the testimony of witnesses, had altered their preliminary recommended sanction. Since neither Provost Brecht nor President Sandoxis had heard this testimony, their decision to terminate was based on incomplete and inclusive evidence. Finally, Venorsky contended that the decision to terminate his tenure status with the university truncated his rights as a faculty member. Specifically, university policy on the termination of appointments of tenured faculty provided that "appeals of termination of tenured faculty for adequate cause shall be made in accordance with university grievance procedures." Venorsky argued that he had been denied "due process" because his termination had not followed the grievance procedures outlined in the *Faculty Handbook* (Attachment B).

The president was not surprised that Venorsky elected to appeal the termination to the board. He was, however, caught off guard by Venorsky's claim that he had been denied his contractual right to due process because his termination had not been issued in accordance with Brockton's grievance procedure. President Sandoxis knew full well that the members of the board would be concerned with, and sensitive to, the issue of contractual rights. The president also knew that the university would soon be given the opportunity to provide a response to the appeal in which he would have to document and explain that indeed Edwin Venorsky had been afforded all rights of due process.

Let's pause here. . .

1. *In terms of university policy, critique the validity of the decisions made at each point in the process—by the dean, the committee, the provost, and finally, the president. For example, was the committee correct to postpone the submission of its final report until Venorsky was well enough to testify? Was the provost correct in her recommendation to the president? Should the president have met with Venorsky and his lawyer? Was the action taken at each level consistent with the provisions of the institution's "Research Misconduct Policy"?*

2. *Do you agree with the provost's recommendation to immediately terminate Venorsky's appointment? What other options were available to the provost? Should the provost have accepted verbatim the altered recommendation for sanction that appeared in the committee's final report? What other factors must the provost take into consideration in making such a recommendation to the president? Have you considered if there is a liability in setting the precedent of retaining a faculty member found guilty of scientific misconduct until he or she finds employment elsewhere?*

3. *Was the president wise to offer to meet with Venorsky and his attorney before making a final decision on the provost's recommendation? What were the advantages and disadvantages to this action? Was the action in keeping with the university's policies? If not, did the action increase the institution's liability in this matter? Should the university's legal counsel have been asked to attend the meeting?*

4. *Given the provisions in the attached grievance policy, evaluate the merit of Venorsky's appeal to the board. What is the strength of each of the three points raised by Venorsky in his appeal to Brockton's Board of Trustees? Anticipate the reaction of the board to each of these arguments.*

5. *The United States Constitution guarantees that an individual not be deprived of liberty or property without due process of law. This right was made applicable to the states by the 14th Amendment to the Constitution. Consider how the board reaction might be different at a public institution when, as state employees, faculty are guaranteed due process by the Constitution.*

6. *Draft the president's written reply to the governing board responding directly to the three points made by Venorsky in his appeal.*

7. *While policy guides actions in a specific instance, the handling of a particular case also provides a methodology to critique the usefulness of the policy. Are there any revisions you would recommend to either the "Research Misconduct Policy" or the "Grievance Procedures for Faculty" based on your experience in working with this case?*

Attachment A

Brockton University
Research Misconduct Policy

Definition of Research Misconduct

The key to defining research misconduct is intent. Research misconduct is an act of deception; it is different from error or from honest differences of interpretation of data. The term "misconduct" includes the following:

A. Falsification of data—ranging from fabrication to deceptively selected reporting, including the purposeful omission of conflicting data with the intent to falsify results;

B. Plagiarism—representation of another's work as one's own;

C. Misappropriation of others' ideas—the unauthorized use of privileged information (such as violation of confidentially in peer review), however obtained; and

D. Formally presented findings based on any other research practices that seriously deviate from those that are reasonable and commonly accepted within the scientific community for proposing, conducting, or reporting research.

Process for Handling Allegations of Research Misconduct

The review process for cases of alleged misconduct consists of two phases: an inquiry and, if it is determined from the inquiry that it is warranted, an investigation. Procedures for both phases are described below. Also described are procedures for reporting to the funding agency (where applicable) and taking interim administrative action when serious circumstances call for immediate precautions. There are also provisions for appealing a determination of research misconduct.

In order to address all allegations of research misconduct expeditiously, the university has formed a standing committee, the Committee on Research Misconduct. The committee will consist of five tenured faculty members appointed by the provost. Committee representation should reflect the broad range of academic disciplines at the university. Committee members will serve for two years; terms will be staggered to further allow for continuity. The committee will interpret the university's policy on research misconduct and will initiate and carry out inquiries and investigations.

Allegations may be reported to the chair of the committee. If the chair determines that the concern does fall under the jurisdiction of the Committee on Research Misconduct, the chair will discuss the inquiry and investigation procedures with the individual who has questions about the integrity of a research project (the complainant). If the individual chooses to make a formal allegation, the matter will be brought before the committee as soon as possible. If the individual chooses not to make a formal allegation but the administrator or committee chair believes there is sufficient basis for conducting an inquiry, the matter will be referred to the committee for appropriate action.

Even if the subject of the allegations (the respondent) leaves the university before the case is resolved, the university will continue the examination of the allegations in accordance with this policy. If there is a finding of misconduct, the university will notify the institution with which the subject of the investigation is currently affiliated. Furthermore, the university will cooperate with other institutions' processes to resolve such questions.

A. Inquiry

    1. Purpose: An inquiry, the first step of the review process, may be initiated by an allegation of misconduct or by information obtained from other sources, such as review of reports. In the inquiry, factual information is gathered and expeditiously reviewed to determine if an investigation of the charge is warranted. An inquiry is not a formal hearing; it is designed to separate allegations deserving of further investigation from frivolous, unjustified, or clearly mistaken allegations.

    2. Structure: The committee must ensure that it has the academic expertise necessary to judge the allegations being made. Therefore, it may call in on- or off-campus consultants as necessary to assist in reviewing a case. If a member of the committee has a real or apparent conflict of interest with a given case, that member will not participate in the review process for the case. In such a case, the committee will recommend to the provost an ad hoc member to substitute. Inquiry proceedings require a majority of the committee in attendance.

    3. Process: To initiate an inquiry, the committee convenes and notifies the respondent of the basis of the inquiry and the process that will follow. Notification will be made in writing and copies will be securely maintained and held confidential in the office of the provost.

    To the greatest extent possible, the inquiry proceedings will be kept confidential in order to protect the rights of all parties involved.

    Whether a case can be reviewed effectively without the involvement of the complainant in the committee proceedings depends upon the nature of the allegation and the evidence available. Cases that depend specifically upon the observations or statements of the complainant cannot proceed without the involvement of that individual in the committee proceedings; other cases that can rely on documentary evidence may permit the complainant to remain anonymous to the committee.

The respondent is obligated to cooperate in providing the material necessary to conduct the inquiry and will be so informed by the committee when the inquiry is initiated. Unco-operative behavior may result in immediate implementation of a formal investigation and appropriate institutional sanctions. The respondent will be given an opportunity to comment on the allegations during the inquiry and to respond to a draft copy of the inquiry findings. If he or she comments on that report, the comments will be made part of the final inquiry record.

Inquiries should be resolved expeditiously. The date the com-mittee convenes to consider an allegation or evidence of mis-conduct marks the beginning of the time period allowed for conducting the inquiry. The inquiry phase must be completed and the final written report of the findings submitted to the provost within 60 days of initiation of the inquiry, unless cir-cumstances clearly warrant a longer period, or within a shorter time period if so specified by a funding agency. If the commit-tee anticipates that the established deadline cannot be met, it shall submit to the provost a report citing the reason(s) for the delay and describing progress to date; it shall also inform the respondent and other involved individuals. Further, the record of inquiry must include documentation of the reason for exceeding the 60-day period.

4. Findings of the Inquiry: The completion of an inquiry is marked by a determination of whether or not an investigation is war-ranted, and by submission of the written report of the inquiry findings to the provost. The report shall state what evidence was reviewed, summarize relevant interviews, and describe the process and conclusion of the inquiry. The respondent and the complainant will be informed by the committee whether or not the allegations will be subject to an investiga-tion. The respondent will be given a copy of the final report of the inquiry.

In the case of the allegations found to warrant an investiga-tion, the provost will notify the director(s) of any funding agen-cies sponsoring the research in question that an investigation will be conducted. In addition, the committee will notify the respondent's department chair and dean of the impending investigations.

If an allegation is found to be unsupported but has been submitted in good faith, no further formal action, other than informing all parties involved in the inquiry, shall be taken. The records and finding of the inquiry, including the identity of the respondent, will be held confidential to the greatest extent possible to protect the parties involved. In such cases the university will undertake diligent efforts to protect the complainant against retaliation. Individuals engaging in acts of retaliation will be subject to disciplinary action and/or grievance proceedings.

Unsupported allegations not brought in good faith shall lead to disciplinary action against the complainant.

B.   Procedures for Reporting to the Funding Component

The agency sponsoring a research project in which misconduct is suspected shall be notified by the provost in writing as soon as the decision had been made to undertake an investigation, and no later than on the date the investigation begins. Agency guidelines for such situations shall be followed. In the case of Public Health Service (PHS) grants, notification is made to the director of the Office of Research Integrity (ORI).

The university also will notify the funding agency at any stage of an inquiry or investigation if it is ascertained that any of the following conditions exist:

1.   There is an immediate health and/or environmental hazard involved;

2.   There is an immediate need to protect federal funds or equipment;

3.   There is an immediate need to protect the interests of the person making the allegations or of the individual who is the subject of the allegations as well as his/her co-investigators and associates, if any; and

4.   It is probable that the alleged incident is going to be reported publicly. [In the case of PHS grants, if the inquiry indicates possible criminal violation, the Office of Research Integrity must be notified within 24 hours of obtaining that information.]

C.   Interim Administrative Action

After the university has notified the funding agency that an investigation is warranted, or that any of the conditions listed in the preceding section exist, the agency may take interim action to protect the rights of involved parties, to protect the welfare of human or animal subjects of research, etc. Such action can range from minor restrictions, requests for assurances, or deferral of a continuation grant application all the way to suspension of the grant.

Interim administrative action also may be taken by the university in the event that any of the conditions listed in the preceding section exist. Interim action does not constitute a finding, but is a precautionary measure necessitated by serious circumstances. The provost may take such action when justified by the need to protect federal funds; the health and safety of research subjects and patients; research data, records, materials, or other information that may be the subject of an inquiry or investigation; or the interests of students, colleagues, and general public. Such action can range from minor restrictions to suspension of the activities of the respondent. Interim administrative action should be taken in full awareness of how it might affect the individuals and the ongoing research within the university.

D. Investigation

1. Purpose: The University Committee on Research Misconduct will initiate an investigation only after it has made an inquiry finding that an investigation is warranted. An investigation is the formal examination and evaluation of all pertinent facts to determine whether misconduct has occurred. Among other things, the investigation shall look carefully at the substance of the inquiry findings and examine all relevant evidence. The investigation findings and recommendations are advisory. They will be submitted to and reviewed by the provost, who will make the final determination on the case.

To the greatest extent possible, the investigation proceedings will be kept confidential. However, it should be noted that complete confidentiality cannot be assured during an investigation, which is a much more formal, wide-ranging proceeding than an inquiry.

2. Structure: Committee members shall be unbiased, have appropriate academic backgrounds for judging the issues being raised, and have no real or apparent conflicts of interest with the case being investigated. The composition of the committee may be challenged for cause by the respondent or by the complainant; the chair of the committee will decide the validity of a challenge for cause. In the event the chair is

challenged for cause, the provost will decide the validity of the challenge.

3. Process: Upon completing an inquiry and finding that an investigation is warranted, the Committee on Research Misconduct will initiate the investigation within 30 days of the date on which its report was submitted to the provost.

To the extent feasible, the committee's procedures in conducting the investigation shall be in compliance with any agency guidelines that must be followed if the research is supported by external funding. The investigation may consist of a compilation of activities including, but not limited to:

a. Review and copying of relevant research data, proposals, correspondence, memoranda of telephone calls or memoranda to file, and other pertinent documents at the university, at the granting agency, or elsewhere;

b. Review of published materials and manuscripts submitted or in preparation;

c. Inspection of offices, laboratory, or clinical facilities, and/or materials;

d. Interviewing of parties with an involvement in or knowledge about the case, including both the complainant and the respondent.

Complete summaries of these interviews shall be prepared, provided to the interviewed party for comment or revision, and included as part of the documentary record of the investigation.

In the course of an investigation, additional information may emerge that justifies broadening the scope of the investigation beyond the initial allegations. The respondent shall be informed when significant new directions of investigation are undertaken.

The committee shall notify the provost of any major developments that could warrant interim action or that must be reported to the funding agency. In the latter case, such developments include disclosure of facts that may affect current or potential funding for the individual(s) under investigation or that the funding agency needs to know to ensure appropriate use of federal funds and otherwise protect the public interest. Significant developments during the investigation will be reported in writing by the provost to the funding agency as necessary, in accordance with agency guidelines.

After conducting the investigation in accordance with the process outlines above, the committee will develop a preliminary report. The preliminary report shall include at least the following: a description of the policies and procedures under which the investigation was conducted; a description of how and from whom, or where information relevant to the investigation was obtained; a specific statement of the committee's preliminary investigative findings relative to possible misconduct in research, or the lack thereof.

A copy of the preliminary report, including all attachments, will be provided to the respondent for the purpose of affording him or her the opportunity to respond. The respondent will be given at least 10 calendar days to respond to the preliminary report. The respondent will be informed that he or she has the right to respond in writing and to request the opportunity to meet with the committee accompanied by an advisor of choice. Should the respondent elect to meet with the committee, he or she will be permitted to make an oral presentation to the committee and to present documentary, testimonial, and rebuttal evidence. A transcript of the meeting will be made available to the respondent.

Following the conclusion of any such meeting held with the respondent and after receipt of the respondent's written response to the preliminary report, the committee will have the responsibility to carefully review and consider the entire record in the matter, to conduct further investigation if necessary, and to prepare a final investigative report setting forth the detailed findings of the committee and any recommended sanctions. The final report shall parallel the preliminary report in format, and shall include the same categories of information. It shall also include the actual text or an accurate summary of the response of the respondent.

The committee then will submit the final investigative report to the provost. The respondent also will receive the final report of the investigation. If the identify of the complainant is known to the committee, he or she shall be provided with those portions of the final report that address his or her role and opinions in the investigations.

The investigation is complete when the provost has reviewed the report, made a determination on the case, and submitted to the funding agency the final report along with a description of any sanctions to be taken by the university.

Investigations shall be conducted as expeditiously as possible. An investigation ordinarily shall be completed within 120 days of its initiation. However, the nature of some cases may render the deadlines difficult to meet. If the committee determines that the full process cannot be completed in 120 days, it must notify the provost of the reason for the delay and ask for an appropriate extension of time.

4. Findings of the Investigation: Findings of an investigation may include the following:

    a. Research misconduct was committed;

    b. No misconduct was committed, but serious scientific errors were discovered in the course of the investigations;

    c. No misconduct or serious scientific errors were committed.

    The provost will review the committee report and make a determination on the case. The section below titled "Resolution" details the follow-up action that must be taken after the determination is made.

    The findings and other records of the investigation will be securely and confidentially maintained, in accordance with pertinent federal and state laws, in a file in the Office of Research Development and Administration.

E. Appeal/Final Review

The respondent may file a written appeal of the determination of the provost with the president of the university in accordance with university grievance procedures. Any appeal should be filed within 30 days after the provost's determination. A time extension, where there is appropriate justification, may be requested of the president. The appeal should be restricted to the body of evidence already presented, and the grounds for appeal should be limited to failure to follow appropriate procedures in the investigation or arbitrary and capricious decision-making. New evidence may warrant a new investigation, in which case the president may reconvene the committee or take other appropriate action.

If the decision of the president affirms the determination of the provost, the respondent may submit an application for appeal to the Board of Trustees, in accordance with the requirements of the Board's *Bylaws*. The decision of any Board review is final.

F. Resolution

1. Finding of No Research Misconduct: All persons and agencies/organizations informed of the investigation must be

notified promptly of the finding of no misconduct. Notification will be made by the provost. The provost will undertake diligent efforts, as appropriate, to restore the reputation of the respondent, when there is a finding of no misconduct.

2. Finding of No Research Misconduct, But Finding of Serious Scientific Error: All persons and agencies/organizations informed of the investigation must be notified promptly of the finding of no misconduct. Notification will be made by the provost.

    The university will need to consider means to correct the scientific record. In the event that the committee discovers serious scientific error, it will include in its final report specific recommendations for action, such as notifying editors of journals in which the respondent's research was published, other institutions with which the respondent has been affiliated, collaborators, professional societies, state professional licensing boards (if applicable), etc. The provost will refer these recommendations to the appropriate administrative official (department chair, dean, or higher administrator) for follow-up action.

3. Finding of Arch-Misconduct: All persons and agencies/organizations informed of the investigation must be notified promptly of the finding of research misconduct. Notification will be made by the provost.

    In its final report, the committee will recommend necessary actions to correct the scientific record and to notify affected individuals or organizations as specified in F.2. above. The provost will refer these recommendations to the appropriate administrative official (department chair, dean, or higher administration) for follow-up action.

    The committee in its report also will recommend specific sanctions to be imposed on the respondent(s), including the reasons thereof. Sanctions can range from a reprimand or removal from the research project to termination of employment. The provost will then be responsible for disposition of the matter.

    The committee's final report will be sent, as appropriate, to affected funding agencies or other organizations, which may impose their own sanctions or take other actions.

Attachment B

Brockton University
Grievance Procedure for Faculty

(excerpted from *Faculty Handbook*, pages 57 to 61)

This document 1) defines the procedures by which a member of the faculty may appeal administrative action or inaction; 2) defines procedures by which charges of unethical conduct may be made; and 3) establishes a Judicial Review Board (JRB).

I. Introduction

    A. Each member of the faculty shall have the right to a hearing and appeal for redress of grievance through established channels. Access to these channels is restricted to faculty or those who were faculty when the action or inaction leading to the grievance occurred. In general, it is preferable that problems be solved within the university at the level at which they arose.

    B. For purposes of this document, "faculty" should be defined as those who hold faculty rank, whether full-time or by joint or cross appointment. Grievances shall be initiated under this document only insofar as the grievance relates to faculty duties or concerns.

    C. Faculty members may initiate a grievance under this document against an action or omission to act by administrators, members of the administrative staff, faculty members, civil service employees, or students which affects the grievant individually. This document shall be construed so that "respondent" shall refer to that person against whom the grievance is lodged.

II. Initiation of a Grievance

    A. Initiation of a Grievance Against an Administrator

        1. Before any formal grievance is filed, there shall be an informal discussion looking toward a settlement between the grievant and the administration officer who made the initial decision which is being grieved. In case of doubt as to the administrator whose decision caused the grievance, the immediate supervisor is the appropriate administrative officer with whom to initiate informal discussion.

        2. If a settlement cannot be reached informally, the grievant may submit a formal grievance, which shall include a statement that informal efforts were made to settle the dispute.

            a. It shall be made in writing, shall provide sufficient detail to allow for a response, and shall state the remedy sought.

    b.   It shall be filed within 20 calendar days of the determination by the grievant of the inability to come to a settlement informally, but in no case later than 60 calendar days after the grievant has become aware of the action which is being grieved.

    c.   It shall be filed with the administrator who made the decision which is being grieved, except in the case of a denial of promotion and/or tenure by the provost when the grievance may be filed directly with the Judicial Review Board (JRB) or the president.

3.   There shall be no formal hearing involving finding of fact at any administrative level.

4.   For the purposes of this grievance procedure, the term "working day" shall be defined as a day during which classes are held during the fall and spring semesters of the school year.

5.   The chair of the JRB shall be apprised of the filing of a formal grievance and shall monitor the progress of the grievance through the grievance process. Failure of the grievant to meet filing deadlines shall result in dismissal of the grievance. Failure of the administrator at each level of the grievance process to respond within specified time periods shall result in automatic appeal to the next higher level.

6.   Within 15 working days after receipt of the grievance, the administrator shall make a written decision either granting or denying the remedy sought in whole or in part.

7.   All proceedings and time limits of this grievance procedure are subject to suspension for the period of time of an approved university leave or of an incapacitating illness affecting a party to the grievance. It shall be the responsibility of the JRB to determine the validity of such suspension and to certify when the conditions of the suspension have ceased, thus restarting the time clock of the grievance procedure.

8.   All "working day" time limits and suspensions or cause may be waived upon agreement of all parties to a grievance, as certified by the JRB.

B.   Charges of Unethical Conduct: Any member of the faculty may file directly with the Judicial Review Board a charge of unethical conduct as defined by the "Code of Ethics." Before filing an official charge of unethical conduct, the grievant shall notify his/her immediate supervisor and together they shall initiate informal discussions with the respondent with the aim of settling the complaint informally if at all possible. If the respondent is the immediate supervisor of the grievant, the complainant shall notify the administrator immediately above the respondent. In the event that the issue is not resolved informally, the JRB shall deal with the charge under procedures defined elsewhere in this document.

III. Appeals from administrative decisions through administrative channels

A member of the faculty objecting to a decision by the administrative officer may make further written appeal through the regular administrative channels.

A. Such written appeal shall be made within 15 working days of the receipt of the decision and shall include the original grievance, the written decision, and the reasons for the appeal.

B. The appeal shall be transmitted to the next level of administration above the source of the decision. At each level of appeal, the administrator who received the appeal shall proceed in accordance with the procedure in Section II.A.

IV. Appeals from administrative decisions through the Judicial Review Board

A. Any member of the faculty who feels that a grievance has not been resolved after appealing to and receiving a decision from the administrative level immediately below the president has the option of continuing the appeal process through administrative channels by appealing to the president, or by filing a formal appeal with the Judicial Review Board. The time limit expressed in Section III.a. shall apply to each level of the appeal process, including the filing of a formal appeal with the JRB.

B. Upon receipt of an appeal, the JRB shall form a panel within 10 working days. The panel shall operate under the provisions of Section VIII. The decision of the panel shall be in the form of a written recommendation to the president. A copy of this recommendation shall be provided to the principal parties on the same day. In the absence of compelling circumstances, the president shall give a written decision as promptly as possible, but within 15 working days. The president shall notify the JRB and the principal parties of the decision. In the event that the president overturns the recommendations of the JRB panel, he/she shall submit a complete report to the JRB and the principal parties to the grievance citing evident and/or procedural grounds upon which the decision was based.

V. Appeals to the Board of Trustees

    A. The grievant may appeal the president's decision to the Board of Trustees.

    B. The Board and the grievant may jointly agree to submit the matter to arbitration and to accept the arbitrator's decision.

        1. The grievant and the Board must both agree on the choice of an arbitrator and the issue being arbitrated. If the parties cannot otherwise agree on an arbitrator, the American Arbitration Association will be asked to supply a panel of arbitrators familiar with the academic environment from which the arbitrator will be chosen.

        2. The arbitration hearing will be conducted under the voluntary labor arbitration rules of the American Arbitration Association.

        3. The arbitrator's fee and expenses, the administrative costs of the American Arbitration Association, and the cost of obtaining a record of the arbitration hearing shall be borne by the university if the arbitrator finds in favor of the university. If a compromise decision is reached, costs should be proportional to the decision reached.

        4. Each party shall bear whatever other costs it may incur.

VI. Right to Counsel

At all stages of appeal the principal parties shall have the right to have present with them an advisor of their choice.

VII. Withdrawal of Grievance

The grievant any withdraw a formal grievance at any stage of the proceedings but may not reinstate it once it is withdrawn. The withdrawal should be made in writing to the individual hearing the appeal.

VIII. The Judicial Review Board

    A. Purpose

    The Judicial Review Board exists to assist the faculty and the administration in resolving grievances and charges of unethical conduct.

    B. Duties of the Judicial Review Board

        1. The JRB shall have the authority to supervise the procedure of the grievance process.

        2. The JRB shall consider all grievances appealed to it.

    C. Procedures of the JRB panels

        1. Upon receipt of a request which necessitates review by a JRB panel, a JRB panel shall be formed. A JRB panel shall consist

of three members. Each party to the grievance shall name a member of the panel who shall be a tenured full professor of a university department not associated with either party to the grievance. The JRB shall name one member of the JRB to the panel who shall not represent a university unit associated with either party of the grievance, and who shall serve as a chair of the panel. Such chair shall instruct the panel in the procedures of JRB hearings and in the history of the particular grievance to that point. Each principal shall be entitled to one peremptory challenge in addition to challenges for cause. The validity of the challenge shall be determined by the JRB.

2. A hearing shall be mandatory in a grievance of dismissal or loss of tenure. In any grievances in which the issues are unclear without finding of fact, a panel shall be formed and a hearing held. The cause of a grievance or charge of unethical conduct must relate directly to the duties and status of the university employee, and shall not be a trivial or an entirely private matter.

3. If the JRB recommends a hearing, the administrator whose decision is being appealed or the respondent shall have the right to submit to the JRB panel a request that the appeal or charge be dismissed as failing to meet the above criteria, and that there are, therefore, insufficient grounds for proceeding to a hearing of the evidence. The grievant may reply with an argument as to why the appeal or charge should stand as written, or may elect to clarify the appeal or complaint. If the JRB decides that the appeal or charge is not actionable, it shall dismiss the appeal or charge.

4. The administrator defending the action or omission which is the subject of the grievance shall be that administrator who made the first negative decision which the grievant is grieving.

5. JRB panel hearings shall be recorded on audio tape.

6. The JRB panel shall hold hearings as promptly as possible, but shall begin no later than 15 working days after receipt of the appeal or charge, and shall report as promptly as possible, but not later than 15 working days after the conclusion of the hearing.

7. The principal parties appearing before the JRB panel shall each have the right to be accompanied by personal legal counsel. The counsel will be permitted to advise clients during the hearing and, with consent of the JRB panel, speak on their behalf.

8. The JRB panel shall require of both the grievant and the respondent a list of witnesses to be called and a copy of any documents that may be introduced into evidence or which may contain evidence that may be introduced by witnesses or which are the basis of professional judgments that may be asserted during the hearing. The JRB panel shall make the information available to all parties.

9. Hearings shall be open unless the JRB panel, upon request of any of the parties, decides a hearing should be closed. If the hearing is closed, only the members of the JRB panel, the principal parties, and other advisors shall be admitted to the hearing, and witnesses for either party shall be present only while they are giving testimony.

10. The principal parties and their representatives shall be permitted to see and hear all evidence, to cross-examine any person giving evidence, and to present their own relevant evidence and arguments.

11. Although the JRB panel may question principals and witnesses, no public statements shall be made by the members of the panel before or during the hearings, or before or during deliberation.

12. In the absence of compelling circumstances the chair, within 15 working days of the close of the hearings, shall send the JRB panels' report to the president, the grievant, the respondent, and the JRB. This report shall contain a specific recommendation regarding relief. In the event of undue delay on the part of the JRB panel, all materials pertaining to the grievance shall be returned to the JRB, which shall review the case and submit a report within 10 working days.

13. After the completion of the JRB panel's action, all documents or copies thereof and tape recordings shall be deposited for safekeeping in the president's office with access to be made available to the principal parties or their designated representatives in case of appeal.

14. The president shall make a decision based on the JRB's report, supporting documents, and in cases where the president chooses to review the testimony, the tape recording of the hearing. Unless both parties are present, the president shall not entertain any new information. The president shall refrain from consulting with either party to the grievance prior to making a decision on the JRB's recommendation.

SELECTED READINGS

Adler, R. S., & Bigoness, W. J. (1992). Contemporary ethical issues in labor-management relations. *Journal of Business Ethics, 11*, 351-360.

The author first offers an analysis of the key elements and values charact-

Written from a corporate perspective, the authors discuss current labor-management issues that pose ethical questions. The authors conclude that ethics means that the interests and rights of all constituencies must be balanced. In higher education, the constituencies would include the administration, faculty, staff, students, alumni, accrediting agencies, and many more.

Austin, A. E. (1990). Faculty cultures, faculty values. *New Directions for Institutional Research, Number 68,* 61-74.

The author first offers an analysis of the key elements and values characteristic of the four primary cultures that influence faculty values and behaviors: the academic profession, the discipline, the academy as an organization within a national system, and the specific type of institution. The author then identifies the tensions and issues that arise from the interaction of these cultures and suggests ways in which an institution can build on its cultural values to enhance organizational performance.

Braxton, J. M. (1991). The influence of graduate department quality on the sanctioning of scientific misconduct. *Journal of Higher Education, 62,* 87-103.

The author reports the findings of a study conducted using chairs of chemistry, physics, psychology, and sociology at 100 randomly selected institutions classified as Research I or II in the Carnegie classification scheme. The study was designed to determine the influence of the graduate school quality on the formality of sanctions taken by department chairs in response to instances of scientific misconduct.

Carland, J. A., Carland, J. W., & Aby, C. D. Jr. (1992). Proposed codification of ethicacy in the publication process. *Journal of Business Ethics, 11,* 95-105.

After a review of the existing problems associated with abuse of the manuscript review process, the authors propose a Code of Ethics for researchers, referees, and editors which is directed toward improving the peer review process.

Carpenter, D. S., Paterson, B. G., Kibler, W. L., & Paterson, J. W. (1990). What price faculty involvement? The case of the research university. *NASPA Journal, 27,* 206-212.

Starting from the premise that teaching is not the only responsibility of faculty at a research institution, the authors examine the obstacles encountered when attempting to enlist faculty in student affairs programming.

Green, M. F., & McDade, S. A. (1991). *Investing in higher education: A handbook of leadership development.* Washington, DC: American Council on Education.

The authors offer strategies and resources for leadership development at all levels of the institution. Of particular relevance to this case study are the chapters on governing boards and presidents.

Hahn, H. G. (1986, April 9). Opinion: Ethics and higher education cannot be separated. *The Chronicle of Higher Education, 21,* p. 47.

The author articulates a rationale for why ethics must be an integral part of higher education if institutions are to fulfill their educational mission.

Trotter, P., & Risdon, P. (1990). Performance counseling. *CUPA Journal, 41*(3), 21-24.

The authors advance the argument that performance counseling should take into account the three components that affect performance: department and professional goals, professional competencies, and factors that impede professional development. They define professional competencies to include: communication skills, interpersonal skills, decision-making and management skills, and skills in working with groups.

Wheeler, D. L. (1992, March 18). U.S. agency proposes trial-like hearings to judge cases of scientific misconduct. *The Chronicle of Higher Education, 38,* pp. A8-A11.

The author summarizes proposed changes on how the Public Health Service would resolve charges of scientific misconduct.

8

Hindsight is 20/20

About the Case

As institutions compete for students and donations, the image of the institution held by certain critical publics becomes more important. The social activities
directed toward courting alumni and members of other external constituencies can
motivate these people to support the institution in very tangible ways. But these
same activities can create and perpetuate a social culture on the campus which may
have a variety of negative implications for the institution. This case specifically
addresses the issue of alcohol on campus—its use at alumni events balanced against
the potential liability incurred for encouraging underage drinking. The case makes
clear the potential problems inherent in decisions made by the president regarding
the serving of alcohol at campus-sponsored activities.

CASE STUDY

Dark skies and heavy rains had descended on Winston University
(WU) making for a very gloomy Monday morning. The weather was
strangely appropriate to the low spirits that engulfed the campus and the
community. This was the Monday after Winston University's annual
homecoming weekend, an event for which many at the university had
spent months planning and preparing.

On the preceding Friday afternoon, spirits and morale on campus
were at a record high as the institution looked forward to a spectacular
homecoming celebration which was to be attended by a record number of
alumni and friends of the institution. However, in a matter of a few hours,
a sunny weekend which was full of promise for the institution transformed into one of the most catastrophic events in the institution's history.

President Richard Brewster sat in his office staring at the headlines in the various newspapers. The headlines in the local paper read: "Coed Dies at Homecoming Party." The nearest major metropolitan newspapers ran headlines which read: "University Employee in Pile-Up," and "Spirited University Students Cause Damage to Campus." No, it had not been a good weekend for Winston University.

The newspaper accounts described three separate incidents all related to the homecoming celebration sponsored by the university. The first story was an account of a student's death. A young woman, age 19, died from an overdose of alcohol when her blood alcohol level exceeded what her body could handle.

The second incident described an automobile accident where a university car driven by the assistant director for alumni relations, with three passengers in the car, failed to stop at a red light causing a three-car collision. Several individuals, including the new president of the alumni association, suffered minor injuries, and one remained hospitalized for observation. The police report revealed that the driver was clearly intoxicated at the time of the accident.

The final account offered a general description of the damage that was done on the campus and throughout the community by a group of roughly 150 to 200 students. These students decided to celebrate the homecoming football victory by partying in the streets, painting signs on private property, blocking traffic, and rolling over at least one car. Scattered among the newspapers on the president's desk were countless phone messages asking him to return calls to reporters at radio and television stations, from news magazines and *The Chronicle of Higher Education*.

The Institution. Winston University is a private institution with an enrollment of approximately 9,000 students. Located in a small rural community, the institution has enjoyed a positive and fruitful rapport with the residents of the surrounding area. The institution is the largest employer in the region and hence the focus of much attention. Winston is primarily an undergraduate institution, but offers a small number of master's degree programs which typically enroll nontraditional students from the region. Roughly 98 percent of the undergraduate student population live in the university's residence halls or in conveniently located off-campus apartments. Commuting undergraduates account for the other two percent of the undergraduate student population.

Winston University has worked diligently during the past five years to gain more visibility for the institution. These efforts, along with an improved recruitment function, were deemed essential to maintaining a healthy student enrollment despite repeated increases in tuition. Greater visibility for the institution was also deemed to be imperative to increasing alumni participation and subsequent financial contributions to Winston. The president couldn't help but wonder how far these positive efforts had been hurt by this news emanating from the events surrounding homecoming.

To Drink or Not to Drink. As President Brewster stared at the rain falling outside his window, his mind drifted back to some of the discussions, indeed heated debates, that took place at his staff meetings during the long months that preceded homecoming. The many discussions about homecoming were always similar and the president could count on each of his various staff members to echo the same points of view from meeting to meeting.

Each time the director of alumni relations and the university's athletic director reported on progress made in the planning of various homecoming activities, the president could count on the university's legal counsel, Michelle Cartier to interrupt with a grave warning about the liability associated with drinking alcoholic beverages on campus and serving alcohol at university-sponsored activities. Anna Goldhill, the dean of students, seemed to be perpetually caught in the middle. In retrospect, these discussions were very vivid in the president's mind. In a kind of slow motion dream, he could hear the staff arguing about the role of liquor at the homecoming event.

Alumni Director: The homecoming planning committee is making great progress in finalizing the schedule of this year's activities. This year the tailgate parties will begin at 11:00 a.m. instead of noon and will close when the game starts at 2:00 p.m.

President: Why start a tailgate party in the morning?

Alumni Director: Responses received from alumni who attended last year's event indicated that they had nothing to do after the morning parade until the tailgate parties opened at noon. Since this seems to be a common theme among the responses we received, the planning committee believes that starting the tailgate festivities one hour sooner will make the weekend run more smoothly and be more appealing to alumni and others.

Athletic Director: The members of the athletic boosters club that I've talked with about this are all in favor of starting at 11:00. But, I want to remind everyone that the game will start at 2:00 and the team needs the tailgaters in the stands to cheer them on to victory through the fourth quarter!

Alumni Director (laughing): Don't worry. Tell the coach that we're going to help keep the fans at the game until it finishes by reopening the tailgate during half-time and again at the close of the game for another hour. That should still give alumni a chance to change before the evening banquet and dance.

University Legal Counsel: Will attendance at the tailgate parties be limited to alumni?

Alumni Director: No, Michelle. Alumni will receive special invitations, but the tailgate area will be open to the general public.

Legal Counsel: Students too?

Alumni Director: Sure. We want alumni to interact with students as much as possible. And besides, how can we keep students out of the tailgate area? Those fields are open to anyone.

Legal Counsel: What measures are being taken to be sure that we don't serve alcohol to underage students? I'm also concerned that you're planning to serve alcohol after the game. These people will be getting into their cars and driving. When the tailgate celebrations were only held prior to the football game, we knew that most people would have several hours for their systems to absorb the alcohol before they attempted to operate a vehicle.

Alumni Director: Not to worry! As always, the campus police will be on the scene and can diffuse any potential difficulty.

Legal Counsel: I totally disagree! I've talked with the chief of campus police and he tells me that this is an impossible situation for them. Without setting up some kind of gate or clearance to check identification cards, the police have no way of being sure they can identify all underage drinkers. Also, I've understand that the police on the scene are directed by staff in the alumni office not to "hassle" returning alumni by suggesting that the more inebriated individuals forego another drink.

Alumni Director (looking to the president for reassurance): Surely, Richard, you understand why we can't have a gate set up with policeman carding guests at an event where we're trying to encourage and bolster support for university activities. Besides, food and nonalcoholic beverages are also available at the tailgate parties. We don't force anyone to drink alcohol. We're all adults and responsible for our own actions.

Legal Counsel (also looking at the president): That's not necessarily true! You and everyone here are well aware of my concerns for the institution's liability at such events. When we sponsor events where alcohol is available to the general public, our liability increases dramatically. In this state, the so called "Dram Shop" laws not only regulate the sale of alcoholic beverages, but also impose specific liabilities on the *seller* if alcohol is sold to an intoxicated person or one who is not of legal age. The law is very clear on this subject.

President: Isn't there anyway that the alcohol could be served in very restricted areas? ...to alumni only? ...and in moderate amounts?

Alumni Director: No, that just won't work. The alumni walk to campus from the parade and head toward the stadium so they can get convenient parking spaces. If we send them someplace else on or off-campus, then they'll have a parking problem when they try to get to the game.

Legal Counsel: Then let's not serve any alcohol at all.

Athletic Director (groaning louder than the others): I'm confident the boosters who are most supportive of the athletic events at this university would not like that at all. Where's your school spirit, Michelle? These events are great opportunities for the institution to build good will.

Director of Development (looking at the attorney in a friendly, but patronizing way): Look, Michelle, I know it's your job to worry about the institution's liability, but it's our job to worry about the institution's financial future and general fiscal health. These fun activities are imperative to our ability to get alumni to support this institution with their checkbooks.

President: I'm looking at the future of Winston as well. Two lost suits in court could sink this institution financially. But my concern goes beyond the institution's legal liability. How do these activities affect our students? What are we, as educators, saying to our young students when we make liquor such an important ingredient in our campus homecoming activities?

Dean of Students: I must confess that I too have had some concern about that. I worry that we often give our students mixed signals. On one hand we have a very aggressive drug education and alcohol awareness program on this campus, but on the other, we host these events where the university may unintentionally and unknowingly serve alcohol to underage students.

President (sounding both parental and presidential): We need to take all necessary steps to avoid any possibility of serving alcohol to underage students!

Alumni Director: No undergraduate student is invited to the alumni's tailgate party where alcohol is served.

Legal Counsel: But you just told us that you couldn't prevent them from coming, and that you, in fact, want them there to interact with alumni.

Dean of Students: I know for a fact that more and more students attend the various tailgate parties each year. Campus police and our regulations can't keep them from attending. These events are open to the public and a student can walk up and be served an alcoholic beverage.

Alumni Director: Don't forget that not all of our students are underage. If an underage student walks up and asks for an alcoholic beverage, that student is breaking the law. That is his or her problem, not ours. Isn't it time we treat our students as adults. We're not their parents. Besides, I thought *in loco parentis* was dead.

Legal Counsel: Not necessarily true. I think Anna and her student affairs people have a very valid point. We *do* send our students mixed messages about the role of alcohol in an enriched social atmosphere.

Athletic Director: Well, it's not like we do this every weekend. Winston sponsors these types of events only at homecoming, the February Ice Carnival, and the Spring Celebration. What can three weekends a year do to undermine the morals and character of our students?

Legal Counsel: It just seems ironic. We try to increase financial support for Winston by drawing students, faculty, staff, alumni and visitors to the campus by hosting such events in order to enhance our reputation with the surrounding community. But in doing so, Winston dramatically increases its legal liability by hosting such events and could irrevocably damage its reputation in the event of a single incident at any one of these events.

Athletic Director: I just don't get it. Remember we're just talking about three weekends a year.

Dean of Students: Well, we do have some research data which suggest that our students do not just view this as three isolated parties a year. It's pretty clear from the student surveys that are conducted by the alcohol awareness staff that a greater percentage of the student body is consuming more alcohol more often than in previous years. In fact, I sent each of you, last week, a copy of two tables (Attachment A) from the most recent survey which compared us with national data and suggest that drinking is a very serious problem on this campus.

Vice President, Academic Affairs: If that's true, Anna, then my own concern increases. I am familiar with the research that shows a clear relationship between a student's alcohol consumption and grade point average. A recent study shows that as the number of drinks per week increases, the student's GPA decreases. As an institution, we have a vested interest in our students doing well as they complete their degree and assume good jobs or go on to graduate schools

Development Director: Well, if students are drinking more, that's a real concern. But it shouldn't affect a homecoming celebration designed to increase alumni support and financial contributions to the university.

Besides, if your data are right it means that students are drinking whether or not we host tailgate parties at homecoming.

President: Well, these are all legitimate issues and we are not going to settle them during the hour scheduled for this meeting. I will want to stay posted on the progress in planning the homecoming celebration. The cautions about institutional liability are worth noting, and I am greatly concerned about students' perceptions of our actions in regard to alcohol availability and usage.

Let's pause here. . .

1. *What issues are central to the disagreement about serving alcohol at university sponsored events? Was the president effective in managing this conflict?*

2. *Would these issues be weighed differently at a public institution or at a community college?*

3. *What is the extent of an institution's liability as defined by your state's "Dram Shop" act or similar legislation governing the use and sale of alcohol?*

4. *Are there precautions which might be taken to insure institutional compliance with the law and safety for those in attendance at campus-sponsored festivities?*

5. *To what extent should institutions be guided by the concept of in loco parentis?*

6. *How do you interpret the data present in Attachment A? Should this information affect the planning of the homecoming activities at Winston University?*

Back to the Present. "Yes indeed, institutional liability needs to be balanced against the potential gains to be incurred by the university," President Brewster mumbled to himself as his eyes darted from one newspaper headline to another. He had not been totally deaf to the cautions echoed by Anna Goldhill, the dean of students, and Michelle Cartier, Winston's legal counsel. He remembered that just two years ago, student drinking at homecoming seemed on the verge of getting out of control, and did result in some damage to a few of the residence halls. In response, the president appointed a special committee to study the issue of alcohol on campus.

After six months of study and deliberation, the committee issued a very well reasoned report with some stiff recommendations. The following were among the committee's recommendations:

1. The university should implement a policy on campus which precludes the serving of alcohol on campus.

2. Students involved in an alcohol violation, even for the first time, should be required to attend a substance abuse workshop sponsored by student affairs.

3. Regular alcohol-free social events should be scheduled on campus so as to present a viable alternative to downtown bars.

4. All university employees should participate in a program designed to address the facts concerning substance abuse and to make the employees aware of the availability of counseling services for staff and students and how to make appropriate referrals to these services.

Upon receiving the committee's report, President Brewster shared it with members of his staff. The vice president for academic affairs and the dean of students were in the process of working together to implement many of the recommendations with regard to drug education. Staff opposition to an alcohol policy which precluded serving alcohol on campus, however, was so great that President Brewster felt that this recommendation could not be successfully implemented.

More Bad News. President Brewster was interrupted by a knock on the door. His secretary announced that Michelle Cartier was here to talk with him regarding the institution's posture following the events of the past weekend. As the legal counsel entered carrying an even larger stack of newspapers, the president looked at her solemnly and said, "Please, Michelle, I don't need to hear 'I told you so.' Just tell me where we go from here."

The attorney clearly had much on her mind. "We'll be too busy to talk about regrets. Richard, my immediate concern is to be sure that any comments which you or other university officials make about the events of homecoming weekend not increase our liability. Can I ask that you call a meeting of all key personnel so we can be sure we are together on this?"

The president picked up his phone and spoke briefly with his secretary, then turned back to the attorney, "Consider it done. Do you anticipate litigation?"

Cartier, looking directly at Brewster, said, "It's probable. I anticipate that the institution will be sued by the individuals injured in the car accident since the driver of the university car was ticketed for running a red light and charged with "driving under the influence" or DUI as the students like to call it. I know that four were treated at the hospital and that one was admitted for observation and is still there. Darlene Hungerford, the newly elected president of the WU Alumni Association, is suffering from pain in her neck and severe headaches."

The attorney consulted her yellow tablet and without pausing said, "I also suspect we will be sued by several property owners who suffered damage at the hands of our students. I don't know yet whether the deceased coed was in attendance at WU's tailgate party, but you can bet that if the excessive drinking that caused her death took place at a university sponsored activity, we'll get a suit on that incident as well."

The president, although devastated, was still thinking. He asked, "Don't we have insurance?"

"Oh yes," said the attorney. "WU's insurance will cover most of the legal liability and damage. You have no insurance, however, on the potential damage to the institution's reputation."

A final pause. . .

7. *Assume the role of the president and devise a strategy for responding to the press on the various events of the homecoming weekend. Would you, for example, consent to an interview or limit your response to a printed statement? Consider the potential risks associated with each approach. Draft a formal press release which summarizes the institution's response to the tragic events of the weekend.*

8. *Learning from the tragedy at Winston University, can you generate some guidelines which might be used to balance the potential liabilities of sponsoring such activities for alumni and development purposes with the anticipated benefits?*

9. *What ethical dimensions should govern fundraising activities? Should an institution have policies and guidelines which regulate all promotional activities sponsored by the institution's alumni office? What parameters would you establish?*

10. *Are alumni and development activities consistent with the general purpose and mission of an institution in higher education?*

11. *What obligation does an institution have to the moral and ethical development of its students? Why might this obligation be different at a public institution or at a community college?*

Attachment A-1

Comparison of student-reported consequences of
substance abuse at Winston University
with other four-year institutions across the nation

	Winston University	Four-year Institutions
Hangover	75%	61%
Nausea	62%	50%
Driving under the influence	49%	35%
Regrets act	48%	41%
Missed class	45%	31%
Fight	41%	32%
Memory loss	38%	29%
Did poorly on test	32%	25%
Criticized	28%	30%
Injury	22%	16%
Taken advantage of sexually	18%	14%

Attachment A-2

Comparison of student-reported consequences of
substance abuse at Winston University with other
four-year institutions with enrollments between 5,000 and 15,000

	Winston University	Four-year Institutions 5-15,000 students
Hangover	75%	61%
Nausea	62%	50%
Driving under the influence	49%	40%
Regrets act	48%	41%
Missed class	45%	28%
Fight	41%	35%
Memory loss	38%	28%
Did poorly on test	32%	27%
Criticized	28%	32%
Injury	22%	18%
Taken advantage of sexually	18%	14%

SELECTED READINGS

American Association of University Professors' Committee A on Academic Freedom and Tenure. (1992). College and university policies on substance abuse and drug testing. *Academe 78(3)*, 17-23.

> A report on the federal requirements for campus anti-drug programs and the subsequent need for institutions to emphasize drug education and rehabilitation intervention to address individual substance abuse problems.

American Council on Education. (1992). *Institutional liability for alcohol consumption: A white paper on institutional liability for consumption of alcohol and drugs on campus*. Washington, DC: Author.

> This third update of the ACE white paper originally issued in 1985 on student alcohol abuse offers a discussion of provisions of various state laws including those imposing financial liability upon the "social hosts" for injuries caused by their intoxicated guests, the 1989 federal law (Drug Free Schools and Communities Act Amendments), and citings of applicable court cases. The concept of *in loco parentis* regarding institutional liability for alcohol is also discussed. Included in the paper are recommended guidelines for institutions to consider as policies are formulated regarding alcohol and drug abuse.

Bernstein, J. (1990, March). The ten steps of crisis management. *Security Management, 34*, 75-76.

> This public relations professional summarizes the ten steps to follow to control negative communications arising out of crisis situations, looking particularly at useful communication techniques, audience identification, assessment of the situation and messages, and evaluative techniques.

Carruth, P. J., & Carruth, A. K. (1991). Education in ethics: The role of higher education. *Journal of Education for Business, 66*, 168-171.

> The authors report on the findings of a study designed to identify those factors that influence the development of, and changes in, student values. A survey instrument was administered to junior- and senior-level university students majoring in business at a regional institution in the South.

Cerio, N. G. (1989). Counseling victims and perpetrators of campus violence. *New Directions for Student Services, Number 47*, 53-64.

> The author discusses various counseling approaches to victims of campus violence and the role of campus police as interventionists in incidents of campus violence.

Cole, S. A. (1991). Professional ethics and the role of the academic officer. *CUPA Journal, 42(3),* 37-41.

The author argues that academic officers should use ethical rather than legal standards for their behavior and offers a series of campus-based examples to illustrate this point.

Curtis, D. B., & Winsor, J. L. (1991). Teaching ethics across the curriculum: A subject for faculty and administrators. *CUPA Journal, 42(3),* 7-12.

This article examines the issues related to instruction in ethical values in higher education and their application to human resource personnel activities. The authors discuss the nature of ethical values, explore issues related to teaching values, and offer specific suggestions to accomplish their purposes.

Davis, J. L., & Hunnicutt, D. M. (1992). Community college student alcohol abuse: An assessment. *Community College Review, 19(3),* 43-47.

A report of a FIPSE-funded project to assess alcohol abuse and drug use among 2,843 community college students from six campuses in one Midwestern state.

Guillebeau, J. (1989, Fall). Crisis management: A case study in the killing of an employee. *Public Relations Quarterly, 35,* 19-21.

This brief article offers an hour-by-hour summary of actions taken by a small college to minimize the potential for unfavorable publicity following the killing of an employee. Guillebeau offers the reader some insight into the utility of a public relations function within an institution of higher education.

Presley, C. A., & Meilmen, P. W. (1992). *Alcohol and Drugs on the American College Campus: A Report to College Presidents.* Produced by Southern Illinois University's Student Health Program Wellness Center by the Drug Prevention in Higher Education Program of the Fund for the Improvement of Postsecondary Education (FIPSE), U. S. Department of Education, Washington, D. C.

Funded by a grant provided by the U. S. Department of Education's Fund for the Improvement of Postsecondary Education (FIPSE), the authors conducted a survey in 1989-91 of FIPSE-funded colleges and universities on the nature, scope, and consequences of alcohol and other drug use by students.

Sherrill, J. M. (1989). Models of response to campus violence. *New Directions for Student Services, Number 47,* 77-88.

Following a discussion of the considerations involved in responding to violence, the author reviews some possible methods of response and identifies some deterrents to campus violence.

9

Supervisor's Dilemma

About the Case

Compassion, empathy, a social conscience, professional responsibilities, and a fear of litigation are a curious mixture of factors to consider when dealing with a delicate office personnel situation. Sooner or later, however, supervisors from department chairs to presidents will find themselves faced with interpersonal situations that require resolution. At such times, questions as to how the situation evolved, why it is surfacing now, who is involved, what are the options available, and most importantly, what is the best solution for all concerned, will need to be answered. This case illustrates the critical nature of both oral and written communication in an interpersonal conflict. The supervisor's private discussions with his administrative assistant serve one purpose; his carefully composed letters to her serve another. Consistent communication plays an important role as the case unravels.

CASE STUDY

The Change. The dean was absorbed in reading the enrollment and credit-hour report for the spring term when he heard a weak knock on his open office door. Standing in the doorway was Mary Alice Martin, his administrative secretary.

"Excuse me, sir, but I thought that you would want to know that Elsie didn't come in again this morning," she said.

Dean Bowyer looked up and took off his reading glasses. "Did she call in?"

"No," his long-time secretary replied, "but she was out all last week and didn't call us every day."

The dean was clearly concerned and said, "Try to reach her at home. I would like to speak with her."

Dean Bowyer tried to go back to reading the enrollment report but found it more difficult to concentrate. This was unusual behavior for Elsie Joiner who had worked as an administrative aide in the dean's office for almost ten years, two with Stanley Bowyer and eight with his predecessor, Alvin Clinton. Although Elsie was often moody, her job performance had been excellent up until about six months ago. Stan Bowyer could recall past instances when Elsie came to work with a fever or other illness because she knew there was a pressing deadline.

However, during the past six months, Elsie seemed to be in a more or less permanent state of depression. Lately, she was quicker than usual to accuse others of hating her or trying to make her look bad. Those who worked with Elsie on a regular basis knew that she preferred not to socialize with her coworkers. Altogether, Elsie was generally cranky and pessimistic about work and life.

The more the dean thought about it, the more he was convinced that events of the last week had signaled a change in Elsie's attitude toward work. Last Monday, Elsie did not show up for work or call in sick. When Mary Alice reached her at home in the late morning, Elsie had explained that she became ill during the night and had slept late. She apologized for not phoning Mary Alice to let the office staff know that she would miss work.

However, on Tuesday and Wednesday of last week, Mary Alice found phone messages from Elsie on the voice mail—called in well before 8 a.m.—indicating that she was still sick. On Thursday and Friday, however, Elsie did not come in and there were no calls to explain her absence. On Friday, at Stan Bowyer's direction, Mary Alice put a get well card from the office staff in the mail to Elsie asking her to please let them know how she was feeling.

Monday brought the start of the new week, but much to Dean Bowyer's dismay there was no word from Elsie. On Wednesday, the dean had Mary Alice phone Elsie. "I've tried Elsie's phone number three times," reported Mary Alice, "and still get no answer. Is there anything else I should do?"

Dean Bowyer, although disturbed, could think of nothing else to get to the heart of the problem and said, "Not right now. Thank you."

The Tension. Dean Bowyer was not sure what to do. Despite his best efforts, he knew that his rapport with Elsie Joiner was not good. Elsie had greeted him two years ago with hostility and suspicion when he was appointed dean. Before becoming dean of the college of engineering, he had been chair of the department of electrical engineering, the college's largest department. He was clearly not a new name or personality to the staff in the dean's office.

From his first day on the job, Elsie seemed intent on believing that she would be fired or summarily dismissed by the new dean. Sensing her discomfort, and in an effort to reassure her, Stan Bowyer had entrusted her with more responsibility which was accompanied by a position upgrade and commensurate pay increase. For two years, he worked carefully and deliberately to demonstrate his complete trust in her competence. He had observed over the last two years, however, that Elsie rarely seemed truly to enjoy her new level of responsibility.

For the most part, Elsie became increasingly depressed and distant from the dean and other members of the office staff. Elsie did not attend office lunches and parties. While the dean's staff appreciated Elsie's strong work ethic and her office skills, they learned to keep their distance.

The dean was genuinely puzzled by Elsie's behavior. He had observed Elsie's rapport with his predecessor to be very uneven. At times, the two could be heard shouting at one another during the middle of the work day. Yet, Dean Bowyer was well aware that his predecessor had counted on Elsie in some significant ways. For example, it was widely known throughout the college that many short deadlines and "crisis" projects were completed only because Elsie was willing to work into the evening hours whenever needed.

No one questioned Elsie's loyalty to the previous dean. In some respects, this made the continued deterioration of Elsie's attitude toward work even harder for Dean Bowyer to understand. He had never requested that either Elsie or Mary Alice stay past normal working hours, nor had he ever raised his voice toward anyone on his office staff. Why then couldn't Elsie feel more secure in an office environment where her work was finally recognized and rewarded?

The Connection. Although loyal to the former dean, Alvin Clinton, Elsie was quick to be critical of him as well. As the newly appointed Director of Development at the same institution, Dr. Clinton continued to interact with the dean's office as he solicited corporate support. Elsie customarily made pointed cynical comments about her former boss whenever correspondence was received from his office.

In particular, Stan Bowyer recalled one conversation with Elsie about six months ago. She was making her usual disparaging comments about Dr. Clinton prompting Bowyer to ask why she didn't feel better about her job since she no longer had to work for Alvin Clinton. Even at the time, Dean Bowyer sensed that Elsie's response might have been one of the few candid and insightful pieces of information he had received from Elsie in two years. Elsie retorted, "He left me. I worked hard for him and made him look good and he should have taken me with him."

The remark dumbfounded the dean. Although it was fairly common for administrators on this campus to take certain office support personnel with them when they were promoted from within, it never occurred to him that Elsie expected to follow his predecessor to the hallowed halls of the central administration building. Based on their heated arguments, most faculty and staff in the college believed that Elsie did not get along well with Alvin Clinton.

Stan Bowyer could not even imagine Elsie in the development office. He didn't think that she had the personality needed to interact with the many people who had business with the director of development and would typically come by that office. He was also quite confident that if it had not occurred to him that Elsie should accompany Alvin Clinton to his new position, then it probably had not occurred to Alvin Clinton either.

The Problem. Clearly something had to be done. On Elsie's ninth consecutive day of absence, Dean Bowyer had Mary Alice try to reach Elsie at her home. Finally, in the late afternoon, Elsie answered the phone. "Elsie," said the dean, "we've all been worried about you." She replied with a surly, "Oh, sure."

Trying another tack, the dean said, "You've been absent from work for more than a week. This is a record for you."

Elsie reacted, "Don't worry, I'll get the data from the Alumni Survey tallied in time for your speech."

Dean Bowyer had almost forgotten about the work she was doing on that material. He said, "I'm not worried about that. If you're ill, we can even get someone else to do it."

He sensed, even over the phone, that he had made a tactical error when he heard her reply. She said, "Oh sure. *Anyone* can do my job."

Dean Bowyer tried to bring the focus of their conversation back to Elsie's health. He asked, "Elsie, have you been to see a doctor?"

"No," she replied, "it's just the flu."

The dean countered, "A flu bug that persists this long probably should be treated by a doctor."

Elsie's familiar accusatory voice said, "I can't afford unnecessary doctor bills."

Dean Bowyer tried not to sound too patronizing over the phone when he said, "Elsie, your medical insurance through the college will cover most of your medical bills. That's no reason to run a health risk." His comment was met with stony silence.

He started anew. "Are you feeling any better, Elsie?"

"No," she replied.

He asked if she had any idea when she might be back at work. "I'll try to come in tomorrow if I'm feeling better."

Dean Bowyer said, "We will sure be glad when you are well again."

Elsie said in a very soft voice, "I have to hang up now."

"Take care of yourself, Elsie." The dean placed the phone in its cradle, doubting that his conversation with Elsie had accomplished anything.

Let's pause here. . .

1. *Given the facts presented to this point in the case, offer your analysis of the situation. What is the personnel problem being faced by the dean? How would you analyze Elsie's behavior? What is within the range of possibilities?*

2. *Assume the position of the college dean and detail what you might do to tackle the problem and correct the situation. Can you determine which of your premises is based on facts as presented in the case study and which are based on inferences?*

More of the Same. The next day, Stanley Bowyer was not too surprised when Mary Alice appeared in his doorway and said, "Elsie did not come to work again."

Without hesitating, the dean picked up the phone and dialed Elsie's home number. To his surprise, she answered the phone almost immediately. He said, "Elsie, I was hoping you'd feel better by this morning."

In her familiar belligerent tone she replied, "Well, I don't."

He asked, "Do you have an appointment with the doctor?"

She replied, "Yes, I made one for later this morning."

Taking a deep breath, the dean said, "Elsie, we need to talk. Do you believe you are well enough to meet with me after your doctor's appointment? If you don't wish to come to the office, I could meet you at the restaurant around the corner from the Doctors' Clinic. I'd be pleased to buy you a bowl of soup or whatever might sound good to you for lunch."

Elsie's reply was much fainter, "I would rather come by the office."

"Good," said the dean, "I'll be looking for you."

Later that day Mary Alice walked into the dean's private office with Elsie following. Mary Alice said, "Dean Bowyer, look who is here. I told her she's looking much better."

Stan Bowyer rose from his chair and said, "We'll all be glad when you are one hundred percent again, Elsie."

Elsie sat down in a chair and didn't say anything in response to either Mary Alice or the dean. Mary Alice rolled her eyes skyward and left the office.

"I appreciate your coming by, Elsie. I know that you're not feeling well." The dean paused allowing Elsie an opportunity for a response, but as there was none, he continued. "What did the doctor have to say about your recovery?"

Elsie stared at the floor and muttered, "Not much. He says that I don't have the stomach flu. But I know I feel sick," countered Elsie.

Dean Bowyer leaned forward and said gently, "Elsie, I'm not an expert, but do you think your increasingly negative attitude toward work is making you ill?"

She stiffened and said, "I get my work done. I work hard."

"Yes, you do," the dean agreed, "but it's been painfully obvious to me that you're simply not happy here."

Elsie went with what she thought was the drift of the conversation and asked, "Am I being fired?"

"No," replied the dean, "but I need every person on my staff to be productive and I would like for all of the people who work here to feel good about their roles in making the office run smoothly. You make a strong contribution, but you also appear to be very depressed about work. That's not fair to you or any of us."

"I just want to be left alone to do my work," she said. "I don't want the student workers bothering me. Besides, they don't like me. What I really want is to be treated fairly."

Bowyer asked for clarification, "What do you mean?"

Elsie said, "I told you about it. I think that I should have been promoted to the development office along with Dr. Clinton. I belong with him in the central administration building."

Bowyer reminded her of past actions in this office. "You did receive an upgrade and pay increase for your excellent work in this office. You understand that a move to the development office might not have resulted in an upgrade in your position classification or an increase in pay."

"Yes, I know," countered Elsie, "but it's a more important place, it's bigger, and I deserve it. I worked hard for Dr. Clinton and he wouldn't be there today if it weren't for my work when he was here!"

Stan Bowyer brought the conversation back to the subject at hand. "I know that you are upset, but there's nothing I can do to change that. Do you think you can still work here?"

Elsie mumbled into her handkerchief; "I have to."

The dean wanted her to see that she had some choices open to her. He said, "No, you could ask for a transfer to a different campus office or you could apply for a job in the private sector. I have a high regard for your capability and would write a positive letter of reference."

Elsie, refusing to hear what he was saying, said, "You just want me out of here, so I wrote a letter of resignation." She handed him a piece of stationery from her handbag.

"That's not true," said the dean, hastily reading the letter. "With your permission, I would like to table your request and hold this letter," he said, putting it in his top desk drawer. "I don't want you to resign, but if you decide to stay I need for you to be one-hundred percent focused on your job."

Elsie said, "I think I need to resign. No one wants me here and I feel too sick to come into work. You all probably think I'm crazy."

"No, Elsie, we don't think you are crazy," replied the dean. "I do believe, however, that you need to work to change the factors which obviously have a negative impact on your health and personal well-being."

Elsie was not persuaded and said, "Yeah, right. How am I supposed to do that?"

"Well," answered the dean, "I've checked with the personnel office, and you have accrued quite a bit of sick leave and vacation time. I would be willing to approve your using accrued vacation and sick leave on the condition that you check in with me by phone and or by mail at least once a week to let me know your progress. Also, I would want your assurance that you would be accessible by phone in case we had questions as we try to cover your work. I would encourage you to use this time to talk with a counselor. As a staff person at the college, you know that you have access to counseling through our employee assistance program without charge."

Elsie, appearing a little brighter, said, "Thanks. I think time away from here will help me to feel better, but what could a counselor do for me? Seems like you *do* think I'm crazy."

Dean Bowyer was ready for that charge. He said, "I think you need someone who can be objective about your situation to help you sort through the issues which have you so angered that they are affecting your health."

Elsie just nodded numbly and asked, "How long could I be off?"

"By my calculations," replied the dean, "you have about three months of time accrued using both your vacation days and sick leave bank."

"Who would do my work?" asked Elsie.

"Well," commented Bowyer, "that's a real problem for us because while you are on approved vacation or sick leave, the college will be unable to hire anyone even part-time to help out, so we'll all be pitching in to cover your work. I'm willing to do that if, in three months or perhaps sooner, you could come back fully charged and renewed in your interest toward work. However, I'll only approve this absence if you agree to keep me informed of your progress at least once a week and if you agree to be accessible by phone. If at the end of three months you find that you are still unable to come back to work, I'll expect that you'll either request a transfer to a different department or be prepared to resign your position so I can replace you. There will be a limit to how long we will be able to manage without being fully staffed. Are these terms agreeable to you?"

Elsie thought for a brief time and said, "Yes, thank you. I believe this will help."

Let's pause again. . .

3. *Evaluate the action taken by the dean. What are the risks and potential gains of the dean's selected course of action?*

4. *Should the dean be consulting with experts in the personnel office? Does he need to talk with an attorney? Should the dean review the matter with the director of development, Elsie's former supervisor?*

5. *Should the dean document any of these discussions in writing? What are the advantages and disadvantages of keeping a written file on the personnel problem with Elsie?*

6. *Would your answers to any of these questions be different if you were told that Elsie was black and both the present and past deans, and Mary Alice, are white? Would your answers be different if you knew that Elsie had, in her ten years with the university, filed two lawsuits against the university for age discrimination? Would your answers be different if you knew that Elsie had been widowed in the past six months?*

Three More Weeks Go By. During the past three weeks, Dean Bowyer received only one telephone call from Elsie. He could plainly see that Elsie was not going to honor her commitment to provide weekly progress reports. Worse yet, the few times that it would have been helpful to seek Elsie's input on a work project by phone, Mary Alice had been unable to reach her. The dean believed that it was now necessary to put his terms to Elsie in writing. He then dictated the following letter and sent it to Elsie at her home.

NORTHEAST UNIVERSITY
College of Engineering

Ms. Elsie Joiner
329 Pine Forest
Emerald Springs, MA

Dear Elsie:

You have been on leave for three weeks now and I've only received one progress report. I remain very concerned about you and, as we agreed, would like to hear from you at least once a week as to how you are doing.

Specifically, I need to know whether your health has improved to a point where you might be able to return to work. I understand that you believe the particular stresses of your present position may have contributed to your health problem. However, that would not preclude a transfer to another position on campus which could be done without jeopardizing your pay scale or your seniority with the institution.

As you know, we have limped along without you for more than four weeks now. I need to do some planning so please let me know of your decision. Has your health improved enough for you to come back to your position? Do you intend to remain an employee of the institution and transfer to another department? If not, I assume you plan to resign.

If you will keep me posted about your progress on a weekly basis, I will honor our agreement for you to utilize all of the sick leave and vacation time accrued. Nevertheless, I do need to know your plans as you make them so I can figure out what I must do to manage your work assignments in this office. I sincerely hope that the time off has allowed you to make progress in battling your health problems and sorting out your alternatives. Please give me a call or write me a note letting me know of your wishes.

> Sincerely,
>
> Stanley W. Bowyer, Dean

Let's pause again. . .

7. *Do you agree with the course of action taken by the dean? If not, specify how you would handle the situation with Elsie at this point in time.*

8. *Critique the letter written by the dean. Does it minimize or increase the institution's liability in the event that this matter ends up in court? Consider whether Elsie could be charged with insubordination for missing so much work.*

9. *If you believe that the time has come (or is past due) for the dean to start a paper trail, draft the document you would write for the file. How far back would you go in making a record of this personnel problem? If your plan for documenting the matter includes a different type of letter to Elsie, please write it. If your plan for documenting the matter includes letters to others (such as the director of personnel), please write these letters as well.*

Two Weeks Later. Dean Bowyer was vaguely aware that two more weeks had passed with no further word from Elsie, so it came as a total surprise when she appeared in his office doorway one day. "Well, Elsie," he said, "I'm pleased to see you. I haven't heard from you in a long time."

She said, "I know, but I'm feeling better and I'm ready to talk with you about the conditions for my return to work."

The dean noticed that the Elsie who now stood before him was much more assertive and firm in her manner than the one he had talked with some five weeks ago. He, however, looked puzzled and asked, "The conditions for your return to work?"

"Yes, you're always telling me that I do good work, right?" said Elsie. He nodded. "Well," said Elsie, "after my three month leave is finished, I'll agree to come back to work if nobody hassles me."

"What?" said the dean, visibly startled.

"I don't want to be hassled about going to office lunches and stuff like that," said Elsie, "and I don't want people making snide comments or talking about me behind my back. I just want to be left alone to do my work."

Dean Bowyer spoke quietly. "We have talked about this on many occasions, Elsie. No one is making snide comments about you. You are too hasty to conclude that people don't like you when, in truth, you don't allow them to get to know you."

"Well," she said, "I'm not going to put up with it anymore. Also, I think I deserve another promotion. Since I didn't get the position in the development office, I want another promotion in the dean's office."

The dean, still flabbergasted by Elsie's tone and manner, replied, "Well, Elsie, you've given me a lot of think about. I'm not sure your conditions are ones that I can honor. I must point out that you did agree to give me progress reports once a week and to be available in the event we had questions as we tried to handle your workload. You have not honored either of these commitments."

She pondered that accusation and finally said, "It wouldn't be much of a leave if I had to sit by the phone all the time and wait for Mary Alice to call. I answered the phone when I was home. Are you sure Mary Alice is calling me when you tell her to? She has never liked me and enjoys getting me in trouble."

The dean said firmly, "Elsie, I am confident that Mary Alice is not trying to get you in trouble with me or with anyone else."

Even as Stan Bowyer spoke, Elsie was up and moving toward the door. Evidently she had said what she had come to say. As the dean watched Elsie leave, his head was spinning. He had no doubt that she was feeling better. She was quite obviously back to her old testy, argumentative self. This was a dramatic contrast to the broken spirit and depression he observed in Elsie just five weeks ago. Given the tenor of the conversation and the nature of the "demands" presented by Elsie, he knew he now needed to take a position in writing. He wrote the following letter and sent it to Elsie at her home a few days later.

NORTHEAST UNIVERSITY
College of Engineering

Ms. Elsie Joiner
329 Pine Forest
Emerald Springs, MA

Dear Elsie:

When we met five weeks ago, you agreed to keep me posted as to the status of your health, but except for your visit to the office today, all contact with you has been at my initiation. You also agreed to remain accessible by telephone to help supply information needed to handle your job duties. However, it has been virtually impossible to reach you by phone. Indeed that is what prompted me to send my first letter to you, seeking some response from you as to the status of your health and your plans with respect to your current position at the institution.

Repeatedly during the past six months, we have talked candidly about the fact that your work performance has not been up to your capability or the level of productivity that I witnessed when I first assumed the deanship two years ago. As you know, your deficient performance has resulted in numerous errors and problems which should have been averted. In the last six months, I have had to monitor your work more closely and intervene more frequently in order to make deadlines or correct errors. When your unplanned absences increased to two or three days each week, much of your work had to handled by other staff in the office.

I hoped that your leave of absence would enable you to think through what you need to do in order to regain the level of performance of which you are capable. It came as a total surprise to learn of your list of demands to return to work. In all candor, I don't understand how you can say that you were doing good work. It's only because of my high regard for your capability and your years of service to the institution that I have resisted documenting the errors and problems created by your poor work performance during the past six months. Nevertheless, we've had numerous discussions about the problems caused and about what you termed as "job burnout."

I must tell you that the conditions you articulated for your return are simply unacceptable. Your first demand was that no one "hassle" you. I'm not in a position to guarantee how others relate to you. This is an old issue and I have spent too much time trying to coach you on how to develop a more effective and productive rapport with office colleagues and staff in other offices. I cannot control or be held accountable for how others relate to you. Given the problems created by your inability to give your job your full effort, I cannot honor your request that you be left alone to do your job without interference. Because I'm accountable for the total productivity of this office, I must intervene to guarantee the work gets done on time and in a quality way. I have spent considerable time thinking about how to restructure your job to better ensure that the work gets done.

If you believe that you are able to return to your present position and give your job full effort, we need to talk about how I plan to restructure the duties which were assigned to you. This would not change your position classification or rate of pay. When you departed five weeks ago, you gave me a signed letter of resignation because you were confident that you would not be returning to this position. Because of the health problems you described, I didn't want you to resign and surrender your health insurance. I suggested that you use your sick leave until your health improved or you had some plan for your next career move. If you have decided to return to this position, you need to start back to work immediately or provide a note from your physician which documents the need for continued sick leave.

Elsie, I believe that I have given you every benefit of the doubt and made available to you every possible benefit. What I cannot do is jeopardize the operation of this office. I need to make plans for getting the work done. Since you have not answered my letter or called me as promised, you leave me no choice but to pursue this matter with the personnel office. Since I am unable to meet the conditions you specified for your possible return, I will assume your intent is to have me process the signed resignation form effective the first day after you have exhausted your vacation and sick leave time. If that is not your intent, please contact me immediately.

Sincerely,

Stanley W. Bowyer, Dean

One final pause. . .

10. *Evaluate the effectiveness of the approach taken by the dean. Should the dean have been more confrontational with Elsie when she presented her list of demands? Explain your answer. Specify how you would have handled the matter.*

11. *Critique the second letter sent by Dean Bowyer to Elsie. Detail any changes you would make. Does the dean's letter minimize or escalate the institution's potential liability? Could Elsie claim that she is a victim of retaliation?*

12. *As the situation unfolded, was the dean correct to encourage Elsie to use available sick leave and vacation time when she was willing, at one point, to resign? Why or why not? Would you have acted on the resignation, once you had her letter resigning from her position? Consider the balance between an administrator's responsibility for office productivity and consideration for the personal needs of the office staff.*

13. *Assume you are the dean, your latest letter is sent, and there is no immediate reaction from Elsie. What would you do? Can you be certain that Elsie received the letter? Would you follow it with another letter or a phone call? Would you then attempt to process the resignation letter after Elsie's sick leave and vacation time are exhausted?*

SELECTED READINGS

Adler, R. S., & Bigoness, W. J. (1992). Contemporary ethical issues in labor-management relations. *Journal of Business Ethics, 11*, 351-360.

Written from a corporate perspective, the authors discuss current labor-management issues that pose ethical questions. The authors conclude that ethics means that the interests and rights of all constituencies must be balanced. In higher education, the constituencies would include the administration, faculty, staff, students, alumni, accrediting agencies, and many more.

Ayres-Williams, R. (1992, March). When managing gets tough: How to handle difficult employees. *Black Enterprise, 22*(8), 63-69.

Although written from the corporate perspective, many of the examples of problem employees are ones that could be found in any office on any campus. The author offers some straightforward prescriptive advice for managing difficult people.

Diaz, E. M., Minton, J. W., & Saunders, D. M. (1987, April). Labor relations update: A fair nonunion grievance procedure. *Personnel, 64*, 13-18.

The authors describe a functioning university-based grievance procedure on a nonunion campus (Duke University) where the process is controlled by management. An unusual feature is the use of students as employee-advocates.

Liedtka, J. (1991). Organizational value contention and managerial mindsets. *Journal of Business Ethics, 10*, 543-557.

The author studied the impact of the signals which organizations send (and the values they hold) to their managers regarding the appropriate behavior in a given situation. Liedtka assumed these different types of organizational value contentions and examined their influence in the manager's responses. Situations described in this article equate easily from business to institutions of higher education. Middle managers can be called deans, but the problems are still the same.

Lindskold, S., Han, G., & Betz, B. (1986). Repeated persuasion in interpersonal conflict. *Journal of Personality and Social Psychology, 51*, 1183-1185.

This article is a report on two studies in which the authors analyzed the effects of repeating and rephrasing a statement of intent to act cooperatively in an interdependent relationship. Repetition and rephrasing of the intention to be conciliatory was found to increase subject cooperation.

Orpen, C., & King, G. (1989). Effects of superiors' feedback, credibility, and expertise on subordinates' reactions: An experimental study. *Psychological Reports, 64,* 645-656.

A brief report of a quantitative research study in which the findings suggest that subordinates' responses are relatively unaffected by the superiors' expertise or credibility, but are significantly influenced by the kind of feedback they receive from these same superiors.

Rahim, M. A., Garrett, J. E., & Buntzman, G. F. (1992). Ethics of managing interpersonal conflict in organizations. *Journal of Business Ethics, 11,* 423-432.

The authors describe specific styles of handling interpersonal conflict: integrating, obliging, dominating, avoiding, and compromising. Each style, depending on the situation, may be used in conflicts with superiors, subordinators and peers. A perspective for the ethical evaluation of conflict management is also provided.

Rampal, K R. (1991). Developing a working code of ethics for human resource personnel. *CUPA Journal, 42*(3), 21-26.

Starting from the premise that ethics deals with standards of personal behavior which are determined by values, Rampal separates ethics from legality and discusses the development of a working ethical code for human resource personnel. A brief description of the various ethical philosophies is provided.

Trotter, P., & Risdon, P. (1990). Performance counseling. *CUPA Journal, 41*(3), 21-24.

The authors advance the argument that performance counseling should take into account the three components that affect performance: department and professional goals, professional competencies, and factors that impede professional development. They define professional competencies to include: communication skills, interpersonal skills, decision-making and management skills, and skills in working with groups.

Tucker, A. (1992). *Chairing the academic department: Leadership among peers (3rd edition).* New York, NY: American Council on Education/Macmillan.

A text for anyone seeking more information about the roles and responsibilities often assigned to department chairs. Of particular relevance to this case are the chapters included in Part V, "Workload assignments, faculty evaluation, and performance counseling."

10

THE NEW MANDATE: ASSESS!

About the Case

Formulating a campus response to a mandate issued by a state board of higher education is difficult and challenging. The power of the board varies from state to state, ranging from a coordinating function only to a more powerful controlling function with direct influence on budget decisions. Regardless of the degree of power held by a given board, institutions have a broad range of significant reactions when an edict is received from a state board. To demonstrate the complexities of the relationship between a state board and a public institution, this case depicts a board which has significant power over both budget and program inventory.

Specifically, the case features the dilemma faced by a provost in responding to the newest mandate issued by that state's Board of Higher Education. This particular mandate involved the design and implementation of a campus-wide initiative which will require a significant investment of time and resources, and which could have important repercussions in terms of future funding support as well as the institution's long-term credibility with the board.

CASE STUDY

Franklin Smith, sitting in his office on a warm September afternoon, was reflecting on how the university might manage its response to the newest mandate received from the state's Board of Higher Education (BHE). Smith was provost on the flagship campus of a multicampus state university system. The institution was one of sixteen public universities within an industrialized northern state. All of the institutions receiving state funds are required by state statute to adhere to the policies and procedures issued by the state's BHE. The BHE is the agency which reviews and recommends all budget requests for the state's public institutions of higher education. For this reason, the BHE wields significant clout over the public institutions within the state. In addition, the state's BHE leadership is appointed by the governor and, therefore, remains sensitive to the wishes of the state legislature and the governor's office. So when the provost received such a mandate, it garnered his full attention.

Already, the BHE was a constant presence for Provost Smith. Each July 1, his office forwards a detailed report to the state capital. The report, called the *Annual Program Report (APR)*, is the largest of several documents mandated by the BHE and the only vehicle by which the institution may request new state funds. This report is the official vehicle by which state institutions transmit to the BHE the results of required academic program reviews, changes in the institution's instructional priorities, and descriptions of new academic initiatives.

The associate provost for planning is responsible for the compilation of this report, which is then carefully reviewed by the provost. Every item included in the *APR* received full constituency review by the relevant academic departments and colleges, the graduate council, and the faculty senate. The data presented in the *APR* are coordinated with data submitted to the BHE via other reports compiled by different campus offices. For example, much of the data requested on cost effectiveness and faculty productivity were compiled in the university's office of institutional research. Other reports, requesting data regarding personnel issues, were compiled by the associate provost for personnel.

The Mandate. Provost Smith had in his hand yet another request from the BHE, also with a July due date. As Smith viewed it, this newest state mandate called for each university to design and implement a campus-wide assessment program to monitor student learning in three areas: general education, baccalaureate-level skills, and the major academic disciplines. The mandate came as no surprise to Provost Smith. The BHE staff had been working on this draft for over a year.

In fact, past practice had been for the BHE staff members to distribute drafts of forthcoming mandates to system-level officers for preliminary reaction. Dr. Smith and his staff forwarded their reactions to the BHE's draft version to the university system's academic officer who, in turn, communicated with the BHE staff. Campus reaction was directed toward trying to influence the BHE personnel toward a longer time frame for the design and implementation phases of the assessment program and to request that the mandate more clearly specify how the information would ultimately be used by the BHE.

The final mandate (Attachment A) was issued last week. Provost Smith was disheartened to discover that it did not incorporate the more important suggestions made by his campus. On a more positive note, he found that the mandate was sufficiently brief and nonspecific as to allow significant discretion for each state institution regarding the actual design of the assessment program. In talking to his counterparts at several of the other public institutions in the state, Provost Smith discovered that they, too, were uncertain how to proceed.

Let's pause here. . .

1. *Review Attachment A. What department or university office should be able to provide the response for the first "guideline" question? What is the most accurate and efficient source for the information requested?*

2. *Who should know the answer to the third "guideline" question about courses and methods to operationalize the objectives? If you believe that the faculty should be able to answer that question, can you be certain that all faculty in a given department would answer in the same way? Could this be a problem and how should it be resolved?*

3. *"Guideline" question five appears to be relatively straightforward. Is it? While the grading system does offer one evaluation of student progress, would any grading system be sufficient to satisfy the BHE mandate for assessment? Why or why not?*

4. *What does the mandate require of the institution? Outline the specific steps that must be taken to comply with the letter and spirit of the BHE guidelines.*

5. *When is the written report due? How many parts will it have? Prepare a succinct outline of the final report. Consider carefully how many audiences the written report may have and how the nature of these audiences or publics should affect the outline and content.*

6. *Will individual student scores have to be reported? Be certain that your decision and practice is consistent with the provisions of the "Buckley Amendment." Under the so-called "Buckley Amendment" of the Family Educational Rights and Privacy Act of 1974 (FERPA), 20 U.S.C. ¶ 1232g, individual student scores would generally be part of the student's educational record which could not be released without the student's written consent. However, the Act does include among the exceptions to this requirement:*

   > *Organizations conducting studies for, or on behalf of, educational agencies or institutions for the purposes of developing, validating, or administering predictive tests, administering student aid programs, and improving instruction, if such studies are conducted in such a manner as will not permit the personal identification of students and their parents by persons other than representative of such organizations*

and such information will be destroyed when no longer needed for pur-
poses for which it is conducted. (20 U.S.C. ¶ 1232g (b)(1)(F).

Note: *The term "organizations" includes, but is not limited to, federal, state,*
and local agencies, and independent organizations. This would not, however,
permit release of personally identifiable records to prospective employers
without the student's written consent.

Funding Support. The most depressing aspect of the new mandate, from Dr. Smith's immediate point of view, was that it had been
issued "dry." In campus jargon, the BHE was asking state universities to
design and implement a comprehensive campuswide assessment program
without any additional state dollars to support the effort. This action was consistent with a recent pattern of similar requests. Overall, with the exception of one year (the last election year), higher education in the state had
experienced five years of continual decline in state budgetary support. The
annual budgets of state universities showed very modest increments ranging from two to four percent increases which never came close to keeping
pace with the rate of inflation.

During the same period, salary increases averaged from three to four-
and-one-half percent per year. Provost Smith recognized the need to retain
good faculty and spare the university the cost associated with recruiting
new personnel to fill vacancies created by faculty who left to assume better
paying positions elsewhere. Therefore, he instituted an internal reallocation
scheme which took funds allocated to vacant or unfilled positions and from
nonpersonnel budget lines to augment salary increases. In this way, the
institution was able to award salary increases which were roughly two to
three percent greater than they would have been without the internal reallocation plan. While that plan had the positive impact on morale anticipated by Dr. Smith, it now meant that fewer reserve dollars were available
to fuel and manage a campus-wide assessment program.

Options and Issues. Beyond the issue of how to assess and how to
fund assessment, Dr. Smith was troubled about the problem of how to
manage such an assessment program. He visualized his place on the university's organizational chart (Attachment B) as he considered his options.

One option for managing the assessment program was to delegate
much of the work to the departments and colleges of the campus. However, the provost was painfully aware that his morale-boosting salary
increase plan had spawned negative management repercussions at the
departmental level. To bolster faculty salaries, some faculty positions that
were "open" through natural attrition, had been "cannibalized" by the
institution to fund the internal reallocation program. Therefore, various

departments across campus were operating with fewer faculty than they had previously. If the assessment initiative was to be orchestrated in such a way that the work was delegated to the academic colleges and departments, the work load of many faculty would significantly increase.

And, before talking with the department chairs, there was another major hurdle for the provost to overcome: the deans. They would be livid about responding to yet another "dry" request. No, Provost Smith was not looking forward to another encounter with that group.

It was evident to Smith that managing a campus-wide assessment program *centrally* would require the addition of new staff. Even if an assessment program could be managed without the creation of a new position (i.e., a director of assessment) additional staff would likely be needed in *any* office that might be given this assignment. This task, for example, might be given to George Beatty, the director of institutional research, but not without the addition of a new staff member in that office. Director Beatty, Smith recalled, was still angry over the need to produce productivity tables each semester in addition to the annual cost effectiveness report required by the BHE.

The possibility remained, Dr. Smith grudgingly admitted to himself, that the complete responsibility for assessment could be assigned to a member of his own staff. He could ask one of the three associate provosts to handle the assignment, but this too was likely to require additional staff or to require the redistribution of duties currently handled by the associate provosts. Clearly, there was no easy or perfect solution for Dr. Smith or his institution.

Let's pause again. . .

7. List the advantages and disadvantages of each of the alternatives being considered by Dr. Smith:

    a.   to delegate the task through the deans to the departments;

    b.   to recommend to the president that the task be assigned to institutional research; or

    c.   to delegate the task to an associate provost.

8. Are there other alternatives not yet considered by Dr. Smith? If so, please name them. You may find it helpful to refer to the university's organization chart, Attachment B.

9. To whom would you assign the assessment project if you were the provost? Please explain in some detail your reasons for selecting this particular approach. Be certain to consider and comment on the personnel as well as fiscal, political and administrative concerns.

10. *Construct a timetable for announcing or communicating the initiative on campus which insures that the task is properly delegated and completed in accordance with the provisions of the state's Board of Higher Education mandate. Remember, it is now early September, and the plan is to be in the July 1 Annual Program Report. As you formulate your plan for implementation, you may decide to alter your previous thinking. You may do so, but be sure to explain why you believe a change is necessary.*

Associate Provost for Planning. Right or wrong, Dr. Smith opted to assign responsibility for the design and implementation of the campus assessment program to his Associate Provost for Planning, Dr. Lawrence Garrison. The job description of this associate provost already included the duties of conducting the academic program reviews, accreditation reviews, finalizing requests for new programs, and overseeing academic planning for the campus.

Dr. Smith had earlier concluded that since assessment activities monitored student learning, these activities should be associated with the curriculum. Therefore, he decided to assign assessment to the associate provost who worked most closely with curricular matters. Smith sincerely hoped that the vantage point held by Associate Provost Garrison would allow for some streamlining in all of the curricular-related initiatives so as to avoid any unnecessary duplication. He continued to harbor the hope that the assessment initiative might be designed and implemented at little or no cost to the institution. Unlike the deans or the director of institutional research, Garrison was a long-time member of Smith's staff and considered to be a good team player. Dr. Smith made the assignment on September 15, giving Garrison responsibility for the mandate without any additional resources.

Faculty Governance. The two administrators talked over their implementation options and decided that the associate provost would take the assessment mandate to the faculty through the faculty senate, a representative body elected by the faculty in each college. They knew that the senate would probably immediately refer the matter to one of its standing committees, most likely the Educational Policy Committee (EPC). As an ex-officio member of the EPC, Garrison was permitted to forward certain materials directly to the membership of the EPC. Usually, following EPC discussion and action, EPC would forward its recommendations to the full faculty senate for review and vote. Rather than go initially to the entire senate, Garrison made the decision to approach the EPC. He would seek the EPC's counsel in drafting both the procedures and the timetable for the university's response to the BHE mandate. As the date of the EPC's meeting approached, Garrison felt like cannon fodder, suspecting that this new assessment initiative would not be well received.

As the associate provost predicted, the faculty on the EPC were totally outraged by the mandate. They perceived that the state's Board of Higher Education was implying that university faculty did not do a good job in teaching students. The mandate was seen as punitive and spiteful. The sentiment was almost unanimous that the associate provost instruct the provost that the campus refused to comply with the BHE mandate for assessment. That scenario could have the effect of jeopardizing the institution's relationship with the BHE, the agency responsible for recommending the institution's budget each year. The one point of comfort for Dr. Garrison was that he was now sure he made the right move in presenting this to the EPC and not to the entire faculty senate.

Let's pause again. . .

11. *Assume the role of Dr. Garrison and script how you would introduce the new mandate to the EPC. Would you distribute copies of the mandate (Attachment A) or paraphrase the provisions of the mandate?*

12. *What would you do now if you were Dr. Garrison? Where does Dr. Smith fit in with Garrison's options?*

13. *Are there other parties who need to be kept informed as progress or lack of progress is made? Who? How? When? Why?*

Committee Support. Before the next EPC meeting, Garrison talked with each of the committee's members individually. He tried to help them understand the costly and dangerous long-term implications for any university that may decide to ignore or refuse to respond to a state Board of Higher Education mandate. He also pointed out the potential benefits of an assessment program to faculty and students and suggested that these activities could be carried out in a way that would be consistent with the faculty's expressed commitment to quality undergraduate education.

At the next meeting of the Educational Policy Committee, the harsh initial reaction had dissipated somewhat. The associate provost was able to switch the issue from *whether* we should do this to *how* might this be done in a way that complements what the institution was already doing.

Over the winter months that followed, Garrison was able to secure the EPC's approval of a document (Attachment C) he created which detailed how the assessment program would be designed and managed at the university. This document was then forwarded to the faculty senate for final approval. Senate approval was obtained in February, about five months after the initial mandate was received. Smith was delighted at what he considered to be a relatively quick response.

The assessment procedure document (Attachment C) called for faculty to assume a leadership role in both the design and implementation of assessment measures. As the provost had hoped, once the faculty viewed the assessment task as one which was related to curriculum, they preferred to be intrinsically involved rather than have the activity conducted by faceless bureaucrats in central administration.

Let's pause one final time. . .

14. *How would you critique the merit of the approach used by the associate provost in communicating the mandate to the faculty?*

15. *Should the provost keep the president apprised of progress? Does the system academic officer need to be kept informed? If yes, specify what information should be forwarded. Consider, for example, whether the system academic officer can be helpful in preparing the BHE to respond favorably to the campus report on the assessment initiative.*

16. *Draft a short note for Associate Provost Garrison to send to Provost Smith keeping him informed of his progress. The memorandum should be drafted in a manner which would allow Smith to forward it to the academic officer in the system office as an "FYI" item.*

17. *What other approach might have been taken to devise a campus procedure for the design and implementation of an assessment program?*

18. *What were the trade-offs that the provost and his staff were willing to make? What were the risks? How were the risks minimized?*

19. *Does the procedures document approved by the faculty senate respond to the BHE mandate? If not, specify why it does not. Be sure to consider the time frame requirements as well as the contact requirements.*

20. *How should the provost respond? Should the procedures document approved by the faculty senate be accepted by the provost unconditionally? If not, explain why. If the provost decides not to accept the procedures document, what actions should he take? For example, how should the provost communicate his acceptance of the faculty senate procedures to the deans? Could the deans argue legitimately that they were "out of the loop" during the planning stage but now have been delegated full responsibility for implementation?*

21. *As provost, you are to draft the provost's response to the faculty senate which articulates your conclusions. What steps remain to ensure proper implementation of the faculty senate proposal?*

22. *As provost, outline your handling of this issue at the next deans' council meeting. Or, if you prefer to inform the deans by memorandum, please draft the memorandum you would send.*

23. *List the anticipated repercussions to your recommended course of action. How would you monitor progress at the college and department levels to be certain that the assessment program was being implemented and that the institution would be in compliance with the BHE mandate by the specified deadline?*

Attachment A

GUIDELINES FOR THE ASSESSMENT OF UNDERGRADUATE
STUDENT LEARNING OUTCOMES

Guideline questions to be answered with annual submission of the
University's Annual Program Report (APR):

1. What are the objectives for undergraduate education? Specify the
    objectives for the general education component of undergraduate edu-
    cation and the development of baccalaureate-level skills in written and
    oral communication, mathematics, and analytical thinking.

2. How are these objectives communicated to students?

3. In what courses, and by what methods, are these objectives taught to
    undergraduate students?

4. What methods are used to assess student progress in general edu-
    cation and in the development of baccalaureate-level skills? How and
    when are these methods evaluated?

5. What methods are used to assess student progress in the major dis-
    cipline? How and when are these methods evaluated?

6. How are the results of assessment measures used to benefit individ-
    ual students and improve the curriculum?

Submission procedures and timetable:

1. The institutional response to these guideline questions must be sub-
    mitted as section IV of the Annual Program Report which is due to the
    Board of Higher Education (BHE) by July I of each year, with the first
    submission due next July.

2. The submission should include a five to ten page summary of follow-
    up action which will be taken before the next annual submission.

3. The submission should incorporate student scores on assessment
    measures in order to demonstrate, in the aggregate, that students
    have mastered the learning objectives of the general education, bac-
    calaureate-level skills, and the major discipline components of their
    undergraduate experience.

4. A complete file of all assessment measures used and student scores
    should be kept by the institution. This information may be requested by
    the BHE as needed to evaluate the strength of existing programs.

Attachment B

UNIVERSITY ORGANIZATIONAL CHART

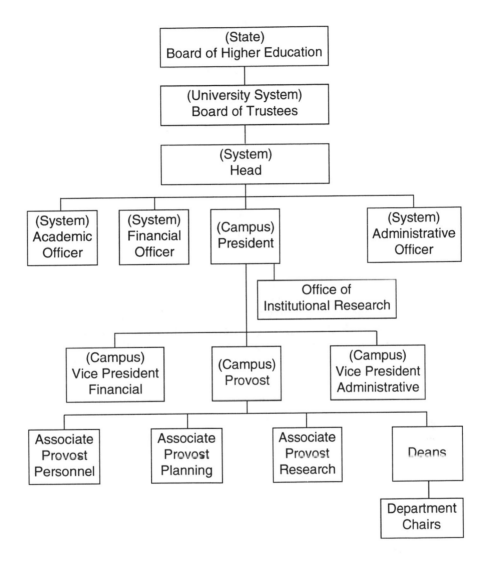

Attachment C

Procedures for Undergraduate Assessment

These guidelines were prepared in response to the state Board of Higher Education (BHE) mandate for assessment. The BHE mandate requires each institution within the state to "assess student progress" in general education, baccalaureate-level skills, and the major disciplines. The following procedures were drafted by the Educational Policy Committee (EPC), approved by the full Faculty Senate, and recommended to the provost.

Assessment of Student Progress in General Education and Baccalaureate-Level Skills

The dean of General Education (GE) currently has responsibility for reviewing the general education program to be certain that learning objectives are appropriate and that the curriculum is relevant for the stated objectives. The GE dean will now assume responsibility for the development of assessment measure which can be used to monitor student progress.

Since the general education program includes the instruction of baccalaureate level skills, the GE dean will be responsible for development of assessment measures which evaluate student progress on both general education and baccalaureate-level skills. The results of assessment will be used by the GE dean to recommend changes for the continued improvement of the general education program. The assessment program, when implemented, will provide a mechanism which is responsive to the following concerns:

1. Continuous monitoring of general education courses and systematic evaluation of the general education program.

2. Standardized assessment of student performance in general education courses, including performance on the baccalaureate-level skills.

3. Increased awareness campus-wide of the university's commitment to improving the quality of undergraduate education.

4. Longitudinal data base for assessing student performance in general education courses.

Assessment of Student Learning in the Academic Major

The academic deans of the respective colleges, in concert with the department chairpersons and faculties will coordinate the review of major programs. Procedures will be developed in each college to provide for an on-going review of learning objectives in developing baccalaureate-level competencies and skills, and evaluation of the relationship between the learning objectives and the curriculum, and the development of multiple measures (other than course grades) for assessing student progress. The assessment program, when implemented, will provide a mechanism responsive to the following concerns:

1. Continuous monitoring of student performance in major degree programs.

2. Standardized assessment of student performance in major degree programs.

3. Increased awareness campuswide of the university's commitment to improving the quality of undergraduate education.

4. A longitudinal data base for assessing student performance in major degree programs.

Timetable for Implementation

All assessment measures should be selected or developed before the close of the next fiscal year. Actual testing will begin no later than two calendar years from the date of the provost's acceptance of this document.

SELECTED READINGS

Aper, J. P., Cuver, S. M., & Hinkle, D. E. (1990). Coming to terms with the account-ability versus improvement debate in assessment. *Higher Education, 20,* 471-483.

Based on an examination of state policies that call for institutions to develop assessment programs, the authors point out that key players do not always hold similar views as to the purposes for assessment. Some perceive assessment as a measure of institution accountability, while other perceive assessment as a tool for program improvement.

Astin, A. W. (1990). Can state-mandated assessment work? *Educational Record, 71,* 34-41.

Astin provides an analysis of the forces driving the assessment initiative in American higher education and the states' "real interest" in higher education to develop the talents of its citizens. A brief description of the basic assessment methodologies as they support or facilitate the objective of assessment is also included.

Astin, A. W. (1991). *Assessment for excellence: The philosophy and practice of assessment and evaluation in higher education.* New York,NY: American Council on Education/Macmillan.

Following an opening chapter on "The Philosophy and Logic of Assessment," the author presents the input-environment-outcome (I-E-O) model as a conceptual guide for assessment activities in higher education. Using this model as a framework for the design of an assessment program, the author suggests methods for assessing outcomes, student inputs, and the environment, analyzing assessment data and using assessment results. Later chapters in the book are devoted to such current topics as "Building a Data Base," "Assessment as Direct Feedback to the Learner," "Assessment and Equity," "Assessment and Public Policy," and "The Future of Assessment."

Banta, T. W. (Ed.). (1988). Implementing outcomes assessment: Promise and perils. *New Directions for Institutional Research, Number 59.* San Francisco, CA: Jossey-Bass.

Banta presents a collection of essays by experts in higher education on the various aspects of implementing assessment measures, including organizational issues, types of measures, and costs and benefits.

Birnbaum, R. (Ed.). (1991). Faculty in governance: The role of senates and joint committees in academic decision making. *New Directions for Higher Education, Number 75.* San Francisco, CA: Jossey-Bass.

This text offers a collection of five essays by various scholars on the roles and influence of faculty governance in decision making, budgetary areas, and policy formation. Governance issues include the use of "joint big decision" committees, the concept of shared authority, principles governing the interaction of faculty leaders and administrators, and campus climates and cultures.

Edgerton, R. (1990). Assessment at half time, *Change, 22,* 4-5.

In this brief editorial, Edgerton comments on the actions taken and progress made in response to the 1986 report of the National Governors' Association, *Time for Results,* which called for an assessment of undergraduate learning. Edgerton urges all institutions working on assessment initiatives to continue their activities and offers five reasons in support of this position.

Erwin, T. D. (1991). *Assessing student learning and development.* San Francisco, CA: Jossey-Bass.

The author places the assessment initiative in some perspective with an opening chapter on "The Emergence and Purposes of Outcome Assessment." The remainder of the book takes the reader through each of the key steps of designing and implementing an assessment program, including establishing objectives, selecting assessment methods, designing new assessment methods, collecting and maintaining records, analyzing information, and reporting and using assessment information. The final chapter examines "The Promise of Assessment for Improving Educational Quality." A sample alumni questionnaire, a student involvement survey, and proficiency guidelines for rating student ability are included in the book.

Ewell, P. T. (1991). *Benefits and costs of assessment in higher education: A framework for choicemaking.* Boulder, CO: National Center for Higher Education Management Systems.

The author discusses the costs and benefits of assessment for institutions of higher education. The analysis takes into account the policy decisions which must be made at each institution such as the advantages/disadvantages of purchasing standardized tests and surveys versus the advantages/disadvantages of using locally-designed assessment measures.

Ewell, P. T. (1991). Assessment and public accountability: Back to the future, *Change, 23,* 12-17.

Ewell provides an analysis of the issues of public accountability that underlie many assessment mandates and notes three current themes or conditions which influence these activities. The interdependent link between assessment and public policy is also described.

Ewell, P. T. (Ed.). (1985). Assessing educational outcomes. *New Directions for Institutional Research, Number 47.* San Francisco, CA: Jossey-Bass.

This book is a collection of eight essays by various experts addressing such issues as the development and use of outcome assessment. Studies conducted at specific institutions are presented as well.

Finifter, D. H., Baldwin, R. G., & Thelin, J. R. (Eds.). (1991). *The uneasy public policy triangle in higher education.* New York, NY: American Council on Education /Macmillan.

The authors discuss the impact of public policy on the issues of diversity, quality, and budget in higher education. Of particular relevance to this case study is Section II on "The tenuous connection: Public policy and higher education quality."

Fleming, J. H., Hilton, J. L., Darley, J. M., & Kojetin, B. A. (1990). Multiple audience problems: A strategic communication perspective on social perceptions. *Journal of Personality and Social Psychology, 58,* 593-609.

Following a lengthy discussion of the research methodology employed, the authors report findings that suggest individuals are capable of conveying accurate information even when they are constrained by having to cope with multiple audiences.

Hutchings, P., & Marchese, T. J. (1990). Watching assessment: Questions, stories, prospects, *Change, 22,* 12-38.

The authors present a summary of their observations and findings from approximately fifty visits to campuses (over a four-year period) where faculty and administrators were struggling with assessment and related issues. Detailed information and comments from persons involved at specific campuses (from Harvard to Seattle Central Community College) allows the reader to observe a broad sweep of the activities and problems.

McClenney, K. M. (1990). Whither assessment? Commitments needed for meaningful change, *Change, 22,* 54.

Five years into the assessment of student learning, McClenney identifies four key issues: the purposes and outcome of undergraduate education; coherence in policy and its implementation; rethink and redesign incentive and reward structures; and expand assessment conversation.

Mentkowski, M. (1991). Creating a context where institutional assessment yields educational improvement, *Journal of General Education, 40,* 255-283.

After discussing the requisite qualities of institutional assessment, the author offers six guidelines for constructing an assessment context which will foster educational improvement. The article contains many examples of institutions' experiences with assessment programs.

Miller, R. I. (1988). Using change strategies to implement assessment programs. *New Directions for Institutional Research, Number 59,* 5-14.

Miller offers suggestions on how to successfully introduce assessment policies and procedures. He discusses change in general before describing five models or strategies for bringing about change, outlines the characteristics of a change model, and concludes with two lists of factors—one found in success-prone change strategies and the other found in failure-prone change strategies.

North Central Association of College and Schools. (1991, Fall). *NCA Quarterly,* 66(2).

Following a statement of the North Central Association of Colleges and Schools regarding the role and importance of assessment to institutional accreditation, the volume contains a collection of essays which offer practical advice and specific case studies in assessing student academic achievement.

Ory, J. C. (1992). Meta-Assessment: Evaluating assessment activities. *Research in Higher Education, 33,* 467-482.

Starting from the premise that assessment activities themselves must be evaluated, Ory describes the standards of the Joint Committee (1981) which were developed for educational evaluation and illustrates their use in conducting assessment activities.

Tierney, W. G. (1983, Summer). Governance by conversation: An essay on the structure, function, and communication codes of a faculty senate. *Human Organization, 42,* 172-177.

The author argues that members of a faculty senate use two principle communications, writing and speaking, to accomplish their governance tasks. He describes how the senate operates, who the actors are, and its five basic functions: ceremonial, directional, news-related, decisional, and conformational.

Underwood, D. B. (1991). Taking inventory: Identifying assessment activities. *Research in Higher Education, 32,* 59-69.

Underwood describes a procedure used at an institution with over 14,000 students to identify those departments interested in participating in a pilot assessment study and educate members of the campus about learning outcome assessment. The author contends that taking inventory of campus assessment activities is an essential step in building an effective assessment program.

Walleri, D., Seybert, J., & Cosgrove, J. (1992). What do students want? How student intentions affect institutional assessment. *Community, Technical, and Junior College Journal, 62*(4), 28-31.

Two-year colleges must obtain data on student educational goals if these institutions are to continue to be effective. Because few students at two-year colleges receive associate degrees, other indices need to be identified. What are the students' educational goals and are these goals achieved?

11

PUZZLE PIECES

About the Case

Most people in higher education accept the reality that promotions require relocation. Intelligent, ambitious people in higher education who want additional power, money, or responsibilities are willing to accept the risk that comes with relocating. However, they do not do so without trying to maintain some measure of control. They gather information before, during, and after the usually intensive and extensive interview process. Then, trusting that they have gathered all relevant data and have accurately assessed the situation, they weigh the advantages and disadvantages of the move and finally make their decisions. Likewise, institutions advertise open positions, describing the assigned duties and requisite skills, searching diligently to fill the vacancy, and ultimately choosing the best available candidate based on carefully crafted criteria. Sometimes the institutions and the people selected meet with success, sometimes not.

CASE STUDY

January 5 was the first working day of the new year. As Anne Herzog sat in her office contemplating the objectives and goals she had set for the coming year, she couldn't help but reflect on how her perception of Westfield College—a prestigious women's college—had changed since she first assumed the position of director of development six months ago.

Anne initially learned of Westfield College the preceding spring when she noticed the college's advertisement (Attachment A) for a director of development in *The Chronicle of Higher Education*. Anne had ten years of experience in higher education development in a variety of positions, including five years as director of planned giving and five years as director of annual giving on a comparable campus. She felt ready to head her own development team and was eagerly searching for such an opportunity. After reading Westfield's advertisement, Anne believed that Westfield College would be a good place for her to assume such responsibility.

When interviewing for the position, Ms. Herzog learned that the newly created director of development position had been deemed essential to the future of the institution by virtually every member of the "president's council." All senior-level administrators reporting directly to the president were, by virtue of their offices, members of that council. Westfield's new organizational chart (Attachment B) would show the director of development likewise reporting directly to the president, and therefore a member of the council.

Let's pause here. . .

1. *Assume the role of Anne Herzog and draft an application letter indicating your desire to be considered for the position of director of development at Westfield College.*

2. *As an applicant for the position of director of development, you have the requisite education and experience, and have just been notified by Westfield that you are one of three finalists being considered for the position. How would you prepare for two days of on-campus interviews? What questions would you expect to be asked and how would you answer them? What questions would you ask the president? What questions would you ask members of the president's council? Are you concerned about the reporting lines as shown in Westfield's organizational chart?*

3. *Assume that you have been offered the position of director of development at Westfield College. What job conditions would you negotiate to receive? Please specify which job conditions would be absolutely essential to your acceptance of the position and which are preferred elements, but not required.*

4. *Assume that you have accepted the position of director of development at Westfield College. How would you go about introducing yourself to the campus and the various constituencies who are interested in, and in some way connected to, the development function?*

5. *In terms of the responsibilities you have just accepted, what might you do before officially assuming the position on July 1? What tasks would you work on immediately? What tasks would have to wait until after July 1?*

In Retrospect. Sitting in her office some six months later, Anne Herzog could still remember how excited she had been the previous summer when she assumed a newly created position that was considered so vital by so many key staff at the college. She had relished the opportunity to hire her own staff and to build a development program from scratch. She had known that this would require much effort, but her enthusiasm was heightened by the fact that the college president, Dr. Patrick McAllister, had told her that he viewed development as critical to the future health of the institution. "Development at Westfield College," he had said, "will be placed on center stage in the decades to come." Anne could not have imagined a better opportunity anywhere which would allow her to utilize all of her experience and talent.

When she accepted the position, Westfield College committed to support the development function with two staff positions and two clerical positions. Any further increases in staff would be funded through revenue generated by the development office. Anne Herzog immediately set to work creating position announcements for two professional staff positions which had been promised. One slot would be in the area of planned giving and major gifts and the other in the area of annual giving and research. Westfield College advertised the positions in early summer, so that a stack of applications were waiting her review on July 1 when she officially began work at Westfield.

The two clerical positions were filled through internal transfers. One experienced secretary moved from the alumnae services office and one secretary transferred from the office of admissions. President McAllister believed that this would equip the newly created office of development with some necessary understanding regarding the admissions and alumnae services offices—two areas in which efforts needed to be coordinated with the activities of the development function.

During Herzog's first month, she successfully interviewed and hired two administrative staff professionals. She chose to hire two young individuals with modest experience but tremendous enthusiasm and energy. She concluded that, in the long run, it would be better (and less costly) to train and cultivate her own staff rather than hire more senior (and more expensive) development professionals.

Reality. By September 1, the development office was fully staffed and in place. While interviewing candidates, Anne Herzog worked long hours to get the office records in place. Lists of alumnae were obtained from the data files of the alumnae services office and matched against a record of gifts made through various administrative offices. At this point it began to dawn on her exactly what type of uphill battle she was expected to wage. In analyzing the records, she could see clearly that Westfield College graduates, by in large, were quite unaccustomed to making financial contributions to the college.

This came as a surprise and shock to her because, during the interview process, everyone had boasted about the strong alumnae support which Westfield enjoyed. If the support was there, she now mused, it was not financial in nature. When she had asked directly about the amount of financial support provided by alumnae, the general response was positive, although all acknowledged that without a centrally administered development office, any records of such gifts were scattered across the various departments benefiting from such activities.

Garnering Alumnae Support. During the fall, Anne spent days analyzing records and interviewing key individuals. By mid-December she was able to piece together the profile of the typical Westfield College woman. The overwhelming majority of Westfield College students were privileged daughters from affluent families who, after graduation, assumed similarly affluent lifestyles. Many of the women worked only until they were married or starting a family. Westfield graduates remained spirited in their love and affection for the institution as evidenced by their attendance at college activities. They flocked to a busy homecoming weekend in the fall, an annual spring festival weekend in April, and a long list of receptions, banquets, and other activities scheduled primarily to allow alumnae to enjoy each others' company and perhaps interact with faculty and students.

In the past, making a financial contribution to the college had not been part of the college's expectation of its alumnae. To be successful, Anne Herzog recognized that she was going to need to alter both the institution's expectations for alumnae and the alumnae's perception of what constituted *support* of their alma mater.

Homecoming seemed like the appropriate place to start. She secured a draft copy of the scheduled events and activities for the homecoming weekend from the director of alumnae services, Stuart Hunt French, and set about determining where and when might be the appropriate place for her to begin interacting with Westfield's alumnae. She considered a reception of some sort or at least the co-hosting of some traditional lunch or dinner event.

Looking back, Anne remembered vividly the shock and dismay she felt when Stuart French initially turned down all her ideas. He felt strongly that homecoming was a "celebration of the college" and believed that he had been successful over the years in "fostering a spirit of goodwill" among alumnae who responded by continuing their support of the college. Further, Mr. French expressed his belief that his rapport with alumnae—which had been carefully built and maintained over many decades—would be significantly weakened and threatened if homecoming degenerated into what he called a "pass-the-collection-plate" activity.

Herzog was confident of her persuasive powers, but found that after several weeks of meetings and conversations with French she was unable to convince him that appeals for financial contributions were not always in poor taste. She also failed to convince him that she did not intend to jeopardize, in any way, the positive relationships he had built with Westfield's alumnae. For whatever reason, French was unable to recognize that alumnae services and development activities could have compatible objectives. If French prevailed, Anne Herzog would be denied virtually all access to the alumnae at the scheduled homecoming festivities.

The President Decides. In early October, when it was clear to Herzog that she and French would not be able to reconcile their disagreement, she suggested that they explore the issue and options with President McAllister. To her utter disbelief, President McAllister sided with the director of alumnae services. President McAllister expressed clearly the tremendous discomfort he would feel personally at the homecoming festivities if "people who had attended out of love for Westfield were pressured into making a financial contribution." When Herzog sought reassurance about the importance of development efforts, the president replied, "We have all made clear our belief that fundraising is critical to Westfield's future, but it must be done in a most graceful manner consistent with the institution's reputation and image." Clearly, Herzog had just lost a major battle and could only hope that she had not lost the war.

Let's pause again. . .

6. *Evaluate Anne Herzog's handling of her disagreement with the director of alumnae services. Could she have predicted this conflict in light of Westfield's reporting lines? What other ways might the issue have been discussed and resolved? What persuasive appeals might she have used to convince the director of alumnae services that his goals were compatible with those of her office? Taking the part of Anne Herzog, role play her interaction with the director of alumnae services.*

7. *Was Anne Herzog correct in taking the disagreement to the president? What could she have done as a middle or interim step? Was there any way that she might have tested the president's reaction before scheduling the three-way meeting in which the president was asked to break the impasse between development and alumnae services?*

A Second Attempt. Unfortunately, the disagreement with Stuart Hunt French was not the only obstacle in the way of a development initiative. Herzog knew from experience that development efforts often were enhanced significantly if students could begin to think of themselves as capable of making contributions to their alma mater—even before they graduated. For this reason, she decided to work more closely with Brenda Sue Jackson, the director of admissions, who was also responsible for the institution's publications. While Herzog was very impressed with the quality of the publications prepared and distributed by Brenda Sue's office, it was obvious to her that none of these publications helped current students view themselves as future financial contributors to the college.

Anne met with the director of admissions to suggest some minor changes that would begin altering this perception in students' minds. However, to her chagrin, she ran up against her second brick wall. Jackson made it very clear that she saw these publications as recruitment and public relations brochures. These publications were, in Jackson's words, "characteristic of the institution's image with the public." Jackson went on to say that Westfield College had a reputation and tradition to protect, and asked Herzog how it would look if people thought that Westfield College was in financial trouble.

Herzog could sense that the Westfield's director of admissions viewed the goal of fundraising from alumnae as a diminution of the institution's image. Given President McAllister's decision with regard to the homecoming activities, Herzog was too fearful to take the publication issue to the president for resolution. If a similar edict were issued on the this matter, she may as well resign.

Herzog's real challenge was now becoming painfully obvious to her. Virtually everyone at Westfield College believed it essential to have a development office because the institution needed to be able to count on the external funds generated by such a office. However, no one seemed to understand or was willing to implement the type of changes that needed to be made in order to generate such revenue. Worse yet, various members of the president's council viewed their own obligations and responsibilities to be in conflict, rather than compatible, with those of the development office.

Now, as she looked out on the gray fog of a gloomy January day, Anne Herzog found it difficult to fathom how much her goals had changed in her first six months as director of development of Westfield College. Six months ago, she saw her challenge to be the tasks of hiring requisite staff, organizing the development function, and setting the stage for a major fundraising effort. Now, she felt further behind than she had been last July. Her immediate challenge was to change attitudes toward development in order to be able to begin to tackle the goals she had set for herself six months ago.

And one final pause. . .

8. *Assume the position of director of development at Westfield College, knowing all that Anne Herzog now knows. Outline a strategy for carrying out your new objectives. Be specific in detailing what you would do in the short term and in the long term and how you intend to deal with each of the key players.*

9. *Could support for campus change be gained from an external source? What source might be used or created to bolster Herzog's efforts to mount a development program at Westfield College?*

10. *Should Anne Herzog consider creating a "development board" to advise her on fundraising and related activities? If so, describe the personal and professional profile of individuals who should be invited to serve on the board. What are the dangers of this action? What are the possible benefits? What, if any, prior approvals should be obtained before constituting a board?*

11. *Are the administrators at Westfield College likely to support an aggressive inquiry into the backgrounds of alumnae (sometimes called "prospect research") to obtain public information regarding land holdings, divorce settlements, stock ownership, etc. if the information gathered is to be used to identify likely prospective donors and the amount that they might ultimately contribute to Westfield? Are there ethical questions that development professionals and institutional leaders must confront regarding their mode of operation?*

Attachment A
Director of Development
Westfield College
Summit, South Carolina

Westfield College, a prestigious women's college, is accepting applications for the newly created position of Director of Development.

Preferred Qualifications:
- Proven success in capital campaign development and major gift fundraising.
- Experience in major gifts and planned giving.
- Strong communication skills.
- Successful management experience in a development office at an independent college or university.
- Bachelor's degree required; advanced degree preferred.

The director will report directly to the college president. The director will design and implement fundraising strategies, extend the college partnerships with nonprofit organizations, and design and execute the annual gifts and capital campaigns commensurate with the college's mission.

Westfield College is an independent, selective admissions institution for women located in a city of 250,000 in South Carolina with a comprehensive program of instruction including the liberal arts, humanities, nursing, and education. Westfield has 3,500 full-time undergraduate students and a small number of graduate and continuing education students.

Nominations and applications complete with resume should be sent to:
Dr. Patrick McAllister, President
Westfield College
Summit, South Carolina

Westfield College is an equal opportunity employer.

Attachment B
ORGANIZATIONAL CHART: Westfield College

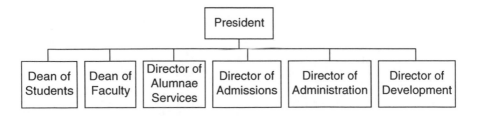

SELECTED READINGS

Bensimon, E. M. (1990). The new president and understanding the campus as a culture. *New Directions for Institutional Research, Number 68,* 75-86.

The focus of this article is on how a new president can understand and become part of the campus culture. The content is organized around the issues of recognizing the institution's culture.

Danko, K. (1991). A survey of attitudes of contributors to business education. *Journal of Education for Business, 67,* 17-20.

This article analyzes a list of items that could influence charitable contributions made to colleges and universities. Factors ranked include teaching quality, geographic proximity, faculty interaction, and reputation of athletic program.

Devault, M. L. (1990). Talking and listening from women's standpoint: Feminist strategies for interviewing and analysis. *Social Problems, 37,* 96-116.

Following a review of the literature on women and languages as it is relevant to four processes of interviewing research (constructing topics, listing to respondents, transcribing and editing interview material, and writing about respondents' lives), the author suggests that traditional paradigms do not account for the feminist perspective.

Haddad, F D., & Hartnett, R. (1989). College student involvement: Alumni fundraising implications. *Journal of College Student Development, 30,* 379-380.

Student involvement in campus activities is shown in this study to be related to alumni donations. In fact, there is a tendency for alumni contributions to increase in direct proportion to the level of student participation in campus activities.

Loessin, B. A., & Duronio, M. A. (1989-1990). The role of planning in successful fundraising in ten higher education institutions. *Planning for Higher Education, 18*(3),45-56.

The authors describe fundraising practices at ten institutions of higher education with successful fundraising programs, dividing their planning into traditional and nontraditional approaches.

Norris, W. (1988, July 1). Questionable science of trapping the greenback. *The Times Higher Education Supplement, 817,* 10.

In this short article from a London newspaper, Norris pokes fun at rich Americans who are the target of "prospect research" activities, and raises questions about the ethics of fundraising by educational institutions.

Reiss, A. H. (1990, May). Bottom line: A working board of directors. *Management Review, 79,* 37-38.

Reiss discusses the positive and negative features of utilizing a board of directors to establish policy, to provide governance, and to offer business expertise in the areas of management, marketing, and finance. He suggests the use of such boards to reach beyond the nonprofit organizations' traditional constituencies.

Rhoads, R. A., & Tierney, W. G. (1990). Exploring organizational climates and cultures. *New Directions for Institutional Research, Number 68,* 87-95.

The authors offer an annotated bibliography divided into three aspects of exploring an organization's climate: understanding culture, methodology, and managing culture.

Stoecker, J. K., & Pascarella, E. T. (1991). Women's colleges and women's career attainment revisited. *Journal of Higher Education, 62,* 394-409.

The authors report findings from a longitudinal study of a national sample of women designed to examine the impact of attending a woman's college on women's postcollege educational, occupational and economic attainment.

Thompson, D. F. (1992). Ethical fundraising: An educational process. *Educational Record, 73,* 38-43.

Arguing that the principles of institutional autonomy and institutional fairness should guide the institution's educational and development programs, the author cites fundraising dilemmas requiring consideration of related ethical issues. He also notes two other areas of ethical concerns: what the fundraiser tries to discover about the potential donors; and what the fundraisers communicate to the donor about the institution.

12

SILENCE GIVES LICENSE

About the Case

From childhood through adulthood, at home and at work, people make decisions which they believe will solve certain problems. Short-term solutions often must be revisited when the problem erupts again. Long-term solutions generally focus on creating an environment or enforcing a policy aimed at eliminating a problem or at least keeping it from resurfacing soon. Sometimes a short-term solution is all that is needed—at that point in time. For example, a quick trip to the local hardware store to purchase a fuse may solve an immediate household emergency. Sooner or later, however, a longer-term solution to the endemic electrical problems of the house may have to be considered so that the homeowners' life does not become a series of quick-fixes ignoring the real and inherent danger of the larger problem.

CASE STUDY

Hillsborough College enjoys a very proud tradition. This private four-year college was founded in 1850 for the purpose of providing a Christian education to male and female students of all races. From its humble beginning, Hillsborough College was perceived as a progressive institution of higher education. Because Hillsborough's original charter was so forward thinking, the leadership at Hillsborough felt spared of any responsibility when affirmative action policies began sweeping institutions of higher education across the nation in the 1970s. After all, how could racial or gender prejudice exist at a college that had been so progressive for more than a century?

Under the leadership of President Lars Peterson, Hillsborough College was content to safeguard the status quo. Women and minority applicants were considered for admission to Hillsborough College as they had always been since its doors opened in 1850. President Peterson believed that the implementation of any special policy targeted to accelerate the recruitment of women and minority students would somehow indict the original integrity of the college. As he once told the institution's governing board, "No special consideration needs to be given to women and minority applicants now because fair consideration has always been given to women and minority applicants and students at Hillsborough College."

Hillsborough College has an enrollment of roughly 4,000 students. Students receive a strong, traditional liberal arts education. While applications for admission are accepted nationwide, most students attending Hillsborough College usually came from the northern Midwest within a radius of 300 miles of the college.

While the college leadership recognized that the enrollment of women and minority students at Hillsborough College was low, this fact was attributed to a belief that women and minority students were more anxious to attend institutions offering technical or more career-oriented associate and baccalaureate degrees. The traditional liberal arts education offered by Hillsborough College was most appropriate for very bright students planning to pursue graduate education. Consequently, the enrollment profile for Hillsborough College did not mirror that region's population demographics, but did not concern the leadership of the college. Without exception, the minority students attending Hillsborough College did so with the support of major scholarship funds.

President Peterson believed that Hillsborough College was, and always had been, an integrated campus. During his 20 years as president, Dr. Peterson had experienced little evidence of racial tension. Occasionally, parents would call to complain when their son or daughter had been assigned a roommate of a different race. Usually, these matters only surfaced when there was an uneven number of minority men or women attending the college and a minority student was paired with a nonminority student in the freshmen residence hall.

Still, President Peterson found that these situations were easily remedied. Hillsborough, like most institutions experienced a modest attrition within the first month of each new academic year. Consequently, it was not difficult to reassign roommates after the first few weeks of the term in a manner that averted any racial difficulties, and it was always possible to give someone a single room, if absolutely necessary.

Minority Faculty Numbers. Two years ago, a small group of minority students had requested a meeting with the president to discuss what they perceived to be a shortage of minority faculty at the college. The students expressed a concern that only three of the college's 200 or so faculty were minority. These three faculty taught courses in cultural pluralism and Afro-American studies, new courses recently added to Hillsborough's mandated distribution requirements.

Dr. Peterson recalled how impressed he was by the students' professional dress and manner as they expressed their concerns to him. They discussed the matter for over an hour and Dr. Peterson remembered vividly how well the students listened to his account of the university's history and perspective. Dr. Peterson had assured the students that Hillsborough would prefer to have more minority faculty and that he hoped more minorities would apply for open faculty positions in the future. The session ended cordially.

Tenure Difficulties. Last year, however, a larger group of minority students visited Dr. Peterson when he announced that one of the three minority faculty would not be granted tenure. President Peterson saw this as a tougher situation because he found it more difficult to explain the institution's tenure policy to these students.

Because there was not a department of "cultural pluralism" or "Afro-American studies" at Hillsborough, faculty teaching these courses held tenure-track positions in one of the more traditional disciplines. The faculty member being denied tenure had his appointment in the department of history. His faculty colleagues in that department voted against his tenure because there was insufficient documentation of continued work in the more traditional discipline of history.

While Dr. Peterson could understand the students' complaint that a faculty member teaching courses in cultural pluralism or Afro-American studies should not be penalized, he stood fast on the need to uphold the Hillsborough's high standard for faculty excellence in the traditional disciplines of the liberal arts. Finally, after two separate one-hour meetings, President Peterson felt confident that the students, though disappointed, understood the larger institutional issue. Dr. Peterson assured the students that every effort would be made to replace the departing minority faculty member with another minority scholar.

Romeo, Romeo. These two seemingly isolated issues during the past two years did not give Dr. Peterson reason for alarm. Consequently, Dr. Peterson was totally surprised and caught off-guard by the events of the past few months.

As usual, the theatre department held auditions in mid-September to cast the annual fall production. This year, the theatre department was scheduled to bring to the college stage a production of Shakespeare's *Romeo and Juliet*. The play's direction was assigned by the department chair to a new non-minority faculty member who had been recruited from a prestigious private college in the Northeast. After a week of auditions and call-backs, the cast was selected and the list was posted. The leading role of Juliet was given to Christine Utgaard, a senior theatre major whose talents had been enjoyed by patrons of the Hillsborough College Theatre for three years. This was no surprise as everyone expected that Christine would be cast as Juliet.

The new faculty member, however, sent shock waves through the Hillsborough College community when he cast an Afro-American male student, Trevone Smith, as Romeo. Trevone was a junior theatre major already recognized as having significant talent. However, he had not been cast in many productions while a student at Hillsborough College because previous faculty directors believed it inappropriate to cast Trevone in such ethnic productions as *Fiddler on the Roof, Brigadoon*, or *I Remember Mama*. Trevone had impressed the audiences, literally bringing down the house, with his performance as Judd, the crazed bad guy, in a recent production of *Oklahoma*.

While the other theatre faculty were surprised by the casting of Trevone in the role of Romeo, they also acknowledged that he was the most talented male student actor on campus. Christine helped ease the theatre faculty's concern when she projected her instant agreement with the selection of Trevone as Romeo. The chair of the theatre department was greatly relieved, but still decided to alert the Hillsborough's administration to the fact that this year's production of *Romeo and Juliet* would be an interracial production.

President Peterson counseled the department chair to have a talk with the new faculty member to help him understand the need to be more sensitive to the Midwestern culture surrounding the Hillsborough College campus. He advised the chair to join him in treating the forthcoming production as "business as usual." There was to be no special publicity. From President Peterson's point of view, it was important to get through the production run—scheduled for the first week in December—without a lot of publicity and to insure more responsible choices in future casting decisions.

Let's pause here. . .

1. *How would you evaluate the president's action regarding the interracial production of* Romeo and Juliet? *Assume the role of President Peterson and describe how you would have handled the discussion with the theatre department chair. If you were the president, would you have responded differently?*

2. *How would you assess the racial climate at Hillsborough College? Does the institution's handling of complaints about roommates offer any insight into the campus climate for minorities? What about the president's personal biases? Specify the basis for your conclusion. Be certain to distinguish between fact and inference.*

3. *Was the new faculty member out of line to cast an interracial production of Romeo and Juliet? Was the department chair negligent in not providing more supervision over the new faculty member during his first term at the college? How does the issue of academic freedom enter this situation?*

The Rehearsals. The department chair agreed to comply with the president's suggestions. However, he decided to postpone his discussion with the faculty director until after *Romeo and Juliet* had completed its run. Everything appeared to be under control until non-cast members started attending the rehearsals. With a small number of theatre majors on the campus, the department often recruited volunteers from the total Hillsborough student population to help with everything from publicity, props and set construction, to box office management. These opportunities for professional experience were deemed to be important for students in other majors. Students majoring in business would help with marketing strategies and advertising, as well as with box office receipts. Students majoring in history would help with the design of period costumes and props. Hence, when non-theatre majors started attending rehearsals, no one was surprised or alarmed.

Faculty present at the rehearsal noticed that the non-major volunteer students were, in general, louder and more disruptive during the rehearsals than they had been in previous years. Still, the behavior was viewed as excessive enthusiasm for the start of a new year and pretty much ignored by the faculty working on the lights and sets. It was not until Trevone and Christine began to rehearse the scene in which they first embrace that a group of white male students transformed their presence from one of annoyance into total disruption. Within minutes, the shouting from the back of the theatre turned the auditorium into a brawl instigated by the hecklers and involving all students present. Faculty had misjudged the amount of tension that had been building and that was released when the overt heckling started.

With the help of campus security and faculty, the fight was brought under control. The next afternoon, all those who were present at the rehearsal the evening before, including those who had participated in the brawl, found themselves seated before the president. President Peterson expressed his outrage and severe disappointment at their behavior and made it clear that this would not happen again. After a full 30-minute lecture, the group was dismissed to return to their residence halls.

A group of theatre majors, however, remained to have a different conversation with the president. This group of students urged the president to take action against those who had heckled and started the fight by suspending them for exhibiting obvious racial prejudice. Their posture surprised the president who had the distinct impression that he was the one being lectured to on how to behave.

He told them that the negative publicity over such a suspension would be harmful to Hillsborough's reputation. After all, Hillsborough College had always had an open door for women and minorities. This single incident of poor judgment on the part of a few was not sufficient reason to tarnish the college's fine reputation. Besides, President Peterson pointed out that some of those who would be first in line for suspension were seniors. In his mind, he explained, it would not be fair to ruin their educational opportunities at Hillsborough College on the basis of one incident.

Let's pause again. . .

4. With the advantage of hindsight, consider if the president was correctly reading the earlier episodes with students. What could the president have done one and two years earlier that might have diffused the racial tension that eventually exploded with the casting of an Afro-American student in the college's production of Romeo and Juliet?

5. Do you agree with the president's treatment of the most recent episode? If not, specify how you would have handled the situation. What risk was the president taking by his actions to protect Hillsborough's reputation and image, as he saw the need? Was the trade-off worth the risk?

The Rehearsals Continue. In the two weeks that followed, the situation escalated. Trevone received almost daily threats to leave the production and the school. Christine, too, received threats of physical harm, most with sexual overtones, if she performed in this interracial production of *Romeo and Juliet* as part of an interracial couple. The faculty director came home one day to find that the trash can outside his home had been set on fire. He too had received several pieces of hate mail suggesting he return to the Northeast before either he or his family was harmed.

The same group of theatre majors, this time accompanied by the faculty director, again talked with President Peterson. They showed the president samples of the hate mail they had received and told of the harassing incidents they all had experienced. The president listened, but remained firm in his belief that he could not place this one incident ahead of the total welfare of the institution. He did suggest as an alternative that the theatre department cancel the show or recast it. The group took great exception to this because all believed that Trevone was the most qualified actor and deserved to play Romeo. How better, they argued, could they illustrate the perceived "inappropriateness" of a Montague and a Capulet falling in love? They further believed that the theatre department would be shirking its educational responsibility to Trevone and others if it succumbed to this racial prejudice.

In one heated moment, the faculty director admonished the president by saying that a true liberal education taught students to resist racial prejudice. The president retorted that this was an easier process when new faculty took the time to learn and be sensitive to the culture within which they were working rather than expecting all cultures to adjust to their imported views. After two hours, the group left with the full realization that President Peterson did not intend to take any action.

The Show Must Go On. Confronted with the choice of canceling the show, recasting it, or proceeding as planned, the group decided unanimously to proceed as scheduled. At the final dress rehearsal that evening, the scene was tense. Instead of heckling or shouting, a large number of visitors and volunteers remained in the back of the theatre and watched the rehearsal in disapproving silence.

The next morning the first faculty member to arrive at the theatre found the set demolished. The stage curtains were slashed, furniture and props were broken, and paint had been poured over the costumes. Later it was discovered that paint had also been dumped on Trevone's car and on the new van of the play's director.

President Peterson met with the theatre faculty to evaluate the situation. Upon surveying the damage, the president elected to cancel the production indefinitely. Now, as he reflected on the events that led up to yesterday's decision, he had deep regrets. Although relieved that Hillsborough's footlights would not illuminate an interracial love story, he was, nevertheless, apprehensive about the violence that brought about the cancellation.

Then, the exodus began. Throughout the day, a few at a time, the college's minority students left the campus in protest of the actions of the administration and fearful for their safety. In addition, several of the non-minority students majoring in theatre who had also received threats for participating in the interracial production of *Romeo and Juliet* had also gone home. The vandalism put the college on the front pages of newspapers in regions where Hillsborough College was virtually an unknown entity. And news of the students' subsequent departures would provide fodder for a follow-up story.

President Peterson sat in his office and began to re-evaluate his posture on the incidents that led up to the destruction in the theatre. He also considered what might be done to restore racial peace at Hillsborough College and to encourage the minority students to return to campus. Moreover, steps had to be taken to ensure that this episode did not hurt the future recruitment of minority students and faculty at Hillsborough

College. And he needed to restore the public's faith in the college as a strong liberal arts institution founded and truly committed to providing an education to students of all races.

A final pause. . .

6. Assume the role of the president and devise a strategy for dealing with this situation. For starters, prepare a press release on the forced cancellation of the college's production of Romeo and Juliet.

7. Assume the role of the college president and field the following questions from the media regarding the exodus of minority students from Hillsborough:

   a. "President Peterson, how do you explain what has happened at Hillsborough?"

   b. "President Peterson, did you have any indication of the amount of racial tension generated on campus by the casting of the roles of Romeo and Juliet?"

   c. "President Peterson, is it true that all of the minority students have left the campus either as a protest against Hillsborough or in fear of their personal safety?"

   d. "President Peterson, how does Hillsborough plan to respond to this sad episode in the institution's history?"

8. Looking to the future, specify your strategy for:

   a. persuading the departed students to return to Hillsborough College, students who are not likely to return unless convinced that the climate will be different for members of racial minorities;

   b. improving the campus climate for minorities and demonstrating a positive change to students, faculty, and the general public;

   c. controlling the damage that might have been done to future recruitment efforts; and

   d. preventing similar incidents in the future.

9. You realize that, as president, you need to telephone Trevone Smith, among others. What are you going to say to Trevone? Who else will you call?

SELECTED READINGS

Ashley, M. E. (1990). *Combating racism on campus: A resource book and model for the 1990s.* Cincinnati, OH: University of Cincinnati.

The author recommends actions to be taken to combat racism on campuses and deals with such topics as the institution-wide commitment, minority faculty and staff, minority students, a campus climate valuing diversity, multicultural training, a multicultural curriculum, community involvement, intervention strategies, and accountability.

Balenger, V. J., Hoffman, M. A., & Sedlacek, W. E. (1992). Racial attitudes among incoming white students: A study of 10-year trends. *Journal of College Student Development, 33,* 245-252.

The authors report the findings of a study designed to analyze the attitudes held by incoming white students toward blacks over the 10-year period from 1978 to 1988, to determine if the racial attitudes held by whites have become more positive or negative.

Bernstein, J. (1990, March). The ten steps of crisis management. *Security Management, 34,* 75-76.

This public relations professional summarizes the ten steps to follow to control negative communications arising out of crisis situations.

Birnbaum, R. (1992). Will you love me in December as you do in May? Why experienced college presidents lose faculty support. *Journal of Higher Education, 63,* 1-25.

The author explores the tension which exists between faculty and presidents, with data from a five-year longitudinal study. He offers some general propositions to explain this often turbulent relationship.

Bishop, T. R. (1992). Integrating business ethics into an undergraduate curriculum. *Journal of Business Ethics, 11,* 291-300.

In this paper, Bishop describes the approach followed in creating a course in business ethics from the identification of the conceptual framework, the issues, and his objectives and strategies.

Bok, D. (1988, Summer). Can higher education foster higher morals? *Business and Society Review, 66,* 4-12.

Bok defines the elements of a comprehensive program of moral education in higher education: courses in applied ethics; discussions of rules of conduct with students and how to fairly administer them; programs of community service; high ethical standards in institutional decision-making; and a campus climate that supports ethical standards. His challenge to the academic community is clear and forceful—and worthy of individual or collective consideration.

Bryden, D. P. (1991, Spring). It ain't what they teach, it's the way that they teach it. *The Public Interest, 103,* 38-53.

This lengthy essay on the curricular and political debate in higher education regarding the traditional core of a liberal education versus a new "multicultural education." He notes that the point of such a new curriculum is not so much to *study* racism as to *eliminate* it through consciousness-raising; he comments on the problems inherent in teaching courses where students find the ideas unpopular; and he concludes with comments on the political persuasion of most college faculty and how that effects the academy.

Cerio, N. C. (1989). Counseling victims and perpetrators of campus violence. *New Directions for Student Services, Number 47,* 53-64.

The author discusses various counseling approaches to victims of campus violence and the role of campus police as interventionists in incidents of campus violence.

Close, J. (1991, February). Speaking out to the public: Ten crisis communication strategies. *Best's Review, 91,* 86f.

Citing a crisis in public confidence, the author challenges corporate leaders to win back the trust of their constituents. He suggests using a combination of communication and actions, noting ten crisis communication strategies to serve as the basis for possible action.

Cramer, S. (1991). Fostering ethical dialogues across campus. *CUPA Journal, 42,* 44-48.

Cramer discusses how the topic of ethics became a stimulus for purposeful, long-term discussion and activities with faculty and staff at a comprehensive college. The Ethics Forum meets monthly and discusses ethical issues faced by adults involved in higher education. The balance of the article focuses on an ethical situational leadership model.

Cunningham, B., & Miller, S. (1991). Racism: Assess the campus and community environment. *Journal of College Student Development, 32,* 181-182.

The authors describe the efforts of a campus task force to rectify the environmental factors which often threaten ethnic minority students who attend predominantly white institutions.

Dalton, J. C. (Ed.). (1991). Racism on campus: Confronting racial bias through peer interventions. *New Directions for Student Services, Number 56.* San Francisco: Jossey-Bass.

A collection of essays on the causes for recent incidents of racial and ethnic hostility on campuses and various uses of peer interventions which can be promoted and used to confront racial bias on campus.

Dennis, E. E. (1992). Freedom of expression, the university, and the media. *Journal of Communication, 42,* 73-82.

The author argues that political correctness and multiculturalism are in conflict with life in the academy. He notes that new courses with new theories of history were often taught by newly recruited faculty and led to predictably explosive results; a modified view of academic freedom questions the use of the classroom "to promote a personal political credo or private religious view."

Ehrlich, R., & Scimecca, J. (1991, Summer). Offensive speech on campus: Punitive or educational solutions. *Educational Record, 72,* 26-29.

Following an account of an incident that took place at George Mason University, the authors discuss the factors inherent in assessing offensive speech. They argue against restrictive campus codes or allowing the group offended to serve as judges, but for determining whether harassment or discrimination *as legally defined* has occurred.

Finifter, D. H., Baldwin, R. G., & Thelin, J. R. (Eds.). (1991). *The uneasy public policy triangle in higher education.* New York, NY: American Council on Education /Macmillan.

The authors discuss the impact of public policy on the issues of diversity, quality and budget in higher education. Of particular relevance to this case study is Section III on "the goals of diversity in higher education."

Fritzsche, D. J. (1991). A model of decision-making incorporating ethical values. *Journal of Business Ethics, 10,* 841-852.

A model to assist persons studying ethical behavior in business is presented which includes the decision-maker's personal values and elements of the organization's culture. The author hypothesizes that this combination produces decisions which may be significantly different than decisions effected by personal values alone. The author's analysis as presented in the narrative and in the model lend themselves as the basis for a lively discussion.

Glenn, J. R. Jr. (1992). Can a business and society course affect the ethical judgment of future managers? *Journal of Business Ethics, 11,* 217-223.

Glenn reports the findings of a four-year study designed to measure the impact of a single course taught in the School of Business at San Francisco State University on the future ethical judgments of students.

Green, M. F. (Ed.). (1989). *Minorities on campus: A handbook for enhancing diversity.* Washington, DC: American Council on Education.

This handbook was written as a practical guide for trustees, presidents, and other higher education administrators. The handbook offers specific strategies for enhancing diversity on campus in seven areas: an institutional audit; undergraduate students; graduate/professional students; faculty; administrators; the campus climate; and teaching, learning, and the curriculum.

Guillebeau, J. (1989, Fall). Crisis management: A case study in the killing of an employee. *Public Relations Quarterly, 35,* 19-21.

This brief article offers an hour-by-hour summary of actions taken by a small college to minimize the potential for unfavorable publicity following the killing of an employee. Guillebaue offers the reader some insight into the utility of a public relations function within an institution of higher education.

Kerr, C. (1984). *Presidents make a difference.* Washington, DC: Association of Governing Boards of Universities and Colleges.

A report based on interviews with more than 800 college and university presidents, spouses of presidents, and others associated with presidents. The focus of the report is on the operational decisions that would help to strengthen leadership in institutions of higher education.

Kerr, C., & Gade, M. L. (1986). *The many lives of academic presidents: Time, place and character.* Washington, DC: Association of Governing Boards of Universities and Colleges.

This report is a sequel to *Presidents make a difference* by Clark Kerr. The focus of this report is an analysis of the academic presidency and how its conduct is influenced by changing times, diverse campus environments, and the varying styles and strategies of its incumbents.

Kuh, G. D., Schuh, J. H., Whitt, E. J., Andreas, R. E., Lyons, J. W., Strange, C. C., Krehbiel, L. E., & MacKay, K. A. (1991). *Involving colleges.* San Francisco, CA: Jossey-Bass.

The authors begin with the premise that two-thirds of a college student's waking hours are devoted to activities other than attending class and studying. The text describes strategies for promoting educationally purposeful out-of-class activities within the context of the campus community.

Levine, A. (Ed). (1992, January/February). *Change, 24*(1).

This issue includes articles by administrators and scholars on the issues associated with integrating multiculturalism into the postsecondary education curriculum. Four articles particularly applicable to this case are: "Three questions for the multiculturalism debate" by Larry Yarbrough; "Signs of a changing curriculum" by the Carnegie Foundation for the Advancement of Teaching; "Beyond politics: The educational issues inherent in multicultural education" by Jerry G. Gaff; and "The quiet revolution: Eleven facts about multiculturalism and the curriculum" by Arthur Levine and Jeanette Cureton.

Levine, A., & Associates. (1989). *Shaping higher education's future: Demographic realities and opportunities, 1990-2000*. San Francisco, CA: Jossey-Bass.

This text contains a comprehensive analysis of the demographic changes in higher education. Separate chapters are devoted to traditional college-age students, Hispanics, Blacks, Asians, and older students. The text concludes with a chapter on the "Uses and misuses of demographic projections: Lessons for the 1990s."

Neumann, A., & Bensimon, E. M. (1990). Constructing the presidency: College presidents' images of their leadership roles, a comparative study. *Journal of Higher Education, 61*, 678-701.

The authors studied the leadership exercised by college presidents, looking at how presidents set goals, construct agendas, communicate and interact, transmit values, and evaluate their own effectiveness. Four presidential types are identified and described by organizational and environmental conditions associated with each.

Pascarella, E. T., & Terenzini, P. T. (1991). *How college affects students: Findings and insights from twenty years of research*. San Francisco, CA: Jossey-Bass.

The authors present theories and models of student change in college. Among the issues discussed are the moral development of students, the formation of students' attitudes and values, and changes in psychological constructs such as identity, self-concept and self-esteem.

Pavel, D. M., & Reiser, M. (1991). Using national data bases to examine minority student success. *New Directions for Institutional Research, Number 69*, 5-20.

The authors review the use of two types of national data bases (student longitudinal surveys and institutional surveys) to determine the level of participation and achievement attained by minority students in higher education.

Rhoads, R. A., & Tierney, W. G. (1990). Exploring organizational climates and cultures. *New Directions for Institutional Research, Number 68*, 87-95.

The authors provide an annotated listing of resources regarding understanding and managing organizational climates and cultures. Culture is presented as a tool for understanding organizational settings.

Sherrill, J. M. (1989) Models of response to campus violence: Responding to violence on campus. *New Directions for Student Services, Number 47*, 77-88.

Violent behavior on a campus requires a response from the campus community. Sherrill discusses various methods of response and factors effecting the response.

Smith, M. C. (1989). The ancestry of campus violence. *New Directions for Student Services, Number 47*, 5-15.

This attorney traces the history of campus crimes and violence from medieval institutions through campus crimes in American institutions in the mid-19th century to the present which he believes started in the post World War II years. The second part of this piece traces the courts' involvement in campus crime including legal theories of liability under tort law and three legal duties regarding campus violence. He summarizes numerous findings in case law involving violence on campuses.

Spotts, B. L. (1991). Creating a successful minority affairs position: Guidelines for institutions and individuals. *The Journal of College Admission, 13*(1), 4-9.

The author argues for the creation of a minority affairs position not as a "quick fix" but as an institutional commitment. She offers five guidelines for the institution and five suggestions for the individual in the position. The reader is left to decide if this is a solution to problems associated with minority students and faculty.

Sullivan, G. M., & Nowlin, W. A. (1990, Summer). Recruiting and hiring minority faculty: Old story, same myths, new opportunities. *CUPA Journal, 41*, 43-50.

Building on the belief that institutions have a vested interest in promoting a campus environment that is comfortable for all students, the authors discuss the critical issues of under representation, need for minority role models, and legal expectations. Five myths that impede the achievement of a multicultural work force are described.

13

AN ATTEMPT TO FINESSE

About the Case

In the game of bridge, a finesse is a strategic move where one player attempts to make a gain without exposing the partnership to any greater possibility of loss than already exists, while maximizing a previously nonexistent chance for possible gain. Central State University, in this case, is strategizing a finesse in terms of the institution's relationship with the state's coordinating board. If the institution's finesse is successful, it will retain its academic program in Russian language. If the institution's finesse does not work, it will lose its Russian program (the result it expects without employing this strategy). Administrators, individuals, corporations, young children, baseball teams, and even babies often use this tactic, without labeling it as a finesse. Communication is the key ingredient, the element on which rests the final result of this approach. Within the framework of communication, word choice and nuance of meaning may spell the difference between success and failure for the institution.

CASE STUDY

Central State University (CSU) is one of eight public regional institutions in this Midwestern state. These state institutions are organized into two systems, each with its own governing board whose members are appointed by the governor. In addition, the governor appoints people to the state's Board of Higher Education (BHE) which retains, by statute, coordinating and regulatory control over all institutions of higher education within the state.

One such regulatory mandate issued by the BHE more than a decade ago is the requirement that all degree programs be reviewed at least once

185

every five years. The results of these reviews are to be reported through the institution's board of trustees to the state's BHE. The BHE reviews these reports carefully and offers suggestions for improving the degree programs. For example, when a program review report indicates that a program is not offering quality instruction or is not healthy as measured by student demand and graduation rates, the BHE recommends that the program be eliminated because it is both educationally and economically unjustified.

Although BHE's reaction to program reviews are couched as *recommendations*, they are difficult recommendations to ignore. The BHE's power to make recommendations in regard to an institution's budget request affords it significant leverage in advancing its own recommendations. Specifically, budget requests prepared by institutions for continued and new funding are submitted first to the BHE. The BHE reviews each budget request and then typically recommends to the state legislature a modified budget request for each institution. Consequently, if the BHE believes that a particular campus is not taking its recommendations seriously, the BHE could decide not to support that institution's future budgetary increase requests. The BHE possesses enough political muscle to maintain ultimate control over the academic program inventory, but not the specific courses which are offered at each of the state's eight regional universities.

Program Review. Central State University had been conducting program reviews long before the BHE required institutions to do so. Consequently, program review at CSU is taken seriously by students, faculty, and the administration. The institution developed elaborate procedures for very comprehensive program review. The process utilizes both an internal review team comprised of faculty from different disciplines on campus and an external review team comprised of experts from the particular discipline being reviewed. These outside experts are brought in from other institutions across the country. For any one program, the entire review process takes slightly more than one calendar year from the time the department begins writing a thorough self-study document to the time the final report is submitted to the institution's board of trustees for approval and forwarding to the BHE.

For the most part, the program review process at Central State works very well. Although the faculty and campus leadership resent the BHE's role in program review, the forced dialogue between the institution and the BHE typically results in clear suggestions for continued programmatic improvement. Occasionally, the institutional leadership believes that the BHE reaction to a specific program review report is made out of context and, therefore, is quite inappropriate for future planning. This usually happens when the student demand and the societal need for individuals trained in certain disciplines moves in a cyclical fashion. The elementary education program provides a clear model of this phenomenon.

For example, if the enrollment in elementary schools throughout the state dips, thus creating less demand for students trained in elementary education, the program review process would document a similar decline in enrollment and in the number of students graduating from the elementary education baccalaureate degree program. The BHE would then use these data to substantiate its recommendation to downsize or eliminate the elementary education program. This recommendation would ignore, for instance, that projected state population demographics suggest that the current poor job market for teachers is temporary and that a tremendous increase in demand for elementary education teachers is in the offing. Those teachers would be needed both to handle growing enrollments in the elementary schools and to cover the number of anticipated retirements in the ranks of the veteran teachers throughout the state.

Such disagreements tended to fuel campus resentment toward the BHE's role in program review. In general, the BHE was perceived as being "out of touch" with reality and incapable of articulating any consistent long-term educational plans for the institution. The BHE was also seen by some more caustic faculty as cost-cutting bureaucrats.

Russian. One of the programs reviewed and reported to the BHE this year by Central State University was the most recent program to face the danger of elimination. The bachelor of arts degree in the Russian language was found by the BHE to be "no longer educationally and economically justified." In its report back to Central's board of trustees, the BHE offered the following analysis.

> Statewide student credit hours generated by foreign language majors decreased by 25% and enrollment dropped by 6% during the last five years. Declining statewide interest in the Russian language is even more apparent. Student credit hours in undergraduate Russian language programs declined by 45% during the last five year period. During the same period, the number of bachelors degrees awarded dropped from 16 degrees to 5 degrees.

> Of the three undergraduate Russian language programs in the state, the program in Central State University has consistently had the lowest enrollment over the last five years. During this period, the program has had an average enrollment of two students per year and an average of 70 program major credits generated. At this time, only one student is enrolled in the program. It is unlikely that sufficient depth and breadth of coursework to support a strong major can be maintained with enrollment at this level. In addition, the university has not provided adequate evidence to indicate that

the program addresses the personal or occupational objectives of graduates.

Elimination of this program would allow the university to redirect funds to other programs for which there is a greater student demand.

Let's pause here. . .

1. *Assume the position of provost and consider your initial reaction to the BHE recommendation to eliminate the bachelors degree program in Russian. Given the well known budgetary risk, would you elect to battle to retain the program? What factors might influence your decision to acquiesce? What factors might move you to take on the state board and fight the recommendation? Are a direct confrontation or total capitulation the only two options available to the institution?*

2. *Evaluate the merits of the BHE recommendation to eliminate the bachelor's degree in Russian. Consider at what point low enrollment adversely affects instructional quality. Would your answer vary with the discipline? Why or why not?*

Central State University's Response. For several sound educational reasons and one large political reality, the university was not anxious to eliminate its bachelor degree in the Russian language. First, the university realized that there would be minimal, if any, cost savings as a result of eliminating the degree program in Russian. Faculty teaching in the program were tenured and would continue to teach courses in Russian whether or not students were afforded the opportunity to pursue a baccalaureate degree major in the Russian language.

Second, the administration believed that dropping the bachelor's degree in Russian would be inconsistent with the mission of the university. As a comprehensive state university, the institution believed that a diverse foreign language component was central to its mission.

Third, faculty in the department of foreign languages were confident that the opening of the iron curtain and increased globalization of society had started a trend toward improved enrollments in foreign languages. They believed that their enrollments would continue to increase during the next decade. Indeed, from the time that the program review report was forwarded to the BHE last July and the BHE recommendation for program elimination was received in October, three more students decided to major in the Russian language degree program.

Lastly, national experts attributed the increase in interest to a growing emphasis on language study as a way of meeting the nation's needs in defense, diplomacy and commerce. Clearly, there is an emerging consensus that the study of foreign languages and cultures is a serious deficiency among American students and a salient component of a baccalaureate education.

While recognizing the oversight role of the BHE, campus leadership was sensing a growing political as well as educational need to establish that matters of program review, evaluation, enhancement and elimination should be left to the discretion of the campus. The administration believed that such decisions should be based on more information than strictly cost data.

Strategizing a Finesse. The dean of the College of Liberal Arts and the university provost agreed with the foreign language faculty that Central State University should retain its baccalaureate degree programs in Russian. However, there was grave concern among those same university administrators as to how best to press this point with the BHE. Central State University wanted its arguments to carry the debate without jeopardizing the institution's rapport with the BHE and without incurring subsequent liability or penalty in future BHE recommendations on forthcoming budgetary recommendations or other academic matters. They wondered if CSU could win the debate and keep the Russian language degree program without jeopardizing the institution's future level of financial support.

After considerable deliberation, the CSU academic leadership decided to advance a recommendation to its board of trustees for review and action. The recommendation would clearly indicate the university's intention to retain the bachelor of arts degree in Russian, but would also evidence the university's commitment to address the program improvement concerns of the BHE. By putting the institution's position in the form of a board resolution, the system's board of trustees would be the agency making the ultimate decision with regard to the BHE recommendation. Two months after receiving the BHE recommendation to eliminate the B.A. degree in Russian, the president of CSU forwarded a draft resolution (Attachment A) to the institution's board of trustees.

Let's pause again. . .

3. *How would you evaluate the action taken by the campus leadership at Central State University? What are the advantages and disadvantages of the course of action being undertaken at Central State University? Do you anticipate that the benefits outweigh the potential risks? Will the compromise be accepted?*

4. Does having the action which flows from the trustees' resolution minimize or increase the risk of retaliation by the BHE? In what position does this resolution place the members of the institution's board of trustees? Having received the resolution, what alternatives are available to the board of trustees? Note that your answer should not be limited to passing or voting down the resolution. Under what conditions is the institution's board of trustees likely to approve the resolution? Consider, for example, whether or not the board of trustees will be active and responsive to the political power struggle.

5. Critique the resolution and accompanying report. Is the BHE the only intended audience? Are the arguments presented effectively? Is the case well-documented? How might the resolution be strengthened?

6. Once such a resolution is approved by the Board of Trustees and word of the action is forwarded to the BHE, what follow-up is needed by the provost? Should there be additional actions taken by the college dean or the department chair or faculty? Your analysis should not be restricted only to actions on the campus.

7. In what ways could Central State University's credibility with the BHE be improved because of its proposed stance regarding the degree program in Russian? In what ways is the institution's credibility with the BHE in greater jeopardy because of the actions the institution is proposing to take?

Attachment A

Central State University

RESPONSE TO THE BOARD OF HIGHER EDUCATION REPORT
ON PROGRAMS REVIEWED DURING 199x-9x

Bachelor of Arts Degree in Russian

Background Summary

On October 1, 199x, the BHE approved a report titled *Programs Reviewed by Central State University during 199x-9x, and Recommendations by the Board of Higher Education.* That report provided that Central State University and its governing Board of Trustees were to be advised that the bachelor of arts degree in Russian were "no longer educationally and economically justified and should be eliminated."

The attached resolution and report appended to it comprise Central State University's response to the BHE recommendation. Specifically, Central State University proposes that these programs be retained for at least three years, during which time they would be monitored against the criteria enumerated in the appended report. The university administration intends to propose to its governing board that the programs be retained or abolished not later than the regular Board of Trustees' meeting three years from this December.

Currently, there are five students majoring in this program. Since this program was reviewed five years ago, modest increases have occurred in the program's enrollments and increased emphasis has been given to foreign language programs in general at state and national levels. The cost of delivering the program is marginal and, in fact, abolishing the program at the present time would result in no appreciable savings in instructional costs, if the university maintained its current level of foreign language instruction offered in the Russian language. Further details are contained in the report appended to this matter.

This proposed response is the result of an administrative examination of the issue by the provost in conjunction with the faculty of the department of foreign languages and the dean of the College of Liberal Arts.

Resolution

BE IT RESOLVED, by the Board of Trustees of Central State University in regular meeting assembled, that Central State University submit the report appended to this resolution to the staff of the state's Board of Higher Education indicating the progress that has been made in assessing the economic and educational viability of the bachelor of arts program in Russian; and

BE IT FURTHER RESOLVED, that Central State University continue to monitor this program and submit to this board a final proposal for retention or abolition of this program not later than the regular Board of Trustees' meeting of December, 199x.

PROGRESS REPORT

Bachelor of Arts Programs in Russian

1. The BHE has recently questioned the level of enrollment in the Russian language program at Central State University. Although the program is small, the national trend in foreign language enrollments is up at the college level where a 4.5 percent increase in enrollment was experienced during the past five-year period. In Russian language enrollment, specifically, the increase is more striking, where an increase of 26.7 percent for the same period occurred.

    Rising interest is also reported on the high school level. One high school in this state recorded a pre-enrollment in Russian language of 180 students this fall. The increased level of activity is only a symptom of increased interest and support on the part of the public, particularly following the major economic and political changes that occurred in the republics that comprise this large part of the world. Most of the recent books, articles, and reports relating to the quality of education have included emphasis on language study among their recommendations; articles and surveys have shown the importance of language study in meeting the nation's needs in defense, diplomacy, and commerce; and prominent educators and national leaders have affirmed its educational value. An emerging consensus places the study of foreign languages and cultures alongside the five "basics" of English, mathematics, computer science, social studies, and the natural sciences as fundamental components of a sound liberal education.

    The study of foreign language and international issues are also widely perceived as among the subjects in which American educational performance has been most seriously deficient. A report prepared by the state's High School Foreign Language and International Studies Committee generally stressed the need for more foreign language study in this state. This report singled out Russian language as one of the most understudied of the critical languages of the modern world. The report noted that the Japanese, Chinese, Russian and Arabic languages are being studied by fewer than five percent of the public high school students in the state, and that these same languages are spoken by over 80 percent of the world's population.

    A statewide association of businesspersons recently issued a report which noted the need for persons interested in world commerce to communicate competently not only in English, but also in other languages as well. Business growth in the state, this report stated, will undoubtedly come from the foreign countries as our governor actively seeks their trade and investments in this state. The report concludes with a strong plea for graduates who are prepared to meet the new job demands.

If the bachelor's degree program in Russian at Central State University was eliminated, access to serious study of the Russian language and Soviet Studies would be in grave danger at one of the state's major comprehensive universities.

2. As to the question of enrollment and degrees awarded, our records show that the credit hours produced in upper-level courses in Russian rose from 27 to 53 during the last five-year period. Although these figures are low, eliminating the bachelor's program would not significantly change the picture; essentially the same courses would have to be taught for those students at the university who are seriously interested in Russian language, Soviet Studies, and international politics whether they are pursuing a degree in Russian language or not. As to the whether there is sufficient depth and breadth in the courses offered, Russian language programs utilize modest-sized faculty and curricular offerings and are less diversified than other language programs. Depth and strength of the major were examined during the last program review. The results were positive.

In the final program review document, the internal review team concluded that "The Russian program should not be deleted if Central State University is to remain a comprehensive university." One of the outside reviewers stated: "If Central State University is to survive as a comprehensive university, it must continue to offer majors in the major foreign languages of the world." Essential but less popular languages such as Russian require limited subsidies from the administration.

As to the occupational objectives of recent graduates, our records show that of the 11 graduates of the last six years who majored in Russian, all but one are either in a job or continuing their education in a program that is related to their undergraduate degree.

Finally, students majoring in engineering, business, political science, anthropology, or any other discipline who wants to do serious work in the area of Soviet Studies should have the same amount of language and cultural studies as a Russian language major. It is essential to realize that students in these disciplines need basically the same courses as a Russian language major. We would, therefore, still need to offer advanced high-level work in Russian whether there is a major or not.

Thus, elimination of the program would have only a negative impact on the institution and its students. The elimination would weaken the position of Russian language in the state. It would contribute to a lowering of student and faculty morale on campus. Additionally, it would make it more difficult to attract and to retain high-caliber faculty in the other foreign languages, but also in any related curricular areas.

3. The university proposes to keep the degree program in the Russian language for the time being because:

    a)   There are a growing number of majors in the program; and

    b)   The program provides a service to other departments, including political science, computer science, and anthropology.

4. The university will closely monitor student demand (as measured by student credit hours) for courses in the Russian language by all students for a period of three years. In addition, the number of graduates with majors, double majors, and minors in Russian language will be tabulated for the three-year period. At the end of this period, the situation will be reevaluated and a recommendation made to Central State University's governing board to retain or abolish the program.

SELECTED READINGS

Abrams, D. M. (1987). Political competition and cooperation between public and higher education agencies of state government. *Journal of Education Finance, 12,* 369-390.

After a brief discussion of political group theory, the author applies this to a case study in organizational competition and cooperation in the state of Utah between the two state departments charged with education. Abrams looks at the structure, dynamics, and actions of education leaders in formulating cooperative budget strategies to deal with the state legislature, and focuses on the problems created outside educational ranks by this cooperative strategy.

Barak, R. J., & Breier, B. E. (1990). *Successful program review: A practical guide to evaluating programs in academic settings.* San Francisco, CA: Jossey-Bass.

This text is a handbook on how to plan, conduct and analyze outcomes for program review. Of particular interest for this case is the chapter on the various roles of administrators, trustees, and state-level staff in tasks related to conducting and interpreting program reviews. The final chapter describes how a program review can and should be linked to institutional assessment, accreditation and planning.

Hossler, D., Bean, J. P., & Associates. (1990). *The strategic management of college enrollments.* San Francisco, CA: Jossey-Bass.

This text is a resource on the general issue of managing enrollment and student recruitment. In particular, the authors detail how marketing strategies can be applied to college student recruitment and retention. In addition, later chapters offer guidance on how information systems can be used for purposes of enrollment management and how enrollment management can be tailored to the needs and parameters of a specific institution.

Kaplan, S. (1989). The quest for institutional excellence: The CEO and the creative use of the accreditation process. *NCA Quarterly, 64,* 379 386.

The author reports on the differences between colleges and corporations in term of control and decision making. Top administrators have the power to set the institution's agenda and to focus its attention. She argues for interactive accreditation where the agency and the college see themselves as partners and not as suspicious adversaries.

Mayhew, L. B., Ford, P. J., & Hubbard, D. L. (1990). *The quest for quality: The challenge for undergraduate education in the 1990s.* San Francisco, CA: Jossey-Bass.

The authors move beyond the issue of economic resources to offer a strategy for restoring and maintaining quality in undergraduate education. The discussion encompasses issues of curricular reform, teaching improvement, academic leadership, and the respective roles of accrediting agencies and governing boards.

Ping, C. J. (1986). Recognizing problems in state universities. *New Directions for Higher Education, Number 55*, 9-16.

Starting from the premise that timely problem recognition is essential to effective policy decisions, Ping offers a model for completing a critical analysis of both the internal and external environments. The focus is on public universities because they are subject to external forces in very direct ways.

St. John, E. P. (1991). A framework for reexamining state resource-management strategies in higher education. *Journal of Higher Education, 62*, 263-287.

Offering an historical review of state strategy in higher education, from the master planning of the '70s through the strategic planning of the '80s, the author develops a framework for the '90s that could be used to influence higher education outcomes. The author outlines the goals, objectives, and outcome measures for higher education resource management, as well as strategies which would be used to improve the capacity of institutions to achieve these goals and objectives.

Uehling, B. (1987). Serving too many masters: Changing the accreditation process. *Educational Record, 68*(3), 38-41.

The author argues that a single accreditation process is hard pressed to accomplish three goals simultaneously: (1) to certify that institutions' programs are meeting minimal standards; (2) to collect information needed by other agencies; and (3) to help institutions or programs improve. She recommends substituting three separate processes, and offers several benefits to support her recommended changes.

THE DOMINO EFFECT

About the Case

This case explores the realities of life in an institution facing reduced resources. The state's economic woes have triggered a response at the institutional level which will eventually have a direct impact at the departmental level. The dean of the College of Arts and Communications has anticipated that the theatre department is particularly vulnerable and may experience difficulties if scrutinized by a university-wide evaluation committee. The role of an acting chair in implementing corrective measures forms the balance of the case study which illustrates change under adversity.

CASE STUDY

The Setting. July 1 signaled the start of a new fiscal year, a year which promised to be fraught with challenges for Southeastern State University (SSU). Southeastern was a publicly supported regional institution with an enrollment of approximately 10,000 students. The university had been founded more than 100 years ago as a normal school in an effort to service the higher education needs of a rural, sparsely populated section of the state.

Absent a strong community college network in the state, Southeastern had gradually evolved from a teachers' college into a comprehensive, though primarily undergraduate, institution. In addition to providing an extensive inventory of baccalaureate degrees, and a dozen master's degree programs, Southeastern had built a strong service component into its mission.

Southeastern encouraged and charged faculty and administrators alike to "provide service to the surrounding area." Service was defined to include such activities as assisting area farmers in solving agriculture-related problems, providing cultural activities for the surrounding community, and supporting local economic growth and development efforts. Largely because of its highly visible service mission, the university enjoyed very strong and positive support from the surrounding community.

The Economy Forces Change. In recent years, however, the economy of the state had taken a turn for the worse. Higher education, in concert with all state supported agencies and activities, had experienced a long series of budget cuts. Worse yet, the economic forecasters and budget gurus promised more cutbacks and a further reduction in fiscal resources over the next five to ten years.

Southeastern State University had benefited from strong leadership in its central administration over the last eight years. The president, George Asher, was hired from the outside five years ago. He hand-picked the vice president for academic affairs, Vincent Picardi, four years ago. Both their styles and philosophies complement one another.

Vice President Picardi was committed to meeting the declining budgets with a combination of creativity and foresight. He determined that the cuts would not be amortized across the board. With the full support of President Asher, Vice President Picardi held to his strong belief that such cuts would only weaken the quality of all programs and services delivered by SSU. Both the president and vice president viewed the more desperate economic conditions as a reason to evaluate the university's curricular offerings and possibly evolve a new mission statement for the institution.

For some time the president believed that the institution's mission statement was too broad. Particularly in light of tightened resources, the president was convinced that it was time to narrow the scope of the institution's academic and service programs. The president found that his efforts to redraft the mission statement were met with resistance from the "long-term natives" who composed about 65 percent of the faculty. No one wanted to give up anything, from noncredit continuing education courses in motorcycle safety and square dancing to master's degree instruction. In this regard, the tightened budget presented an opportunity for the president to streamline the university's academic and service program inventories and position the institution for the economic changes of the coming decade.

The Committee for Program Evaluation and Prioritization (CPEP). After a full year of discussion, the vice president received the support of the faculty's representative body, the faculty senate, to conduct an evaluation of all degree programs and service activities to determine the relative merit of each in accordance with the mission of the university. The faculty senate worked with the vice president to establish criteria for the proposed evaluations. Each criterion was weighted and rank ordered in importance as follows:

1. *Centrality*. How central is the degree program or service activity to the mission of the institution?

2. *Quality*. Is the degree program or service activity of high quality as measured by such standards as faculty credentials, student/participant evaluations, and other qualitative reviews or reports?

3. *Productivity*. What is the productivity of the degree program as measured by such objective standards as credit hour production, number of majors, graduation rate, and cost per credit hour? What is the benefit of the service activity as measured by such standards as number of participants, visibility, or enhancement of the university's reputation?

4. *Demand*. Who and how many are served by the degree program or service activity?

5. *Cost*. What is the cost of the degree program or service activity and is the benefit to the institution worth the investment?

The evolution of these criteria involved the full participation of the faculty senate members who represented the faculty and consulted throughout the process with their respective academic deans. All involved understood that one of the results of this process would be the elimination of some degree programs and service activities. Faculty and administrators agreed that it was better to maintain quality in fewer academic programs and service activities than to risk rendering the existing menu of degree programs and services mediocre.

With consensus regarding the evaluation criteria and a faculty senate resolution recommending that a campus-wide evaluation of all degree programs and service activities be undertaken, the vice president for academic affairs constituted a "blue ribbon" committee last spring made up of well respected distinguished faculty. All appointed had the full endorsement of the academic deans and the faculty senate. Each of the six colleges had one representative on the committee, with all members being tenured associate or full professors. In addition, the director of the "President's Scholars Program" and the director of "Student Recruitment and Admissions" were appointed by the vice president to the committee.

During the coming fiscal year, this eight-person group, named the Committee for Program Evaluation and Prioritization (CPEP), would begin the work necessary to fulfill its charge to evaluate all degree programs to determine the relative merits of each to the university.

Meanwhile in the College of Arts and Communications
(CAC). Dr. Maria Montez, dean of the College of Arts and Communications, was apprehensive about the activities scheduled for the coming

fiscal year. While Dean Montez was in full agreement with the vice president's plan to reduce the degree program inventory rather than inflict budgetary reductions across all programs, she was anxious about the prioritization review of her college to be conducted by the CPEP. This elite committee would be using rather traditional criteria to evaluate the relevant merits of all degree programs (number of majors, number of credit hours generated, number of faculty publications, and program cost effectiveness).

Several of the programs in the College of Arts and Communications, however, were very nontraditional. Dean Montez's fear was that some programs, particularly those in the performing arts, would not fare well when held up against the long-accepted traditional academic criteria.

The College of Arts and Communications was comprised of six academic departments: art, music, theatre, speech communication, journalism, and radio/television. College enrollment had remained steady despite a decline in overall university enrollment. The enrollment increases experienced in the departments of speech communication, journalism, and radio/television offset the modest declines experienced in the departments of art, music, and theatre. Among the programs in the fine arts, the department thought to be the most vulnerable to a CPEP review was theatre.

The theatre department found itself in a vulnerable position for several reasons, of which two were related to personnel issues and one to curricular matters. Recently, the chair of the theatre department, who had held the position for ten years, had resigned suddenly in order to accept a deanship at another state university. Second, the faculty were unable—in the wake of the chair's departure—to function as a unified department, and were continually disagreeing over virtually every decision that was required of the department. And finally, the curriculum offered by the department was too diverse for the size of its faculty and a direct result of the department's lack of philosophical unity, that is, mutually accepted departmental mission.

Dean Montez was now considering her options. She felt the two-month notice given by the departing chair did not allow enough time for a national search for a replacement. She considered the makeup of this relatively small department as she contemplated her next move. University policy required that only tenured faculty be eligible for appointment to department chair positions. Policy did not require that the chair hold tenure in the department discipline. University practice was to hire chairs through national searches.

The theatre faculty was comprised of three tenured full professors, all of whom had been at Southeastern State University for 17 or more years, and three untenured assistant professors who had been at the university less than five years. Each of the assistant professors had a continuing appointment and was working toward tenure. This dichotomy was made more dramatic by the fact that the senior full professors perceived themselves as "scholars" of theatre and engaged in publishing activities while the more junior untenured professors identified themselves as "performing" artists.

Consequently, neither faction fully respected the credentials and accomplishments of the other group, or for that matter even understood their talents and motivation. The department operating procedures (Attachment A) were written in such a way that the full professors controlled all personnel decisions made and voted on by the department. In addition to the six faculty members, the department had the equivalent of three full-time staff positions: a costume shop manager, a director of technical theatre, a half-time box office manager, and a half-time publicity specialist.

After considering the personnel involved, Dean Montez reviewed the curricular makeup of the departmental offerings. To accommodate the interests of both faculty factions, the department offered undergraduate degrees for both performance and non-performance oriented majors. At the undergraduate level, students could pursue any one of five performing specialties (acting, directing, costume design, technical theatre, and theatre business). Non-performance majors could choose specializations in playwriting, theatre history, and theatre education. Clearly, the size and credentials of the department faculty did not support such diverse program offerings. With six faculty and eight program specializations, students pursuing any of the specializations usually took all of their coursework from just one or two faculty members.

Let's pause here. . .

1. *What options are available to the dean for filling the vacant chair position? List the advantages and limitations of each alternative. What factors should be considered in the short-term and in the long-term to solve this personnel problem?*

2. *Describe the culture of the theatre department. Explain how the department climate will impact the dean's list of alternative solutions.*

3. *As dean, would you appoint one of the department's full professors as the new chair of the department—either on a temporary or permanent basis? Why or why not?*

4. *As dean, would you immediately initiate a national search? What are the positives and negatives in this decision? If you decide to proceed with a national search, how would you manage the department throughout the search process?*

The Understudy. Dean Montez made her decision. Rightly or wrongly, she concluded that the selection of any internal candidate would carry severe negative repercussions. In the first place, the institution's policy requiring that only *tenured* faculty be considered for administrative appointments impacted her decision. Her choice from present theatre faculty narrowed to one of the three full professors. Given the current conflict between the untenured assistant professors and the tenured full professors, the selection of any one of the three full professors would have resulted in a less than democratic environment.

The former chair had managed to keep the peace by standing between the two faculty factions. Since the department operating paper (Attachment A) precluded any untenured faculty from serving on the department's personnel committee, the tenured full professors controlled many important decisions. The chair balanced this inequity by appointing the untenured faculty to the department's curriculum committee. Hence, the full professors controlled the personnel decisions, but the assistant professors controlled the curriculum. This delicate system of checks and balances would be destroyed if one of the department's full professors were named chair, and in turn, appointed a new curriculum committee. At the moment, the dean was not prepared to use her time to referee the split between the tenured "scholars" and the untenured "performing artists."

Therefore, from the dean's perspective, the selection of any faculty member from within the department to serve even as an acting chair would be a mistake. The dean chose to appoint one of her two associate deans to the position of acting chair of the Department of Theatre. Dean Montez made it clear to the theatre faculty that the acting appointment would be for 12 months only while the department geared itself for a national search.

Since the associate dean appointed to the acting chairship was held in high regard by the faculty of the department, there was some degree of positive consensus regarding their acceptance of the dean's decision. The only one, in fact, to voice any disagreement was a full professor who felt that the chairship should be given to the full professor who was nearest retirement age. He reasoned that because the job was a 12 month appointment (instead of a standard nine month academic appointment), it could be used to bolster the retirement benefits received by that full professor. Since the other two full professors did not share the same opinion, this disagreement was easily diffused by Dean Montez who then named the associate dean, Quentin Blake, as acting chair of the Department of Theatre. Having served as associate dean for six years, Dr. Blake had a professional rapport with the members of the theatre department and was greeted with some enthusiasm by the faculty.

Let's pause again. . .

5. Write a charge for the dean to give to the associate dean. Now review your draft and determine whether copies could be distributed to the faculty as written. If not, draft a second statement that might be presented to the faculty as a collective department agenda for the coming year. What is the dean's agenda for the acting chair and this department given the dynamics within the department, considering the department's position in the college and the upcoming CPEP evaluation?

Moving *Down* the Ladder. Dean Montez outlined a very clear and specific agenda for Associate Dean (and acting chair) Blake. Specifically, he was to strengthen those factors which made the department particularly vulnerable to the review of the CPEP. This would involve preparing the documents to be used by the CPEP committee for its review, preparing a divisive faculty for a review in which such factionalism could become a serious liability, fostering a more congenial spirit of collegiality among faculty and staff for the sake of the department, initiating discussions regarding the broad scope of the academic program in relation to faculty credentials, and conducting a national search for a permanent chair.

With the appointment made, and the new fiscal year underway, both the dean and the acting chair were ready to fine-tune and implement their game plan for the theatre department.

Let's pause again. . .

6. Assume you are the associate dean and newly appointed acting chair for the Department of Theatre. Outline your strategy for accomplishing each of the goals set by the dean for the coming year. List each of the specific objectives you would try to accomplish in order to affect the overall change sought by the dean. Would these strategies need to be sequenced in any particular order?

7. For each objective you would attempt, map out an approach complete with a timetable for accomplishing each step in the activity.

8. To what extent would you involve the Dean Montez in your efforts? Consider how and with what frequency you would report to the dean regarding your progress.

9. How would you evaluate your success?

10. *Did your agenda include the following items? If not, explain why.*
    a. *Revising department operating procedures;*
    b. *Improving faculty relationships;*
    c. *Fostering the acceptance of a department identity among the faculty;*
    d. *Revising the curriculum to eliminate some specializations;*
    e. *Drafting a position description for the chair search;*
    f. *Conducting a search for next department chair;*
    g. *Working with each faculty member regarding a personalized professional development plan.*

11. *Did your agenda include any other items? What? Why?*

The First Encounter. Associate Dean Blake was about to conduct his first theatre department faculty meeting following his appointment as acting chair. Tensions among the faculty, Dr. Blake realized, were even more strained than Dean Montez had perceived. The department secretary showed up at the meeting with a tape recorder. As one of the full professors explained, "The meetings are taped so no one can deny or refute what was said at the meeting." This was the first time that the associate dean learned that department minutes have been full transcriptions of everything said, complete with profane language, name calling, and accusations.

As Blake was contemplating what to do about the tape recorder positioned ominously in the middle of the table, and whether to allow this practice to continue even through his first meeting, his thoughts were interrupted. Another of the full professors was reminding him in a loud voice that the untenured faculty would have to leave the room when agenda item three is discussed because it was a topic on which they could have no input. Upon glancing at the agenda, Dr. Blake realized that item three on the agenda was the personnel committee's recommendation on the use of student workers in the department. One of the untenured assistant professors objected lightly by commenting that she would find it helpful to know what student worker support was assigned to production as she was to direct the season's first show.

And one last pause. . .

Assume the role of the acting chair.

12. *How would you handle this faculty meeting? For example, in terms of getting off to a good start with the faculty, is it better to adhere to previous practice or to change it? What license can an "acting" chair take? You may wish to review the roles typically assigned to the department chair to determine how each might be altered for an acting chair.*

13. *Which of your objectives for the year are already in jeopardy at this first encounter with the faculty?*

14. *If you decide to deviate from previous practice, how might you present that to the faculty? Script your comments to those present at the meeting. If you decide to adhere to previous practice, how and when will you begin to effect a change in the practice among the faculty?*

15. *Are you bound to follow the procedures outlined in the department's operating paper? Please explain your conclusion.*

16. *What actions might you have been taken in advance of the first meeting to result in a different scenario? How can a new chair (acting or permanent) test the department climate before walking into such a confrontation?*

17. *Based on the performance of the faculty at the first department meeting, do you think it's more advisable to discuss issues in a group meeting or to implement your game plan with more one-on-one conversations? Explain why.*

Attachment A

Operating Paper: Department of Theatre

Department mission: The Department of Theatre accepts as its mission two important challenges which are in keeping with the reputation and direction advocated by Southeastern State University. First, the department, through its academic degree programs, will strive to offer excellent instruction to undergraduate students pursuing the Bachelor of Arts degree in Theatre and to the graduate students pursuing the Master of Fine Arts Degree. Second, as the only theatre of its size and caliber within a radius of 200 miles, the department commits to providing high quality theatrical performances for the residents of the surrounding region.

Department organization: The department meets and votes as a faculty of the whole. The major business of the department, however, will be handled through a structure of three department committees:

1. Personnel Committee: The Personnel Committee will be comprised of three tenured faculty elected by the full faculty. The Personnel Committee will vote and recommend on any decision relative to personnel, including promotion and tenure decisions, merit pay awards, new faculty hires, the use of graduate assistants and student workers, and the reappointment of faculty on term appointments.

2. Curriculum Committee: The Curriculum Committee is comprised of three faculty appointed by the department chair. The Curriculum Committee will vote and recommend on any proposed change in the curriculum, including new courses, course modifications, and revision in the degree specializations.

3. Production Committee: The Production Committee is comprised of the following individuals: Director of Technical Theatre, Costume Shop Manager, Box Office Manager, Publicity Specialist, and the Department Chair. The committee membership will change as the department moves through the production season to allow for the Director and, if appropriate, the Choreographer of each production to join the Production Committee throughout the production's run. The Production Committee decides the budget for each production, monitors the production process, and evaluates the success of each production.

SELECTED READINGS

Bennett, J. B., & Figuli, D. J. (Eds.). (1990). *Enhancing departmental leadership: The roles of the chairperson.* New York, NY: American Council on Education/Macmillan.

This text contains 26 essays which offer strategies and concrete guidance on many of the tasks and responsibilities typically assigned to the department chair. Part One of the book which presents essays on the roles and responsibilities of chairs, and Part Five, which focuses on determining departmental priorities and directions, are of particular interest for this case study.

Bennett, J. B. (1988). Department chairs: Leadership in the trenches. In M. F. Green (Ed.), *Leaders for a new era: Strategies for higher education.* New York, NY: American Council on Education/Macmillan.

Bennett contends that the "core academic success" of institutions of higher education rests upon the quality and capabilities of the chairs. Working from this premise, the author discusses the ambiguous but important role of the chair, the rewards and frustrations associated with the position, and the leadership opportunities for chairs.

Creswell, J. W., Wheeler, D. W., Seagren, A. T., Egly, N. J., & Beyer, K. D. (1990). *The academic chairperson's handbook.* Lincoln, NE: University of Nebraska.

This handbook contains specific strategies for department chairs in working with faculty and in developing their own leadership capabilities. The strategies presented evolved from interviews with 200 successful academic chairs from 70 campuses. Of particular interest to this case is the discussion of the chair's role as an academic leader (Chapter 3).

Ehrle, E. B., & Bennett, J. B. (1988). *Managing the academic enterprise: Case studies for deans and provosts.* New York, NY: American Council on Education/Macmillan.

In this text, the authors present 25 original case studies and multiple solutions to the most common problems faced by deans and provosts. The specific issue of strengthening departmental responsibility and preserving an essential department are addressed in chapters two and three.

Green, J. S., Levine, A., & Associates. (1985). *Opportunity in adversity: How colleges can succeed in hard times.* San Francisco, CA: Jossey-Bass.

The authors begin with the premise that institutions facing fiscal austerity also have opportunities to turn themselves around as they emerge from these difficulties. The text is a collection of chapters written by experts in higher education who discuss how institutions can grow during hard times to be strong financially, educationally, and in their own understanding or sense of the institution's purposes.

Kaplan, S. (1989). The quest for institutional excellence: The CEO and the creative use of the accreditation process. *NCA Quarterly, 64,* 379-386.

The author talks about differences between colleges and corporations in term of control and decision-making. Administrators have the power to set the institution's agenda and to focus its attention. She argues for interactive accreditation where the agency and the college see themselves as partners and not as suspicious adversaries.

Mayhew, L. B., Ford, P. J., & Hubbard, D. L. (1990).*The quest for quality: The challenge for undergraduate education in the 1990s.* San Francisco, CA: Jossey-Bass.

The authors move beyond the issue of economic resources to offer a strategy for restoring and maintaining quality in undergraduate education. The discussion encompasses issues of curricular reform, teaching improvement, academic leadership, and the respective roles of accrediting agencies and governing boards.

Tierney, W. G. (1983, Summer). Governance by conversation: An essay on the structure, function, and communication codes of a faculty senate. *Human Organization, 42,* 172-177.

The author argues that members of a faculty senate use two principle communications, writing and speaking, to accomplish their governance tasks. He describes how the senate operates, who the actors are, and its five basic functions: ceremonial, directional, news-related, decisional, and conformational.

Watts, E. S. (1991). Governance beyond the individual campus. *Academe, 77*(5), 28-32.

The author discusses the reasons for a perceived decline in senate effectiveness and how senate leaders are finding unique ways to come together through: conferences or councils of separate senates in a multicampus institution; regional consortia; and statewide consortia—all in an effort to revitalize the role and importance of faculty governance.

Wolvin, A. D. (1991). When governance is really shared: The multi-constituency campus. *Academe, 77*(5), 26-28.

The author describes the important role that a governing body can play, particularly when it is representative of all constituents on the campus and is perceived as credible. He also notes the problems associated with such a multiconstituency senate.

WHO'S ON FIRST?

About the Case

Student-faculty conflicts typically start with a disagreement involving two persons and then escalate to absorb the time and attention of many others. This particular conflict will ultimately involve three levels of institutional administrators—the vice president, the dean, and the department chair—and encompass both vertical and horizontal tensions. Faculty and students have long revered the social values of collegiality and democracy. Without strong economic or operational incentives, administrators at institutions of higher education laboriously work through decisions in ways that differ from those employed by managers in the private business sector. In higher education, edicts and instantaneous judgments are rare. Administrative efficiency in that environment requires patience, tact and time.

CASE STUDY

Vice President Marilyn Johnson was pleased to see that the stack of incoming mail this Monday was lighter than usual so early in the fall semester. After three years as vice president of academic affairs at a respected public university, she had a good sense of the relationship between the volume of her mail and her discretionary time. She believed that the 18,000 students, seven colleges, and 85 major programs of study at Riverbend University were a challenge to her administrative skills but did not preclude the option for personal involvement—as her own form of an internal audit—in any particular situation. Her brief moment of calm was ruined as she began to read the first letter in the pile of mail in front of her.

September 25, 199x

Dear Vice President Johnson:

I am writing to file a formal appeal of the grade I received in Information Systems (IS) 263. Professor Schmidt gave me a grade of "F" which I feel is very unfair.

I followed all the steps suggested by my academic advisor for presenting my complaint. I first talked with Professor Bernard Schmidt who told me that he had more important things to do than recalculate my grade. So I talked with the head of the Information Systems department, Dr. Wilson. He told me that he had known Professor Schmidt for a very long time and was sure that my grade had been calculated correctly. This made me very upset because without a passing grade in IS 263, I can't enroll in the next course that is required for my major.

I went back to my advisor who suggested that I write a letter to the dean of the College of Arts and Sciences explaining my side of the story. I did that, and Dean Krebs wrote me a letter telling me that he agreed with Professor Schmidt and Dr. Wilson. I feel that they are all being very unfair!

I've kept all papers returned to me, and the scores on these papers prove that I should not have a failing grade in the course. Right before the final exam, Professor Schmidt told me that if I got an 80% on the final, the lowest grade I could get for the course would be a "C." Now he says that he never told me that! He's trying to say that I heard him wrong. Also, Professor Schmidt got so angry when he found out that I wrote a letter to the dean that he went to the dean and filed some kind of charges against me!

Things can't get much worse so I'm writing to you in hope that someone on the outside will look at my papers objectively and see that I've been treated unfairly. Thank you for you time.

Sincerely,

Angela Taylor

When the vice president finished reading Angela Taylor's letter, she sighed and put a note on the letter asking her assistant to request Angela's file from the dean's office in the College of Arts and Sciences. As she placed the item in her out-box, she added a request for a copy of the student grievance procedures of the College of Arts and Sciences and a copy of the university's student conduct code.

More Information. A few days later Vice President Johnson once again found Angela Taylor's letter of September 25 in her in-box. This time, however, the letter and copies of certain policies were clipped to a file folder which had just arrived from the College of Arts and Sciences. The folder contained copies of the following items (Attachment A, 1-5):

- September 30 transmittal memorandum from Dean Krebs to Vice President Johnson (Attachment A-1);

- July 4 letter from Angela Taylor to Dean Krebs appealing her grade in IS 263 and summarizing her initial discussion with Professor Schmidt (Attachment A-2);

- July 15 memo from Professor Schmidt to Dr. Wilson, the department chair, officially filing charges of academic dishonesty against Angela Taylor (Attachment A-3);

- July 19 memo from Dr. Wilson to Dean Krebs informing the dean of Professor Schmidt's formal complaint against Angela Taylor, charging her with academic dishonesty (Attachment A-4); and

- July 25 letter from Dean Krebs to Angela Taylor informing her of his decision to uphold her grade of F (Attachment A-5).

Removing the large clip, Dr. Johnson found copies of the grievance procedures of the College of Arts and Sciences (Attachment B), and Riverbend University's Student Conduct Code (Attachment C).

After a quick reading of the letters in the file, it was obvious to the vice president that there was a major communication gap between Angela Taylor and Professor Schmidt (and other college administrative officers). Marilyn Johnson focused on a number of key sentences that she felt epitomized the differences in their perceptions and interpretations.

Although not mentioned directly in any of the correspondence, Vice President Johnson believed that the basic question, at least for her, was whether or not the provisions of the college's Student Grievance Procedures had been followed. She wondered if Angela or her advisor or Professor Schmidt were even aware of these procedures. Vice President Johnson also had a second concern. She was bothered about the question of academic dishonesty. From the limited information available in the student's file, she found it difficult to determine whether or not Professor Schmidt had a legitimate basis for filing charges of academic dishonesty against Angela Taylor.

Let's pause here. . .

You are to assume the role of the vice president and decide on your own plan for handling this matter.

1. *After reviewing the policies in Attachments B and C and the correspondence provided in Attachment A, determine whether the actions taken to date are consistent with the time frame and review provisions specified by the college's Student Grievance Policy and the university's Student Conduct Code. When were the provisions followed and when were they ignored?*

2. *Now make a list of the alternatives available to the academic vice president and identify the trade-offs associated with each alternative. For example, Vice President Johnson could decide to initiate a fact-finding hearing and make a decision on Angela Taylor's grade and on Bernard Schmidt's charge of academic dishonesty. What possible liabilities might she incur in terms of setting precedent or damaging her working relationship with the dean of the college? Would such an action give the appearance that Vice President Johnson is not supportive of the current institutional policies regarding grievance resolution?*

   a. *What is the trade-off if the matter is returned to the college?*

   b. *What is the trade-off if Vice President Johnson alone decides on the student's guilt or innocence?*

   c. *What is the trade-off if Vice President Johnson upholds the student?*

   d. *What is the trade-off if Vice President Johnson upholds the instructor, the chair, and the dean? But, is this an "all or nothing" situation? Can Marilyn Johnson decide that one (or two of the three) is right and the other wrong? Where can a line be drawn?*

3. *Would your plan for handling this matter change if you knew that Angela Taylor carried an overall grade point average of 3.25 (on a 4.0 scale)?*

4. *Would you alter your plan for handling this matter if your administrative assistant reminded you that Angela Taylor was one of a very few minority students at Riverbend who had been recruited to attend the university on a scholarship that covered her tuition, room and board?*

5. *Inherent in this and most student grievances over grades is the issue of the faculty's prerogative to assign grades. Give some thought to what role, if any, academic administrators should play in the process of reassessing assigned grades.*

The Vice President's Decision. Vice President Johnson considered a variety of options and finally elected to send the matter back to the college for a second review. The vice president telephoned Dean Krebs and reviewed her rationale for having the matter reconsidered at the college level. She told Krebs that she had considered holding a fact-finding hearing at the vice presidential level but decided to give the dean a second chance to "do it right."

Although not pleased with the prospect of looking further at this student's grievance and the faculty member's counter-charge, Krebs preferred to have the matter reconsidered at the collegiate level rather than to have a fact-finding hearing at the vice presidential level that might result in overturning a college decision. He asked the vice president to send it back. Johnson, therefore, drafted the following letter to the student:

RIVERBEND UNIVERSITY
River Valley, AR

October 23, 199x

Dear Ms. Taylor:

I have reviewed your letter to me dated September 25, and other correspondence related to your appeal of the grade received in IS 263 last spring.

While you contend the grade of "F" was incorrect based on scores received on exams and class assignments, the course instructor has, as you know, initiated a formal complaint against you charging that you falsified grade information on documents submitted to university officials with the intent of obtaining a higher grade in the course. Such conduct would be in violation of the academic dishonesty provisions of the Student Conduct Code which prohibit "knowingly furnishing false information to a university official relative to academic matters."

I have determined that a hearing is necessary to consider both your appeal of the grade and the charges brought against you by the instructor. Furthermore, I have asked Dean Krebs to appoint a hearing committee to review all available information and make recommendations to the dean on the matter. Since the complaint of academic dishonesty carries with it the possibility of disciplinary sanctions, the hearing will be conducted in accordance with the procedures outlined in Riverbend's Student Conduct Code. You will be afforded all procedural rights provided under the Student Conduct Code applicable to the charges of academic dishonesty.

Upon completion of the hearing process at the dean's level, you will then have the opportunity to initiate an appeal to this office if you are not satisfied with the decision. If you have any questions concerning the determination and process described in this letter, please do not hesitate to contact me.

Sincerely,

Marilyn A. Johnson
Vice President for Academic Affairs

cc: Dean John Krebs

Let's pause again. . .

6. *Do you agree with the decision made by the vice president to return the matter to the college dean for further consideration? Why?*

7. *What are the potential advantages and liabilities of this decision for the vice president? What are the potential advantages and liabilities for the dean? Have you considered, for example, how well the chair and dean followed university policy to afford the student proper due process?*

8. *Assume that you agree with the vice president's decision. Now, take a second look at her letter to Angela Taylor. What were the vice president's objectives in terms of the message(s) in the letter? Have these objectives been met? Is the letter likely to diffuse the intensity of the student's grievance against her instructor?*

9. *Given your own analysis, would you make changes in the letter being sent by Vice President Johnson to Angela Taylor? If so, rewrite the letter.*

10. *As vice president, do you intend to write a separate letter to Dean Krebs to clarify your reasons for returning the matter to the college? If so, draft that letter and indicate whether you would send the student a copy of your letter to the dean.*

11. *Speculate as to why Vice President Johnson decided to phone the dean and to write the student? Now, assume the role of the college dean and think through how you intend to handle this matter, given your recent communication with the vice president.*

12. *What special consideration should be given in the formation of a hearing panel? What special directions or guidance would you offer the hearing panel?*

13. *As dean of the largest college at Riverbend, are there other actions which should be taken to prevent such confusion and escalation of future student-faculty conflicts? Please specify what action you might take. How you would notify parties of your concern and your intentions? How would you implement your decision? For example, would you send a memorandum to all department chairs reminding them to read the policy? Would you personally conduct a two-hour workshop on handling student grievances? Would you arrange for someone else to conduct such a workshop? Would you involve the faculty in these retraining efforts?*

14. *Would the resolution of this case be different if the student grievance took place on a campus where all department chairs report directly to a "dean of the faculty" who, for all practical purposes, functions as the academic vice president? How might the outcome differ?*

Attachment A-1

MEMO TO: Dr. Marilyn Johnson
Vice President for Academic Affairs

FROM: Dr. John Krebs
Dean of the College of Arts and Sciences

SUBJECT: Student Grievance

DATE: September 30, 199x

Per your request, enclosed is a copy of Angela Taylor's file including correspondence from our office concerning her claim that Professor Schmidt unfairly graded her work in Information Systems 263. Also enclosed is a copy of Professor Schmidt's intent to file charges of academic dishonesty against this student. I believe you'll find that Professor Schmidt has a very solid case against her. It is regrettable that we must spend so much of our time on a few students who have difficulty accepting their shortcomings.

cc: Dr. Roger Wilson, Chair, Information Systems
Professor Bernard Schmidt

Attachment A-2

July 4, 199x

Dear Dean Krebs:

Professor Schmidt gave me an "F" in Information Systems (IS) 263 this past spring. This grade was *not* deserved. Therefore, I have been protesting it since finals week of the Spring semester.

When I first told Professor Schmidt that my grade had been calculated incorrectly, he told me he would make the correction. However, when the final grade sheet was posted, the correction was not made. Professor Schmidt was not in his office that day or the remainder of finals week. I did not get a chance to talk with him again. He also told me earlier that if I got 80% on the final, the lowest grade I could get for the course would be a "C."

When I told my academic advisor that Professor Schmidt had said that he would correct the grade, my advisor talked with him. My advisor told me that Professor Schmidt now thinks that I altered the grades on my papers. Professor Schmidt told my advisor that he has no intention of changing my grade of "F." I then went to the head of the department, Dr. Wilson. I showed him my assignments with the scores on them. The chair looked at them briefly, but told me he had to agree with Professor Schmidt.

He said that it was a matter of Professor Schmidt's word against mine, and he had known Professor Schmidt for over ten years.

With all respect, the fact that he's known Professor Schmidt for ten years is not an issue here. I've tried all summer to resolve this situation. I hope it can be resolved before the end of the fall semester. I need a passing grade in IS 263 in order to take the next course required in the program. With your help, I hope to get it.

Sincerely,

Angela Taylor

Attachment A-3

MEMO TO: Dr. Roger Wilson, Chair
Information Systems Department

FROM: Bernard G. Schmidt, Professor
Information Systems

SUBJECT: Student Grievance

DATE: July 15, 199x

I wish to bring student disciplinary charges against Angela Taylor for falsifying records during an appeal in an attempt to acquire a higher grade in IS 263. I realize the seriousness of the charge I am making; the consequences of the student's behavior, however, have such wide-reaching implications that I feel disciplinary action must be taken now. I have given Angela every opportunity to withdraw her claim, but since she persists in taking her appeal to the dean, I must demand disciplinary action.

Attachment A-4

MEMO TO: Dr. John Krebs, Dean
College of Arts and Sciences

FROM: Dr. Roger Wilson, Chair
Information Systems Department

SUBJECT: Complaint of academic dishonesty against Angela Taylor

DATE: July 19, 199x

The Student Conduct Code states in Section C.I.: "Any member of the university community may initiate disciplinary proceedings by filing a complaint within 20 days of a discovery of an alleged violation of the Student Conduct Code. The complaint must be made in writing with all available evidence attached. The complaint shall be filed with the department chair in the unit in which the alleged violation occurred."

Professor Schmidt has submitted a formal complaint in writing against the student for submitting falsified documents to the academic advisor, the department chair, and the college dean. These photocopied documents included quizzes, assignments, and a final examination answer sheet. The student stated in her letter to you that Professor Schmidt would not meet with her. However, Professor Schmidt's grade book indicated a change in the score 18/20 (being questioned by the student) to a score of 19/20. Also, one document submitted was done so on lined paper. Professor Schmidt requires ALL work be submitted on plain computer paper. The two scores of 60 and 65, which are marked in heavy print, had been scored as 30 and 35 respectively in Professor Schmidt's grade book. The final examination answer sheet indicate a 99/109 - 90%; however, Professor Schmidt's computer program, used to calculate final examination scores, rounds up and does not drop fractions. The student's score would not have indicated 90% but 91%. Professor Schmidt's grade book indicated a score of 73% for the student's final examination.

Based upon the documentation submitted by the student, a complete review of her scores, my review of Professor Schmidt's grading procedures, and a visual inspection of Professor Schmidt's grade book, I recommend the student be notified in writing concerning the charges of academic dishonesty being initiated. I further recommend disciplinary suspension as the sanction for the offense. This recommendation is in keeping with the Student Conduct Code (Section B.2.).

cc: Dr. Bernard Schmidt
Dr. Roger Wilson

Attachment A-5

Riverbend University
College of Arts and Sciences

July 25, 199x

Ms. Angela Taylor
1005 Briarwood
Apt. 5-B
River Valley, AR

Dear Angela:

I received your letter dated July 4, 19xx, concerning a grade you were given in IS 263, this last spring semester. I have completed an examination of the situation and concur with the grade given by Professor Schmidt.

Furthermore, Professor Schmidt initiated a formal complaint of academic dishonesty with substantial documentation for knowingly furnishing false information to university officials relative to an academic matter. The alleged violation would lead to unconditional academic suspension. If you do not agree with this decision to suspend you from the program, please make an appointment to see me. Prior to your appointment, please review the enclosed Student Conduct Code, specifically the section on academic dishonesty and the sanctions which will be imposed.

Sincerely,

John Krebs, Dean
College of Arts and Sciences

Attachment: Copy of Student Conduct Code

cc: Dr. Bernard Schmidt
Dr. Roger Wilson, chair

Attachment B

COLLEGE OF ARTS AND SCIENCES
Procedures for Handling Student Academic Grievances

A matter relating to academic evaluation is the responsibility of the department or the program in which a grievance initiates and the office of the college dean. Every effort should be made to resolve such academic evaluation disputes quickly at the program level.

Grades may be appealed only on procedural grounds and not on substantive grounds. Matters pertaining to the evaluation of a course in which the student is or has been registered that are not resolved between the persons directly involved will be adjudicated in the following manner:

1. A student who has a reason to be aggrieved will file the complaint in writing with the department chair.

    a. The complaint must be presented in sufficient detail that a proper response may be made.

    b. The complaint must be received by the department chair within 30 days after the discovery of the issue or incident being grieved.

2. The department chair will submit a copy of the complaint to the other party named in the compliant within three working days.

3. The other party will respond in writing to the complaint to the department chair within 15 days of receipt of the copy of the complaint.

4. The department chair will, within seven working days of the receipt of the response to the complaint, transmit a written decision in the matter to both parties along with notification of appellate procedures. A copy of the response to the complaint will be sent to the appropriate dean. Failure of either party to respond through the appropriate appellate channels within 15 working days will be interpreted as acceptance of the decision and its implementation by the appropriate office.

5. Should either party be unwilling to accept the decision of the department chair, an appeal may be made to the college dean. Such appeal must be submitted in writing within 15 working days within the receipt of the decision by the department chair. The appeal must specify:

    a. The original charges;

    b. Specific action or actions being appealed; and

    c. Grounds for appeal.

6. The appellate, after consultation with the college dean, will select one of the following procedures for adjudication:

    a. Administrative: The college dean will review the matter with each of the parties involved and render a decision within 30 days of the review;

    b. Panel: The college dean will appoint a panel consisting of three faculty members with no administrative appointment and three students to review the matter and render a decision within 30 days of the review. Written records of the review proceedings will be placed in the student's permanent record in the college.

7. When a decision is reached by one of the above methods, the college dean will notify each of the parties of the decision in writing. A copy of

the decision will be filed with the student's permanent record in the college.

8. Appeals of any action taken at the level of the dean of the college will be made to the vice president for academic affairs. A written request for such an appeal must be submitted within 15 working days after the aggrieved has received the final decision from the dean of the college. The written appeal must contain the reasons for which the appeal is made. The vice president for academic affairs will notify the appellate of her/his decision in writing within 10 working days following receipt of a written appeal.

Attachment C

RIVERBEND UNIVERSITY
Student Conduct Code

Section IV. Policies and Procedures Applicable to Academic Dishonesty

A. Judicial Structure

1. Department-Level

   The department chair shall have initial jurisdiction over complaints of academic dishonesty and may adjudicate the case if the student accepts responsibility for the violation(s). In any case where the student does not accept responsibility for the violation(s) the chair shall review the complaint of alleged academic dishonesty and decide whether there are sufficient grounds to formally charge the student with a violation of the code. When social misconduct is also involved in an incident(s) of academic dishonesty, the chair shall charge the student with all violations. All charges shall be adjudicated under the provisions for academic dishonesty.

2. College-Level

   a. Each dean has the responsibility for the formal resolution of charges against a student.

   b. Charges of falsifying information on applications for admission shall be adjudicated by the director of admissions. The director of admissions, for the purpose of administering this code, shall operate at the level of other deans.

3. Vice Presidential-Level

   This level has jurisdiction to hear appeals.

B. Informal Disciplinary Procedures

1. Informal Hearing

    In cases where the student admits to a violation of the code relating to academic dishonesty, the matter may be adjudicated at the department level. An informal discussion between the instructor and the student shall be held. If the student admits to a violation of the code, the instructor shall inform the departmental chair and the student whether, as a sanction for the violation, the instructor will assign a failing grade for the work and/or course. The instructor shall also recommend to the chair any other sanctions that may be imposed, pursuant to B.2. The chair shall meet with the instructor and the student, receive the acknowledgment of responsibility from the student, receive the recommendations from the instructor, and apprise the student of the sanction.

2. Sanctions

    The full disciplinary history of the student shall be considered in determining the sanction. Sanctions which may be imposed when the student accepts responsibility for the conduct are:

    a. The student may be removed from the class for the remainder of the testing period.

    b. The instructor may assign the student a failing grade for the work and/or course.

    c. The student may be placed on disciplinary probation.

    d. Any combination of the above.

    e. The department chair may recommend to the dean that the student be suspended from the university. The department chair shall also inform the student in writing that a disciplinary suspension is recommended as an appropriate sanction for the student's violation of the code.

        1) If the student elects to challenge the severity of the recommended suspension, the student may request an informal hearing on the proposed sanction(s) before the dean.

        2) The student may submit a request in writing for an informal hearing on the proposed sanction(s) within 5 days of receipt of the chair's recommendation.

        3) In such cases the dean (or that officer's designee) shall meet with the student, the chair and/or instructor, and apprise the student of the sanction(s).

3. Notification

    The department chair shall send written verification of the

sanction(s) to the student. Such notification will normally be sent within five days of the meeting with the instructor and the student.

4. Appeal

    The student may appeal the severity of the sanction or failure to follow prescribed procedure, pursuant to C.8. A student may not appeal the question of guilt.

C. Formal Disciplinary Procedures

1. Initiation of a Complaint

    Any member of the university community may initiate disciplinary proceedings by filing a complaint within twenty days of discovery of an alleged violation of the Student Conduct Code.

    a. The complaint must be made in writing with all available evidence attached.

    b. The complaint shall be filed with the department chair of the unit in which the violation is alleged to have occurred.

    c. The complaint may include a recommendation concerning the appropriate sanction(s) to be imposed if, following formal adjudication, the student is found in violation of the code.

    d. In any case initiated by an instructor, the complaint shall state whether or not the instructor will assign a failing grade for the work and/or course if, following formal adjudication, the student is found in violation of the code in the manner alleged in the complaint. In any such case the instructor shall assign a "deferred" in lieu of a letter grade pending adjudication and final resolution of the complaint.

2. Formal Charges

    The department chair shall review the complaint and, within ten days, determine whether there are grounds to believe a violation may have occurred.

    a. If there are sufficient grounds to believe a violation may have occurred, within five days of such determination the chair shall notify the student in writing of the violation with which the student is charged. A copy of the charges shall be submitted to the appropriate academic dean.

    b. If there are no grounds for disciplinary charges, the complainant shall be notified. If the complainant wishes to proceed with a disciplinary charge, a written request must be submitted to the appropriate academic dean within ten (10) days of the receipt of the notification. The dean shall review the request, the complaint, and the departmental chair decision and decide whether to allow the complainant to pursue formal charges of the alleged violation set forth in the complaint.

3. Formal Adjudication

    In cases of alleged academic dishonesty where guilt is disputed by the student, the case will be adjudicated at the dean's level with a formal hearing. The dean shall notify the student in writing regarding the date, time, and place of the hearing. The notification will be considered to have been delivered if the notice is sent to the current local address of the student. Thus, failure to notify the university of changes in address could result in a hearing being held *in absentia*.

    a. The student has the right to:
        1) Be apprised of all evidence.
        2) Hear and question available witnesses. Sworn statements will be accepted from those persons unable to attend the hearing.
        3) Not be compelled to offer evidence which may be self-incriminating.
        4) Receive a written decision specifying judicial actions.

    b. The student has the option to have:
        1) Advisory assistance. The responsibility for selecting an advisor is placed on the charged student. The advisor may be any individual except a principal in the hearing. The advisor shall be limited to advising the student and shall not participate directly in the hearing.
        2) An open or closed hearing.
        3) Witnesses testify in his/her behalf. Sworn statements shall be accepted from those persons unable to attend the hearing. Character witnesses may be excluded by the hearing agent.

    c. Hearing Agent
        The charged student may submit a preference for a hearing before a judicial board or the dean or his/her designee. The dean shall decide the hearing agent.

4. Judicial Hearing Agents

    a. Judicial Board Directives
        1) Size: A judicial board shall be comprised of seven members. A quorum required to conduct a hearing shall be five members. A decision shall be reached by majority vote.

2) Membership:
   a) Student members shall meet the following standards: full-time as defined by the director of admissions; good disciplinary standing since matriculation; minimum grade point average of 2.5 (undergraduate).
   b) Faculty members may include any person under faculty appointment, excluding administrators.
   c) All appointments shall be reviewed by the office of the vice president for academic affairs to ensure that candidates meet the minimal requirements. A list of judicial board members will be available upon request from the office of the academic dean.
3) Judicial Board Operating Papers: Each judicial board may develop its own operating paper. Each operating paper shall be reviewed by the office of the vice president for academic affairs to ensure consistency with the provisions of this code.
4) Administrative Advisors: Each judicial board shall have an administrative advisor from the office of vice president for academic affairs. The advisor's role shall be limited to providing guidance and clarification.
5) Terms: Each judicial board shall be in session for twelve weeks during the fall and spring terms and for four weeks during the summer term. A board is not expected to meet during the first two nor the last two weeks of a term. Disciplinary cases shall be adjudicated by an administrative hearing officer when a board is not in session or is defunct.
6) Powers: A judicial board shall make a decision of guilt or innocence and shall make a recommendation on the sanction to the dean.

   b. Administrative Hearing Officer: The administrative hearing officer shall be the academic dean or that officer's designee.

5. Judicial Hearings
   a. Time limitations:
      1) A student electing formal adjudication shall have a minimum of five days written notice prior to a hearing.
      2) A student shall have five days after receiving notification of the decision in which to submit an appeal.
   b. Failure to appear: Initial jurisdiction hearings shall be held *in absentia* when the charged student fails to appear. An appeal shall be dismissed when the student fails to appear.

    c. Tape recordings: All formal judicial hearing shall be tape recorded. After the appeal period has expired the tape may be erased.

    d. Challenge for cause: A student may challenge panel members for cause. The decision to remove a panel member will be made by the other panel members.

    e. Peremptory challenge: A student may challenge one panel member without assigning any cause. A peremptory challenge will be automatically honored by the chair of the panel.

    f. Confidentiality: All evidence, facts, comments, and discussion at a closed hearing and all executive sessions shall be held in strict confidence. Failure to maintain confidentiality may result in removal of judicial board members by the dean.

6. Sanctions

A student's disciplinary history shall have no bearings on the question of guilt or innocence. If, however, a student is found to be in violation of the code, the full disciplinary history shall be considered in determining the sanction. The academic dean shall request the student's disciplinary record from the office of admissions and records. Sanctions which may be imposed are:

    a. The instructor may assign the student a failing grade for the work and/or course.

    b. The student may be placed on disciplinary probation.

    c. The student may be suspended from the university.

    d. Any combination of the above.

7. Notification

The dean shall send written notification of the decision of the hearing and sanction(s) to the student. Such notifications will normally be sent within five days of receipt of the judicial board's recommendations or within five days of the administrative hearing.

8. Appeals

Any disciplinary determination or sanction involving academic dishonesty may be appealed from the dean's level by submitting an application for appeal to the vice president for academic affairs within five days after receiving notification of the prior decision. However, the right of appeal does not guarantee that an appeal will be granted nor does it entitle the student to a full rehearing of the case. An appeal hearing, if granted, will be limited to the issues set forth in subparagraph c. below.

a. The student may submit a preference for an appeal hearing before a judicial board or an administrative hearing officer. The vice president for academic affairs shall decide the hearing agent.

b. The burden of proof at the initial jurisdiction level is on the university. At the appeal level, however, the student bears the burden of demonstrating error as defined in the following item (c).

c. Three issues constitute possible grounds for an appeal:
   1) Were judicial procedures correctly followed?
   2) Did the evidence justify a decision against the student?
   3) Was the sanction(s) imposed in keeping with the gravity of the violation? Previous violation(s) of the code and the accompanying sanction(s) will be considered in determining a proper sanction for a current violation.

d. The appropriate committee of the judicial board or the administrative hearing officer will review the appeal to ascertain whether there are sufficient grounds for a hearing.

e. If an appeal hearing is granted, the agent hearing the appeal will not rehear the case. The agent will limit the review to the specific points of the appeal that were accepted at the screening review.

f. The agent hearing the appeal may:
   1) Affirm the decision(s) of the initial jurisdiction.
   2) Affirm the decision(s) and reduce the sanction.
   3) Modify the decision(s) of violation and reduce the sanction.
   4) Reverse the decision(s) of violation, remove the sanction, and dismiss the case.

g. A student dissatisfied with the decision on appeal may seek review by the vice president by submitting such a request in writing within five days after receiving notification of the prior decision. Review by the vice president shall also be limited to the issues specified in subparagraph c. above.

h. Further appeal may be made to the president, and then the board of governors by filing an application for appeal.

SELECTED READINGS

Aaron, R. M. (1992, winter). Student academic dishonesty: Are collegiate institutions addressing the issue? *NASPA Journal, 29*(2), 107-113.

This article summarizes the results of a survey of 257 chief student affairs officers at four-year private and public community colleges. Data are compiled on institutions with academic integrity codes and adjudication guidelines, the institutions' methods for disseminating academic integrity information to students and to faculty, the institutional officer responsible for adjudicating acts of student academic dishonesty, and other institutional activities that address student academic integrity matters.

Dannells, M. (1991, March). Changes in student misconduct and institutional response over 10 years. *Journal of College Student Development, 32*, 166-170.

The author reports on the results of a longitudinal study of changes in student misconduct cases and institutional response over ten years, comparing the results of two national surveys in such areas as incidence of disciplinary cases, sanctions, and rehabilitative actions.

Ferguson, M. (1990, winter). The role of faculty in increasing student retention. *College and University, 65*, 127-135.

After presenting statistics on student attrition, the author discusses the important role of faculty in student retention. Findings from interviews with 112 students enrolled at Buffalo State College are reported.

Green, M. F., & McDade, S. A. (1991). *Investing in higher education: A handbook of leadership development.* Washington, DC: American Council on Education.

This text offers strategies and resources for leadership development at all levels of the institution. The chapters on leadership development for faculty, department chairs, and academic deans would be helpful in preventing the scenario of this case study.

Jendrek, M. L. (1992). Students' reaction to academic dishonesty. *Journal of College Student Development, 33*, 260-273.

The author examines the reactions of university students who acknowledged witnessing a student cheating during an examination, their attitudes toward the offending student, and their feelings about academic dishonesty in general. The researcher further provides attitudinal responses by demographic variables including observers' grade point average, sex, and membership or pledging of a sorority or fraternity.

Kuh, G. D. (1990). Assessing student culture. *New Directions for Institutional Research, Number 68*, 47-60.

The author summarizes literature on student cultures and reviews approaches to assessing student culture which is believed to have a significant impact on many aspects of college life, including student learning.

Smith, D. L. (1992). Validity of faculty judgments of student performance: Relationship between grades and credits earned and external criterion measures. *Journal of Higher Education, 63*, 329-340.

Smith's statistical research found, in all five academic departments, consistently positive and often strong correlation between grades assigned and student performance on an external standardized measure of academic achievement in the field. Smith's findings were contrary to the opinions offered by some national reports in which grades and credits earned were seen as inadequate measures of academic achievement.

Tucker, A. (1992). *Chairing the academic department: Leadership among peers (3rd ed.).* New York, NY: American Council on Education/Macmillan.

A text for persons seeking more information about the roles and responsibilities typically assigned to department chairs. Of particular relevance to this case study are the chapters on students and managing conflict.

Weaver, K. A., Davis, S. F., Look, C., Buzzanga, V. L., & Neal, L. (1991). Examining academic dishonesty policies. *College Student Journal, 26*, 302-305.

These researchers report on a study of 200 college catalogs, at least four from each state, from both two-year and four-year institutions, to examine the content of institutional policies on academic dishonesty. Eight themes were identified, with material on each theme compiled into a comprehensive sample policy.

Wines, W. A., & Napier, N. K. (1992). Toward an understanding of cross-cultural ethics: A tentative model. *Journal of Business Ethics, 11*, 831-842.

Starting from the premise that ethics is the systematic application of moral principles to concrete problems, the authors describe the ethical dilemma that results when moral values are applied to decisions made in cross-cultural settings.

WHOSE DECISION
IS THIS ANYWAY?

About the Case

As front line managers, department chairs are typically expected to imple-ment the policies and directives of the central administration. At the same time, department chairs are the primary advocates for the faculty and department majors. This "middle" position between faculty and central administration is especially challenging when faculty/department goals are incompatible with the goals and objectives of the central administration. The following case illus-trates this complexity and the impasse created when the dean of the college makes a decision which appears to be totally incompatible with the depart-ment's objectives.

CASE STUDY

The Dean and the Budget. Early May heat enveloped the bucolic campus of Middleburg College, a public institution with an enroll-ment of 4,000 students. The dean of the college, Frederick "Fritz" Schaefer, was in his office reviewing budget data to determine where additional cuts might be made in the college budget in the event that the next fiscal year's budget, which was to be announced by July 1, was reduced still fur-ther. As the second ranking administrative officer, reporting directly to the president, he knew that morale at Middleburg was low, but he also knew what few others did, that if the budget outlook did not improve, morale was going to drop even further.

Middleburg College had been hit hard by statewide budget cuts in higher education. Three years ago, every public institution within the state received a "flat" (i.e., no increase) budget. The last two years brought midyear rescissions which required Middleburg College to return to the state roughly five percent of its initial budget—which was "flat" in the first place. Worse yet, with each subsequent fiscal year the rescission amounts were subtracted from the budget for the following year and ultimately became a permanent reduction. This, in fact was what happened during the last two fiscal years. The dean of the college had budget figures on his desk which were ten percent less in actual dollars than the budget he implemented three fiscal years ago. Likewise, he was well aware that increases in the consumer price index and the inflation rate had further reduced the buying power of those dollars.

Dean Schaefer's train of thought was interrupted when his secretary buzzed him on the intercom to say that the director of admissions was on the telephone. He was greatly relieved when he picked up the phone and heard the up-beat tone of the director's voice. "Good news," said Maria Herrera. "We've been watching the admissions data for the coming Fall semester and it looks like total college enrollment will be up despite the 15 percent increase in tuition." (In a desperate self-help measure, the board of Middleburg College approved a 15 percent tuition increase effective with the coming fall semester. This increase was the single largest tuition increase ever approved in the history of the institution. It also marked the second tuition increase within the past four years.)

• Dean Schaefer responded, "That's great, but are we sure that these students will show up in the fall?"

The director of admissions knew well that scenario, and agreed saying, "That's always a risk, but I'm basing my projections on those students who have already scheduled advisement appointments to get their class schedules ready for the Fall semester. That means that they've paid their deposit, have reserved a room in the residence halls, and are coming to campus to meet with their academic advisor."

Dean Schaefer agreed, "In that case, Maria, your enrollment figures sound good."

"Yes," interjected the director of admissions, "but we've hit one snag that could unravel the whole effort."

Dean Schaefer, while trying to remember the last time he heard good news that was not delivered with a concurrent difficulty or coupled with a loud "however," said, "What is that?"

Maria Herrera took a deep breath and then aired her concern, "The biggest increase in enrollment for the fall semester is in incoming freshman rather than transfer students. With a tight job market for students graduating from high school, more of them seem to have decided on college as a good alternative. However, our problem will become apparent when these students meet with their academic advisors, and discover that some of the key freshman courses are filled. The biggest bone of contention is likely to be English Composition. Particularly with the increased tuition, incoming freshman and their parents do not understand why entering students cannot enroll in a *required* freshman course during their freshman year. Actually, it may not be an insurmountable problem. My figures show that we could manage the overflow with an additional five sections of English Composition."

Dean Schaefer, sounding more relieved, commented, "That seems like an easy solution. Go ahead, find the classroom space, and add the five new sections. I'll call the chair of the English department and tell her what we've had to do."

Let's pause here. . .

1. *Was adding five new sections of English Composition an "easy solution"? Easy for whom? What are the potential liabilities that accompany this "quick fix"?*

2. *What other alternatives are available to the dean of the college? Specify the potential advantages and disadvantages of each alternative.*

3. *What general authority is typically delegated to the dean of the college on budget matters, personnel matters, and curricular matters?*

4. *Clearly motivated by the budget crunch, Dr. Schaefer felt obligated to act unilaterally in adding the five new sections. Did he overstep his authority?*

5. *Assume the role of the dean of the college and indicate how you intend to inform the chair of the English department of your decision to add five sections of English Composition to the fall schedule. Would you, for example, schedule a meeting, write a memo, or use the telephone? List the points you intend to make and specify the order in which you want to make them.*

The English Department. Rachel Berkowitz, the chair of the English department, was contemplating the morale at Middleburg, or rather the morale of the faculty of the English department. Three months ago when the dean of the college announced that there was some likelihood of an increase in freshman enrollment, morale among the department's faculty plummeted. A departmental program review conducted four years earlier documented that the English department was woefully understaffed. Given the budgets of the last three years, the situation had become much more acute. Full-time English faculty teach at least 12, and sometimes 15, credit hours each semester. While the institution does not have a campuswide policy on faculty workload, Dr. Berkowitz knew from the annual reports that the course load carried by the faculty in the Department of English exceeded the college average of nine credit hours per faculty per semester.

She knew that in many departments, faculty taught nine credit hours a semester in order to allow them time for service activities and some research. She was somewhat alarmed by recent public statements by the dean of the college encouraging faculty to do more research because he believed that active researchers made better teachers. Further, the dean of the college had made clear to the chairs his conviction that a small college known only for its teaching was at a distinct disadvantage in the recruitment of students and faculty.

However, Berkowitz sympathized with the present English faculty who had found it difficult to devote time to research. The department chair felt a sense of true accomplishment when this semester, for the first time, she was able to keep the course loads of all full-time, untenured faculty on continuing, tenure-track appointments to 12 credit hours. The chair deemed this to be important since the department had not been fairing well in recent promotion and tenure decisions. English department faculty simply could not demonstrate a sufficient record of research and publications to get tenured and/or promoted. The chair was able to hold the course loads of nontenured faculty to 12 credit hours because the tenured full professors agreed to assume 15 credit hour workloads. Motivating the tenured full professors was their fear that unsuccessful tenure reviews for the more junior faculty would ultimately result in the department losing more faculty positions. All in all, Berkowitz concluded that, while morale may be low, *esprit de corps* was high.

The English department had been hurt badly by the budget cuts. Because the budget reductions came as midyear rescissions on top of zero-increase budgets, Dean Schaefer had decided to amortize the pain across the college by reducing the existing budgets within each department by the same percentage. The dean of the college was adamant that contracts would be honored and that no faculty member or staff working at the college would be given a pink slip. Consequently, the midyear rescission could only be taken from nonpersonnel (i.e., support costs) budget items. The dean of the college made cuts across all programs without any consideration of the number of majors, the total credit hour production, the program quality, the centrality of the program to the institution, or recent program review findings which documented whether or not departments were over- or under-staffed.

The dean was not insensitive to these differences. However, he truly believed with the rescission funds coming from the support costs budget that all departments were probably at the same level of spending for the year and so an across-the-board cut seemed the fairest way to share the pain. From one fiscal year to the next, however, there was no internal reallocation and so the across-the-board percentage surrendered to mid-year rescission became an across-the-board permanent reduction in each department's base budget for the following year.

When the rescissions became permanent base reductions, the department faculty voted unanimously to take the cuts in a way which would preserve instructional quality. The Department of English surrendered a civil service position with the understanding that faculty would now type their own course materials. The department also surrendered all support for faculty travel and long distance telephone privileges.

The faculty were committed to preserving the quality of instruction. Five years ago, the department had received a favorable recommendation from the state's Board of Higher Education on its request for a state grant to enhance the quality of instruction in its freshman-level English Composition course. This course is a central component of the college's general education program, and is required of all students. The proposal was favorably reviewed by the Board of Higher Education and some additional funds were received to hire part-time faculty to teach sections of the English Composition course. The department faculty deemed it very important that these funds not be returned as part of the rescission or base budget reduction. If supported, this decision would allow the Department of English to honor the provisions specified in the proposal advanced to the state's Board of Higher Education, such as limiting the enrollment of all such courses to 20 students per section.

Let's pause again. . .

6. With this amount of information about the English department, would you, as dean of the college, alter your approach to the chair? If so, how and why?

7. Does any of the information presented about the Department of English alter your assessment of the dean's decision to add five more sections of English Composition?

8. What parameters should be used by the dean of the college to order the institution's priorities at this time of budget crisis? Clearly what is in the best interest of the Department of English may not be in the best interest of the total institution. How should such competing priorities be managed by the dean of the college?

The Council of Chairs. The English department chair, Rachel Berkowitz, was also chair of Middleburg College's Council of Chairs. This group, comprised of all department chairs, met on a monthly basis to discuss issues they had in common and to respond to any item of business forwarded to them by the dean of the college for their reaction. Two years ago, after the first midyear rescission, the Council of Chairs passed a resolution requesting that the dean of the college work toward the establishment of criteria which might be used in the event of any further budget cuts. While none of the department chairs relished the possibility of having his or her program cut any further, all were in agreement that across-the-board cuts were devastating to program quality and to the overall reputation of the college.

The dean chose not to act on the resolution. By the time Schaefer met with the Council of Chairs to explain his thinking, the budget for the next fiscal year had already been received and put in place. Although the budget incorporated the preceding year's midyear rescission as a base budget reduction, there was no clear indication from the state that there would be further cuts. The dean explained that midyear rescissions were the result of cash flow problems within the state and emphasized the difficulty in trying to plan for such uncertain events.

The dean, whose discipline was chemistry, explained that planning during uncertain budget times was simply impossible. He used the analogy of a chemistry professor who could not decide which experiments he wanted students to work with until he knew what chemical supplies were available. As dean of the college, he could not plan for the college until he knew what level of budget support was coming to the college. The chairs, the majority of whom were supportive of the dean of the college, chose not to press the issue.

However, unhappiness increased and morale dropped when a second midyear rescission came only a few months later. Now the chairs were facing a new fiscal year with a further reduced base budget and no clear criteria for how additional budget reductions might be made in the event they were imposed by the state.

Let's pause again. . .

9. *Consider the merits of managing budget cuts as across-the-board reductions where every unit is asked to surrender the same percentage of its base budget regardless of size, productivity, and importance to the institution. Then review the merits of differential cuts where some units lose more than the average percentage so that other programs can be spared the full impact of the budget reduction. What parameters might be used to determine the ideal method for a particular institution?*

10. *With the information you now have about the Council of Chairs would you, as dean of the college, alter your approach to the chair of the English department? If so, how and why?*

The Telephone Call. Dr. Berkowitz was contemplating the tight fall teaching schedule in her department when she received a telephone call from the dean of the college.

"I've just been on the phone talking with the Maria Herrera, the director of admissions," said the dean. "First good news I have had in days. Finally, it looks like we're going to get a break from the budget cuts we've been experiencing. She tells me that enrollment for this coming fall semester is up despite the 15 percent increase in tuition. I don't have to tell you what that means to Middleburg."

Dr. Berkowitz couldn't decide why she was the recipient of this good news, but echoed the dean's positive tone, "Wonderful. Does that mean that you'll be able to restore some of our budget?"

Chuckling slightly, the dean moved into the reason for his call, "Well we're not that far along yet and we need to see what our actual income is before we could contemplate distributing any of the increased revenue among the departments, but we'll certainly consider that. What is imperative is that we see these increased applications and admissions carried through matriculation. Maria tells me that the increase is mostly in the category of incoming freshman. Unfortunately, we don't have enough sections of English Composition to guarantee that these incoming students can take freshman comp during their freshman year. Maria and her people are worried that when students learn this they will be inclined to matriculate at a different institution—feeling that Middleburg is overcrowded. I agree and told her to open five new sections of English Composition. I wanted to call you as soon as possible so you could work with her regarding scheduling the times for these additional sections and think through how you might want to assign faculty."

Rachel Berkowitz was immediately defensive saying, "I don't have any faculty left to assign to five new sections. As you know, English faculty carry among the heaviest course loads in the college. If the faculty in English are expected to meet the research as well as teaching criteria for promotion and tenure, I'm hard-pressed to increase their work loads beyond what they already are."

"Well, I understand that you would champion the cause of your faculty," said the dean smoothly, "but the college is in a crisis situation and I need your support on this."

"The English department faculty," said the chair, "are perfectly willing to support the college during this time of budget crisis. If you'll notice in the budget cuts we have made, the faculty have been making personal sacrifices to finance their own travel, long distance telephone privileges, and clerical support in order to preserve instructional quality. I cannot, however, ask them to do something that is so detrimental to their personal and professional future at this institution."

The dean, becoming a little more firm and heated, raised his voice slightly and said, "Well, we are going to teach school. I'm not going to allow any department faculty to cost us enrollment which can provide some relief to the state budget cuts we're experiencing. I know budgeting is a complex concept and somewhat obscure, but believe me, we need these courses taught because we need these new enrollees to pay their tuition. If you can't face your faculty and explain to them that their obligation is to teach courses for this college, I will tell them."

"Well you're welcome to meet with my faculty at any time," Berkowitz countered, "but I believe you'll find them to be a group strongly committed to quality education who have been working hard for this institution for many years."

"Good, then we shouldn't have any disagreement," said the dean. "You know, there is another way to handle this overload of incoming freshmen. I could simply tell the director of admissions to remove the cap on those sections already on the books and instead of 20 students per section, we'll put 35 in each class."

"Wouldn't that be violating the agreement the college made with the state's governing Board of Higher Education," asked Berkowitz, "when we received the state grant to improve the quality of the English Composition course at this college?"

"Look, you let me handle the state's Board of Higher Education," said the dean, beginning to lose his patience. "All I need you to do is get your faculty in line. The bottom line is while the state may have given us a grant to improve English Composition five years ago, they've continued to reduce our base budget ever since. We will order our own priorities and I'm telling you that a priority for this college must be increasing our enrollment in order to make up some of the deficit in the state budget."

Let's pause one last time. . .

11. *Critique the dean's approach to the department chair. Was the dean's communication style effective? Was his communication style appropriate for the problem at hand? How might your strategy and style differ (for better or worse) from the one selected by the dean of the college? Edit and rescript the dean's telephone conversation with Dr. Berkowitz in an attempt to manage the conflict more effectively.*

12. *Who is right? Who should have control of course quality? Who should be allowed to set course enrollment limits which can help ensure course quality? Who should have control over the college budget for the delivery of the academic programs?*

13. *If you were the chair, what action would you take? If you were the dean of the college, what action would you take? In either role, what is the price of*

backing down? Is there a middle position which preserves program quality without jeopardizing institutional enrollment?

14. *Is the chair of the English department overstepping her authority in her statements in this matter? Is the dean of the college overstepping his authority and responsibility in his comments regarding his perception of the problem? Whose decision is it anyway?*

SELECTED READINGS

Bennett, J. B. (1988). Department chairs: Leadership in the trenches. In M. F. Green, (Ed.) *Leaders for a new era: Strategies for higher education*. New York, NY: American Council on Education/Macmillan.

Bennett contends that the "core academic success" of institutions of higher education rests upon the quality and capabilities of the chairs. Working from this premise, the author discusses the ambiguous but important role of the chairperson, the rewards and frustrations associated with the position, and the leadership opportunities for chairs.

Duffy, F. M. (1991). Q2 Leaders—powerful, political, and ethical. *CUPA Journal, 41*(3), 1-6.

Duffy provides background material on power, politics and ethics, and argues that effective leadership in a university is the result of the proper exercise of power and politics in an ethical manner. He utilizes a model in which Q2 is the quadrant when powerful political behavior overlaps with ethical behavior.

Green, J. S., Levine, A., & Associates. (1985). *Opportunity in Adversity : How colleges can succeed in hard times*. San Francisco, CA: Jossey-Bass.

The authors begin with the premise that institutions facing fiscal austerity also have opportunities to turn themselves around and emerge from adversity. The text is a collection of chapters written by experts in higher education which discuss how institutions can grow during hard times to be stronger financially, educationally, and in their sense of institutional purpose.

Levin, H. M. (1991). Raising productivity in higher education. *Journal of Higher Education, 62*, 241-262

The author offers an analysis of the issues associated with the need to improve productivity in higher education and proposes a systematic approach to raising productivity that requires a clear statement of goals and priorities, established incentives, and an information generating system that encourages the search for effective alternatives.

Morris, V. C. (1981). *Deaning, middle management in academe*. Urbana, IL: University of Illinois Press.

Based on personal experience, Morris provides a realistic portrayal of the "middle manager" position of the academic dean. Written with wit and clarity, Morris analyzes the inner structure of campus management to depict the human side of personnel management, public and student relations, budget planning, affirmative action, faculty politics, salary disputes, and tenure decisions.

Reilly, B. J., & DiAngelo, J. A. (1990). Communication: A cultural system of meaning and value. *Human Relations, 41,* 129-140.

The author argues that a positive trusting corporate or institutional environment gives additional meaning or insight to communications within that culture. Executive management, he suggests, must attempt to provide an environment of trust and security to facilitate optimum communications.

Tucker, A. (1992). *Chairing the academic department: Leadership among peers (3rd edition).* New York, NY: American Council on Education/Macmillan.

A text for anyone seeking more information about the roles and responsibilities often assigned to department chairs. Of particular relevance to this case is the chapter entitled "Dealing with deans and university administrative officers."

Tucker, A. (1991). *The academic dean. Dove, dragon, and diplomat (2nd edition).* New York, NY: American Council on Education/Macmillan.

This text offers a description of the roles and responsibilities assigned to academic deans. Specific chapters are devoted to the relationship of the dean to department chairs, to provosts and vice presidents, and to the faculty and students.

Walker, D. E. (1986). Administrators vs. Faculty: How to change the good guys-bad guys scenario. *Change, 18,* 9.

This brief essay examines the campus environment where high numbers of faculty (75%) consider administrators (who often came from the ranks of that very faculty) at their schools to be mediocre or worse. Walker suggests some causes for this phenomena: unrealistic expectations, organizational breakdowns, and lack of involvement in decision-making.

BIBLIOGRAPHY

Aaron, R. M. (1992, Winter). Student academic dishonesty: Are collegiate institutions addressing the issue? *NASPA Journal, 29*(2), 107-113.

Abrams, D. M. (1987). Political competition and cooperation between public and higher education agencies of state government. *Journal of Education Finance, 12,* 369-390.

Adams, W. C. (1992, Spring). Helping your organization triumph over negatives. *Public Relations Quarterly, 37,* 12-16.

Adler, R. S., & Bigoness, W. J. (1992). Contemporary ethical issues in labor-management relations. *Journal of Business Ethics, 11,* 351-360.

American Association of University Professors' Committee A on Academic Freedom and Tenure. (1992). College and university policies on substance abuse and drug testing. *Academe 78(3),* 17-23.

American Council on Education. (1992). *Institutional liability for alcohol consumption: A white paper on institutional liability for consumption of alcohol and drugs on campus.* Washington, DC: Author.

Aper, J. P., Cuver, S. M., & Hinkle, D. E. (1990). Coming to terms with the accountability versus improvement debate in assessment. *Higher Education, 20,* 471-483.

Ashley, M. E.. (1990). *Combating racism on campus: A resource book and model for the 1990s.* Cincinnati, OII: University of Cincinnati.

Astin, A. W. (1990). Can state-mandated assessment work? *Educational Record, 71,* 34-41.

Astin, A. W. (1991). *Assessment for excellence: The philosophy and practice of assessment and evaluation in higher education.* New York,NY: American Council on Education/Macmillan.

Astin, H. S., & Leland, C. (1991). *Women of influence, women of vision.* San Francisco, CA: Jossey-Bass.

Atkinson, R. C., & Tuzin, D. (1992). Equilibrium in the research university. *Change, 24,* 21-31.

Austin, A. E. (1990). Faculty cultures, faculty values. *New Directions for Institutional Research, Number 68,* 61-74.

Ayres-Williams, R. (1992, March). When managing gets tough: How to handle difficult employees. *Black Enterprise, 22*(8), 63-69.

Balenger, V. J., Hoffman, M. A., & Sedlacek, W. E. (1992). Racial attitudes among incoming white students: A study of 10-year trends. *Journal of College Student Development, 33,* 245-252.

Banta, T. W. (Ed.) (1988). Implementing outcomes assessment: Promise and perils. *New Directions for Institutional Research, Number 59.* San Francisco, CA: Jossey-Bass.

Barak, R. J., & Breier, B. E. (1990). *Successful program review: A practical guide to evaluating programs in academic settings.* San Francisco, CA: Jossey-Bass.

Belenky, M. F., Clinchy, B. M., Goldberger, N. R., & Tarule, J. M. (1986). *Women's ways of knowing: The development of self, voice, and mind.* New York, NY: Basic Books.

Bennett, J. B. (1983). *Managing the academic department: Cases and notes.* New York, NY: American Council on Education/Macmillan.

Bennett, J. B. (1988). Department chairs: Leadership in the trenches. In M. F. Green (Ed.), *Leaders for a new era: Strategies for higher education.* New York, NY: American Council on Education/Macmillan.

Bennett, J. B., & Figuli, D. J. (Eds.). (1990). *Enhancing departmental leadership: The roles of the chairperson.* New York, NY: American Council on Education/Macmillan.

Bensimon, E. M. (1990). The new president and understanding the campus as a culture. *New Directions for Institutional Research, Number 68.* San Francisco, CA: Jossey-Bass.

Bernstein, J. (1990, March). The ten steps of crisis management. *Security Management, 34,* 75-76.

Bieber, J. P., Lawrence, J. H., & Blackburn, R. T. (1992). Through the years—Faculty and their changing institution. *Change, 24,* 28-35.

Birnbaum, R. (Ed.). (1991). Faculty in governance: The role of senates and joint committees in academic decision making. *New Directions for Higher Education, Number 75.* San Francisco, CA: Jossey-Bass.

Birnbaum, R. (1992). Will you love me in December as you do in May? Why experienced college presidents lose faculty support. *Journal of Higher Education, 63,* 1-25.

Bishop, T. R. (1992). Integrating business ethics into an undergraduate curriculum. *Journal of Business Ethics, 11,* 291-300.

Blackburn, R., & Wylie, N. (1990). Current appointments and tenure practices. *CUPA Journal, 41*(3), 9-21.

Bok, D. (1988, Summer). Can higher education foster higher morals? *Business and Society Review, 66,* 4-12.

Bok, D. (1991). The improvement of teaching. *Teachers College Record, 93*(2), 236-251.

Bossman, D. (1991). Cross-cultural values for a pluralistic core curriculum. *Journal of Higher Education, 62,* 661-681.

Boyer, E. L. (1987). *College: The undergraduate experience in America.* New York, NY: Carnegie Foundation for the Advancements of Teaching/Harper & Row.

Boyer, E. L. (1990). *Scholarship reconsidered: Priorities of the professoriate.* Princeton, NJ: Carnegie Foundation for the Advancement of Teaching.

Braxton, J. M. (1991). The influence of graduate department quality on the sanctioning of scientific misconduct. *Journal of Higher Education, 62,* 87-103.

Brown, R. S. (1986, September/October). Can they sue me? Liability risks from unfavorable letters of reference. *Academe, 72,* 31-32.

Bryden, D. P. (1991, Spring). It ain't what they teach, it's the way that they teach it. *The Public Interest, 103,* 38-53.

Bryson, J. M. (1989). *Strategic planning for public and nonprofit organizations: A guide to strengthening and sustaining organizational achievement.* San Francisco, CA: Jossey-Bass.

Carland, J. A., Carland, J. W., & Aby, C. D. Jr. (1992). Proposed codification of ethicacy in the publication process. *Journal of Business Ethics, 11,* 95-105.

Carpenter, D. S., Paterson, B. G., Kibler, W. L., & Paterson, J. W. (1990). What price faculty involvement? The case of the research university. *NASPA Journal, 27,* 206-212.

Carruth, P. J., & Carruth, A. K. (1991). Education in ethics: The role of higher education. *Journal of Education for Business, 66,* 168-171.

Cerio, N. C. (1989). Counseling victims and perpetrators of campus violence. *New Directions for Student Services, Number 47,* 53-64.

Clagett, C. A., & Huntington, R. B. (1992). Assessing the transfer function: Data exchanges and transfer rates. *Community College Review, 19,* 21-26.

Close, J. (1991, February). Speaking out to the public: Ten crisis communication strategies. *Best's Review , 91,* 86f.

Cohen, A. M. (1992, February). Calculating transfer rates efficiently. *Community, Technical, and Junior College Journal, 62*(4),32-35.

Cole, S. A. (1991). Professional ethics and the role of the academic officer. *CUPA Journal, 42*(3), 37-41.

Colvin, T. J., & Kilmann, R. H. (1990). Implementation of large-scale planned change: Some areas of agreement and disagreement. *Psychological Reports, 66,* 1235-1241.

Cooper, D. A. (1992, January). CEO must weigh legal and public relations approaches. *Public Relations Journal, 48,* 39-40.

Cramer, S. (1991). Fostering ethical dialogues across campus. *CUPA Journal, 42,* 44-48.

Creswell, J. W., Wheeler, D. W. Seagren, A. T., Egly, N. J., & Beyer, K. D. (1990). *The academic chair's handbook.* Lincoln, NE: University of Nebraska.

Cross, K. P., & Fideler, E. F. (1989). Community college missions: Priorities in the mid-1980s. *Journal of Higher Education, 60,* 209-216.

Cunningham, B., & Miller, S. (1991). Racism: Assess the campus and community environment. *Journal of College Student Development, 32,* 181-182.

Curtis, D. B., & Winsor, J. L. (1991). Teaching ethics across the curriculum: A subject for faculty and administrators. *CUPA Journal, 42*(3), 7-12.

Dalton, J. C. (Ed.). (1991). Racism on campus: Confronting racial bias through peer interventions. *New Directions for Student Services, Number 56.* San Francisco, CA: Jossey-Bass.

Danko, K. (1991). A survey of attitudes of contributors to business education. *Journal of Education for Business, 67,* 17-20.

Dannells, M. (1991, March). Changes in student misconduct and institutional response over 10 years. *Journal of College Student Development, 32,* 166-170.

Davis, J. D. (Ed.). (1993). *Coloring the halls of ivy.* Bolton, MA: Anker Publishing.

Davis, J. L., & Hunnicutt, D. M. (1992). Community college student alcohol abuse: An assessment. *Community College Review, 19*(3). 43-47.

Deegan, W. L. (1992, April/May). Proven techniques: The use and impact of major management concepts in community colleges. *Community, Technical, and Junior College Journal, 62*(6), 26-30.

Dennis, E. E. (1992). Freedom of expression, the university, and the media. *Journal of Communication, 42,* 73-82.

Devault, M. L. (1990). Talking and listening from women's standpoint: Feminist strategies for interviewing and analysis. *Social Problems, 37,* 96-116.

Diaz, E. M., Minton, J. W., & Saunders, D. M. (1987, April). Labor relations update: A fair nonunion grievance procedure. *Personnel, 64,* 13-18.

Dougherty, K. J. (1992). Community college and baccalaureate attainment. *Journal of Higher Education, 63,* 188-213.

Dressel, P. L. (1987). Mission, organization, and leadership. *Journal of Higher Education, 58,* 102- 109.

Duffy, F. M. (1991). Q2 Leaders—powerful, political, and ethical. *CUPA Journal, 41*(3), 1-6.

Eble, K. E., & McKeachie, W. J. (1986). *Improving undergraduate education through faculty development.* San Francisco, CA: Jossey-Bass.

Edgerton, R. (1990). Assessment at half time, *Change, 22,* 4-5.

Editors of the *Chronicle of Higher Education.* (1991). *The Almanac of Higher Education: 1991.* Chicago, IL: University of Chicago Press.

Ehrle, E. B., & Bennett, J. B. (1988). *Managing the Academic Enterprise: Case studies for deans and provosts.* New York, NY: American Council on Education/Macmillan.

Ehrlich, R., & Scimecca, J. (1991, Summer). Offensive speech on campus: Punitive or educational solutions. *Educational Record, 72,* 26-29.

Erwin, T. D. (1991). *Assessing student learning and development.* San Francisco, CA: Jossey-Bass.

Essex, N. L. (1990). When administrators evaluate: Precautions to take when recommending job applicants. *Educational Horizons, 68*(3),158-160.

Ewell, P. T. (1991). Assessment and public accountability: Back to the future, *Change, 23,* 12-17.

Ewell, P. T. (1991). *Benefits and costs of assessment in higher education: A framework for choicemaking.* Boulder, CO: National Center for Higher Education Management Systems.

Ewell, P. T. (Ed.). (1985). Assessing educational outcomes. *New Directions for Institutional Research, Number 47.* San Francisco, CA: Jossey-Bass.

Ferguson, M. (1990, Winter). The role of faculty in increasing student retention. *College and University, 65,* 127-135.

Finifter, D. H., Baldwin, R. G., & Thelin, J. R. (Eds.). (1991). *The uneasy public policy triangle in higher education.* New York, NY: American Council on Education /Macmillan.

Fleck, R. A., Jr., & Shirley, B. M. (1990, Winter). Expert systems for transfer credit evaluation: Problems and prospects. *College and University, 65,* 73-83.

Fleming, J. H., Hilton, J. L., Darley, J. M., & Kojetin, B. A. (1990). Multiple audience problems: A strategic communication perspective on social perceptions. *Journal of Personality and Social Psychology, 58,* 593-609.

Fritzsche, D. J. (1991). A model of decision-making incorporating ethical values. *Journal of Business Ethics, 10,* 841-852.

Garrett, R. L. (1992). Degree of centralization of governance of state community college systems in the United States, 1990. *Community College Review, 20*(1), 7-13.

Gibson, G. W. (1992). *Good start: A guidebook for new faculty in liberal arts colleges.* Bolton, MA: Anker Publishing.

Glenn, J. R. Jr. (1992). Can a business and society course affect the ethical judgment of future managers? *Journal of Business Ethics, 11,* 217-223.

Gmelch, W. H., & Miskin, V. D. (1993). *Leadership skills for department chairs.* Bolton, MA: Anker Publishing.

Green, J. S., Levine, A., & Associates. (1985). *Opportunity in Adversity: How colleges can succeed in hard times.* San Francisco, CA: Jossey-Bass.

Green, M. F. (Ed.). (1989). *Minorities on campus: A handbook for enhancing diversity.* Washington, DC: American Council on Education.

Green, M. F., & McDade, S. A. (1991). *Investing in higher education: A handbook of leadership development.* Washington, DC: American Council on Education.

Grubb, W. N. (1991). The decline of community college transfer rates: Evidence from national longitudinal surveys. *Journal of Higher Education, 62,* 194-217.

Guillebeau, J. (1989, Fall). Crisis management: A case study in the killing of an employee. *Public Relations Quarterly, 35,* 19-21.

Haddad, F. D., & Hartnett, R. (1989). College student involvement: Alumni fundraising implications. *Journal of College Student Development, 30,* 379-380.

Hahn, H. G. (1986, April 9). Opinion: Ethics and higher education cannot be separated. *The Chronicle of Higher Education, 21,* p. 47.

Hall, R. M., & Sandler, B. R. (1982). *The classroom climate: A chilly one for women?* Washington, DC: Association of American Colleges, Project on the Status and Education of Women.

Hambrick, D. C., & Fukutomi, G. D. S. (1991). The seasons of a CEO's tenure. *Academy of Management Review, 16,* 719-742.

Harper, L. F., & Rifkind, L. J. (1992). Competent communication strategies for responding to sexual harassment. *CUPA Journal, 43*(2), 33-40.

Harris, J., Silverstein, J., & Andrews, D. (1989). Educating women in science. In C. S. Pearson, D. L. Shavlik, & J. G. Touchton (Eds.), *Educating the majority: Women challenge tradition in higher education* (pp. 294-310). New York, NY: American Council on Education/Macmillan.

Hartman, S. J., Griffeth, R. W., Crino, M D., & Harris, O. J. (1991). Gender-based influences: The promotion recommendation. *Sex Roles, 25,* 285-300.

Henry, S. D. (1991). Higher education and cultural pluralism: A reawakening of ethics. *CUPA Journal, 41*(3), 13-19.

Hickson, M. III, & Stacks, D. W. (1992). *Effective communication for academic chairs.* Albany, NY: State University of New York Press.

Higgerson, M. L., & Rehwaldt, S. S. (1993). *Complexities of higher education administration: Case studies and issues.* Bolton, MA: Anker Publishing.

Hollingsworth, A. T., & Boone, L. W. (1990). Decision time: The dilemma for institutions of higher education. *CUPA Journal, 41,* 1-10.

Hossler, D., Bean, J. P., & Associates. (1990). *The strategic management of college enrollments.* San Francisco, CA: Jossey-Bass.

Hurst, P. J., & Peterson M. W. (1992). The impact of a chief planning officer on the administrative environment for planning. *Research in Higher Education, 33,* 1-17.

Hutchings, P., & Marchese, T. J. (1990). Watching assessment: Questions, stories, prospects, *Change, 22,* 12-38.

Jendrek, M. L. (1992). Students' reaction to academic dishonesty. *Journal of College Student Development, 33,* 260-273.

Jones, J. C., & Lee, B. S. (1992). Moving on: A cooperative study of student transfer. *Research in Higher Education, 33,* 125-140.

Kaplan, S. (1989). The quest for institutional excellence: The CEO and the creative use of the accreditation process. *NCA Quarterly, 64,* 379-386.

Keller, G. (1983). *Academic Strategy: The management revolution in American higher education.* Baltimore, MD: The Johns Hopkins University Press.

Kerr, C. (1984). *Presidents make a difference.* Washington, DC: Association of Governing Boards of Universities and Colleges.

Kerr, C., & Gade, M. L. (1986), *The many lives of academic presidents: Time, place and character.* Washington, DC: Association of Governing Boards of Universities and Colleges.

Knoell, D. M. (1990, October/November). Guidelines for transfer and articulation. *Community, Technical, and Junior College Journal, 61,* 38-41. [Excerpted from *Transfer, articulation, and collaboration: Twenty-five years later.*]

Knouse, S. B. & Giacalone, R. A. (1992) Ethical decision-making in business: Behavioral issues and concerns. *Journal of Business Ethics. 11,* 369-377.

Kuh, G. D. (1990). Assessing student culture. *New Directions for Institutional Research, Number 68,* 47-60.

Kuh, G. D., Schuh, J. H., Whitt, E. J., Andreas, R. E., Lyons, J. W., Strange, C. C., Krehbiel, L. E., & MacKay, K. A. (1991). *Involving colleges.* San Francisco, CA: Jossey-Bass.

Levin, H. M. (1991). Raising productivity in higher education. *Journal of Higher Education, 62,* 241-262.

Levine, A. (Ed). (1992, January/February) *Change, 24*(1).

Levine, A., & Associates. (1989). *Shaping higher education's future: Demographic realities and opportunities, 1990-2000.* San Francisco, CA: Jossey-Bass.

Liedtka, J. (1991). Organizational value contention and managerial mindsets. *Journal of Business Ethics, 10,* 543-557.

Lindskold, S., Han, G., & Betz, B. (1986). Repeated persuasion in interpersonal conflict. *Journal of Personality and Social Psychology, 51,* 1183-1185.

Loessin, B. A., & Duronio, M. A. (1989-1990). The role of planning in successful fundraising in ten higher education institutions. *Planning for Higher Education, 18*(3),45-56.

Magnusen, K. O. (1987). Faculty evaluation, performance, and pay: Applications and issues. *Journal of Higher Education, 58,* 516-529.

Manning, K., & Coleman-Boatwright, P. (1991). Student affairs initiatives toward a multicultural university. *Journal of College Student Development, 32,* 367-374.

Mayhew, L. B., Ford, P. J., & Hubbard, D. L. (1990). *The quest for quality: The challenge for undergraduate education in the 1990s.* San Francisco, CA: Jossey-Bass.

McClenney, K. M. (1990). Whither assessment? Commitments needed for meaningful change, *Change, 22,* 54.

Mentkowski, M. (1991). Creating a context where institutional assessment yields educational improvement. *Journal of General Education, 40,* 255-283.

Miller, R. I. (1986). Academic promotion and tenure. *The Journal of the College and University Personnel Association, 37*(4), 19-26.

Miller, R. I. (1988). Using change strategies to implement assessment programs. *New Directions for Institutional Research, Number 59,* 5-14.

Morris, V. C. (1981). *Deaning, middle management in academe.* Urbana, IL: University of Illinois Press.

Moses, Y. T. (1989). *Black women in academe: Issues and strategies.* Washington, DC: Association of American Colleges, Project on the Status and Education of Women.

Mouritsen, M. M. (1986). The university mission statement: A tool for the university curriculum, institutional effectiveness, and change. *New Directions for Higher Education, Number 55,* 45-52.

Neumann, A., & Bensimon, E. M. (1990). Constructing the presidency: College presidents' images of their leadership roles, a comparative study. *Journal of Higher Education, 61,* 678-701.

Norris, W. (1988, July 1). Questionable science of trapping the greenback. *The Times Higher Education Supplement, 817,* 10.

North Central Association of College and Schools. (1991, Fall). *NCA Quarterly, 66*(2).

Ommeren, R. V., Sneed, D., Wulfemeyer, K. T., & Riffe, D. (1991, Fall). Ethical issues in recruiting faculty. *CUPA Journal, 41*(3), 29-35.

Ormrod, J. E. (1986). Predictors of faculty dissatisfaction with an annual performance evaluation. *The Journal of the College and University Personnel Association, 37*(3), 13-19.

Orpen, C., & King, G. (1989). Effects of superiors' feedback, credibility, and expertise on subordinates' reactions: An experimental study. *Psychological Reports, 64,* 645-656.

Ory, J. C. (1992). Meta-Assessment: Evaluating assessment activities. *Research in Higher Education, 33,* 467-482.

Pascarella, E. T., & Terenzini, P. T. (1991). *How college affects students: Findings and insights from twenty years of research.* San Francisco, CA: Jossey-Bass.

Pavel, D. M., & Reiser, M. (1991). Using national data bases to examine minority student success. *New Directions for Institutional Research, Number 69,* 5-20.

Pearson, C. S., Shavlik, D. L., & Touchton, J. G. (1989). *Educating the majority: Women challenge tradition in higher education.* New York, NY: American Council on Education/Macmillan.

Phelps, D. G. (1990/1991, December/January). Access, equity, and opportunity. *Community, Technical, and Junior College Journal, 61,* 34-37.

Ping, C. J. (1986). Recognizing problems in state universities. *New Directions for Higher Education, Number 55,* 9-16.

Prager, C. (Ed.). (1988). Enhancing articulation and transfer. *New Directions for Community Colleges, Number 61.* San Francisco, CA: Jossey-Bass.

Presley, C. A., & Meilmen, P. W. (1992). *Alcohol and Drugs on the American College Campus: A Report to College Presidents.* Produced by Southern Illinois University's Student Health Program Wellness Center by the Drug Prevention in Higher Education Program of the Fund for the Improvement of Postsecondary Education (FIPSE), U. S. Department of Education, Washington, D. C.

Rahim, M. A., Garrett, J. E., & Buntzman, G. F. (1992). Ethics of managing interpersonal conflict in organizations. *Journal of Business Ethics, 11,* 423-432.

Rampal, K R. (1991). Developing a working code of ethics for human resource personnel. *CUPA Journal, 42(3),* 21-26.

Reilly, B. J., & DiAngelo, J. A. (1990). Communication: A cultural system of meaning and value. *Human Relations, 41,* 129-140.

Reiss, A. H. (1990, May). Bottom line: A working board of directors. *Management Review, 79,* 37-38.

Reynolds, A. (1992) Charting the changes in junior faculty: Relationships among socialization, acculturation, and gender. *Journal of Higher Education, 63,* 637-652.

Rhoads, R. A., & Tierney, W. G. (1990). Exploring organizational climates and cultures. *New Directions for Institutional Research, Number 68,* 87-95.

Ringle, P. M., & Capshaw, F. W. (1990). Issue-oriented planning: Essex Community College. *New Directions for Institutional Research, Number 67,* 69-82.

Roueche, J. E. (1988). The university perspective. *New Directions for Community Colleges, Number 64,* 53-60.

Russo, C. J., Ponterotto, J. G., & Jackson, B. L. (1990, Summer). Confidential peer review: A supreme court update and implications for university personnel. *Initiatives, 53,* 11-17.

Sandler, B. R. (1986). *The campus climate revisited: Chilly for women faculty, administrators, and graduate students.* Washington, DC: Association of American Colleges, Project on the Status and Education of Women.

Schmidtlein, F. A., & Milton, T. H. (Eds.). (1990). Adapting strategic planning to campus realities. *New Directions for Institutional Research, Number 67.* San Francisco, CA: Jossey-Bass.

Seldin, P. (1991). *The teaching portfolio: A practical guide to improved performance and promotion/tenure decisions.* Bolton, MA: Anker Publishing.

Seldin, P. (1993). *Successful use of teaching portfolios.* Bolton, MA: Anker Publishing.

Seldin, P., & Associates. (1990). *How administrators can improve teaching: Moving from talk to action in higher education.* San Francisco, CA: Jossey-Bass.

Sexual harassment: Issues and answers. (1992). *CUPA Journal, 43*(2), 41-52.

Sherrill, J. M. (1989) Models of response to campus violence: Responding to violence on campus. *New Directions for Student Services, Number 47,* 77-88.

Smith, D. L. (1992). Validity of faculty judgments of student performance: Relationship between grades and credits earned and external criterion measures. *Journal of Higher Education, 63,* 329-340.

Smith, M. C. (1989). The ancestry of campus violence. *New Directions for Student Services, Number 47,* 5-15.

Spotts, B. L. (1991). Creating a successful minority affairs position: Guidelines for institutions and individuals. *The Journal of College Admission, 13*(1), 4-9.

St. John, E. P. (1991). A framework for reexamining state resource-management strategies in higher education. *Journal of Higher Education, 62,* 263-287.

Stimpson, C. R. (1992, July/August)). Some comments on the curriculum: Can we get beyond our controversies? *Change, 24,* 9-11, 53.

Stoecker, J. K., & Pascarella, E. T. (1991). Women's colleges and women's career attainment revisited. *Journal of Higher Education, 62,* 394-409.

Sullivan, G. M., & Nowlin, W. A. (1990, Summer). Recruiting and hiring minority faculty: Old story, same myths, new opportunities. *CUPA Journal, 41,* 43-50.

Summers, R. J. (1991). Determinants of judgments of and responses to a complaint of sexual harassment. *Sex Roles, 25,* 379-392.

Sykes, C. J. (1988) *ProfScam: Professors and the demise of higher education.* Washington, DC: Regency Gateway.

Taback, H. (1991, October). Preventing a crisis from getting out of hand. *Risk Management, 38,* 64-69.

Thompson, D. F. (1992). Ethical fundraising: An educational process. *Educational Record, 73,* 38-43.

Tierney, W. G. (1983, Summer). Governance by conversation: An essay on the structure, function, and communication codes of a faculty senate. *Human Organization, 42,* 172-177.

To-Dutke, J., & Weinman, E. (1991). Developing articulation agreements between two-year and four-year colleges: A program to program curriculum based approach. *College Student Journal, 25,* 524-528.

Touchton, J. G., & Davis, L. (Eds.). (1991). *Fact book on women in higher education.* New York, NY: American Council on Education/Macmillan.

Townsend, B. K. (Ed.). (1989). A search for institutional distinctiveness. *New Directions for Community Colleges, Number 65.* San Francisco, CA: Jossey-Bass.

Trotter, P., & Risdon, P. (1990). Performance counseling. *CUPA Journal, 41*(3), 21-24.

Tucker, A. (1992). *Chairing the academic department: Leadership among peers (3rd edition).* New York, NY: American Council on Education/Macmillan.

Tucker, A., & Bryan, R. A. (1991). *The academic dean: Dove, dragon, and diplomat. (2nd edition).* New York, NY: American Council on Education/Macmillan.

Turner, C. S. V. (1992). It takes two to transfer: Relational networks and educational outcomes. *Community College Review, 19,* 27-33.

Uehling, B. (1987). Serving too many masters: Changing the accreditation process. *Educational Record, 68*(3), 38-41.

Underwood, D. B. (1991). Taking inventory: Identifying assessment activities. *Research in Higher Education, 32,* 59-69.

Vander Waerdt, L. (1987, October 7) How to maintain your integrity and avoid liability for giving honest references. *The Chronicle of Higher Education, 34,* B2-B3.

Vineyard, E. E. (1993). *The pragmatic presidency: Effective leadership in the two-year college.* Bolton, MA: Anker Publishing.

Walker, D. E. (1979). *The effective administrator.* San Francisco, CA: Jossey-Bass.

Walker, D. E. (1986). Administrators vs. Faculty: How to change the good guys-bad guys scenario. *Change, 18,* 9.

Walleri, D., Seybert, J., & Cosgrove, J. (1992). What do students want? How student intentions affect institutional assessment. *Community, Technical, and Junior College Journal, 62*(4), 28-31.

Watts, E. S. (1991). Governance beyond the individual campus. *Academe, 77*(5), 28-32.

Weaver, K. A., Davis, S. F., Look, C., Buzzanga, V. L., & Neal, L. (1991). Examining academic dishonesty policies. *College Student Journal, 26,* 302-305.

Wheeler, D. L. (1992, March 18). U.S. agency proposes trial-like hearings to judge cases of scientific misconduct. *The Chronicle of Higher Education, 38,* A8-A11.

Wines, W. A., & Napier, N. K. (1992). Toward an understanding of cross-cultural ethics: A tentative model. *Journal of Business Ethics, 11,* 831-842.

Wolvin, A. D. (1991). When governance is really shared: The multi-constituency campus. *Academe, 77*(5), 26-28.